Integrating D3.js with React

Learn to Bring Data Visualization to Life

Elad Elrom

Apress®

Integrating D3.js with React: Learn to Bring Data Visualization to Life

Elad Elrom
New York, NY, USA

ISBN-13 (pbk): 978-1-4842-7051-6   ISBN-13 (electronic): 978-1-4842-7052-3
https://doi.org/10.1007/978-1-4842-7052-3

Managing Director, Apress Media LLC: Welmoed Spahr
Acquisitions Editor: Louise Corrigan
Development Editor: James Markham
Coordinating Editor: Nancy Chen

Cover image designed by Freepik (www.freepik.com)

Distributed to the book trade worldwide by Springer Science+Business Media LLC, 1 New York Plaza, Suite 4600, New York, NY 10004. Phone 1-800-SPRINGER, fax (201) 348-4505, e-mail orders-ny@springer-sbm.com, or visit www.springeronline.com. Apress Media, LLC is a California LLC and the sole member (owner) is Springer Science + Business Media Finance Inc (SSBM Finance Inc). SSBM Finance Inc is a **Delaware** corporation.

For information on translations, please e-mail booktranslations@springernature.com; for reprint, paperback, or audio rights, please e-mail bookpermissions@springernature.com.

Apress titles may be purchased in bulk for academic, corporate, or promotional use. eBook versions and licenses are also available for most titles. For more information, reference our Print and eBook Bulk Sales web page at www.apress.com/bulk-sales.

Any source code or other supplementary material referenced by the author in this book is available to readers on GitHub via the book's product page, located at www.apress.com/9781484270516. For more detailed information, please visit www.apress.com/source-code.

Printed on acid-free paper

This book is dedicated to the readers who learn from failures,
gain experience, and keep questioning.

Table of Contents

About the Author

 **Elad Elrom** is a React d3 full stack expert. Additionally, he is a technical coach and a coder. As a writer, he has authored and co-authored several technical books. Elad has consulted for a variety of clients, from large corporations such as AT&T, HBO, Viacom, NBC Universal, and Weight Watchers, to smaller startups. Aside from coding, Elad is a PADI diving instructor and a pilot. Visit him at EliElrom.com.

About the Technical Reviewer

Alexander Chinedu Nnakwue has a background in mechanical engineering from the University of Ibadan, Nigeria, and has been a front-end developer for more than three years working on both web and mobile technologies. He also has experience as a technical author, writer, and reviewer. He enjoys programming for the Web, and occasionally, you can find him playing soccer. He was born in Benin City and is currently based in Lagos, Nigeria.

Introduction

Congratulations! You have decided to integrate D3.js with React. There are plenty of ways to learn, such as training courses, YouTube videos, and blog posts, among others. In fact, I am offering an interactive course for integrating React and D3 and it compliments this book very well, as it expands and gives more examples on the topic in this book, check out the course here: `https://elielrom.com/BuildSiteCourse`.

Much of this information is of good quality; however, each piece is usually based on a different technology stack, and you need to adjust to a different author style or piece the information together to understand it. For these reasons, using this book is a great choice when you want to learn how to integrate D3.js with React, and it will help you understand the concepts deeper. Additonally, we all learn differently, and reading from a book has advantage as you can follow at your own phase and better understand key concepts.

The book teaches you how to work seamlessly with D3.js and React alongside other libraries such as TypeScript. I explain how all these technologies work together and show lots of examples.

This book is set up logically, so you should read the chapters in chronological order. I will build on each topic as you move through the book, and it will be an exciting development journey.

Additionally, there are thousands of libraries that can help expedite your development effort and make your life easier. It can get confusing to pick what libraries to learn and use. In this book, one of my goals was to ease the pain and help you not only pick the best and most popular library but also to give you a rundown of the other options.

My aim is not just to teach you how to integrate D3.js with React. You will learn about tools and libraries that will help you integrate charts to get the job done, and you'll learn about other technologies and how to join the React community that utilizes the latest and best libraries.

Human nature is choosing the easy way out and learning tools that are easy to master. From my experience, the tools that have a steep learning curve, such as D3.js, are the ones that usually offer more value. They are worth the extra effort you put in to learning them, as knowing these tools makes you a valuable resource.

Choosing D3.js over libraries that are built on top of D3.js is worth the effort. By learning D3.js with React, you can improve the quality of your code as well as potentially earn more as a developer and help tell your "story" better.

You should be comfortable with HTML, JavaScript, and CSS when reading this book, and it's helpful to have some knowledge of React. That said, I made an effort not to require these proficiencies in the book, and it's possible to read this book without any prior knowledge; feel free to research the concepts that you are unfamiliar with. A good way to do this is to purchase my other React.js book, *React and Libraries* (www.apress. com/gp/book/9781484266953). This book can be considered as a continuation of that one. Additionally, I have online courses that I encourage you to take https://elielrom. com/BuildSiteCourse.

In terms of organization, we will create an actual project that includes D3.js and other commonly used components and architecture. I will give you helpful examples, showing you the complete full development cycle. You will learn how to publish your app on a server as well as ensure the quality of the code.

The book code examples can be downloaded from https://github.com/Apress/ integrating-d3.js-with-react.

Make sure to read this book and work on the examples to completion. You will become a better React developer, able to complete projects and publish them to the wild, as well as integrate charts with confidence.

Lastly, as a bonus to you and as a thank-you for purchasing this book, you can reach out to me and receive a free ebook that includes many typical React interview questions. You can use these questions to increase your knowledge as well as practice for an interview. See https://elielrom.com/ReactQuestion.

Lots of effort was put into this book from myself, and the editiorial team, however, If you find errors, do not hesitate to point them at https://github.com/Apress/ integrating-d3.js-with-react/blob/main/errata.md. Additionally, I would love to hear about any interesting React and D3.js projects. I am available for consulting, coaching, or tutoring: https://elielrom.com/CoachingHourly.

Thanks again for purchasing this book, and let's get started on your React and data visualization development journey today.

CHAPTER 1

Setting Up Our Technology Stack

Integrating interactive data visualization (aka *data viz*) components can help you tell your story better. React is already set up to be able to animate Scalable Vector Graphics (SVG), HTML, and Canvas; this is nothing new. We've had the ability to animate SVG, Canvas, and HTML for years with HTML and pure JavaScript. React has HTML, CSS, and JavaScript capabilities and can play nicely with other libraries to help create charts and animate views.

Why use data visualizations?

- Business intelligence with data visualization capabilities is becoming more popular because it offers an return on investment (ROI) of $13.01 on every dollar spent (https://nucleusresearch.com/research/single/analytics-pays-back-13-01-for-every-dollar-spent/).

- As they say, a picture is worth a thousand words.

- Ninety-three percent of communication is nonverbal (https://ubiquity.acm.org/article.cfm?id=2043156).

- Our brain processes an image at a speed of 13 milliseconds. Ninety percent of information transmitted to our brain is visual (https://news.mit.edu/2014/in-the-blink-of-an-eye-0116).

- Our brains process visuals 60,000 times faster than text (https://carlsonschool.umn.edu/faculty-research/mis-research-center).

- High-quality infographics are 30 times more likely to be read than text (https://blog.kissmetrics.com/your-brain-on-visualization/).

- Ninety-seven percent of people believe information is more reliably shown by a graph than words and numbers (Cornell University).

© Elad Elrom 2021
E. Elrom, *Integrating D3.js with React*, https://doi.org/10.1007/978-1-4842-7052-3_1

1

React's biggest advantage over other web platforms is that it uses the virtual DOM (VDOM), which speeds up performance. We can take advantage of what React has to offer as well as other third-party libraries, such as the D3 library and data management, to crunch our data and not just build compelling charts components, but also increase performance. At the same time. Sometimes we want to take control and have our components control the elements instead of React.

Adding other libraries and technologies to the mix, such as Recoil, Material-UI, TypeScript, unit testing, Sassy Cascading Style Sheets (SCSS), and others, will require more knowledge, but it is a small price to pay in exchange for what we get.

In this book, I will give you the tools to learn how to create data visualizations with React, and we will get help from extensive D3 libraries as well as other libraries that are standard in the world of React.

This first chapter serves as an introduction. We will review the tools we'll use in this book to create animations and charts, as well as set up our first "Hello World" D3/React/TypeScript project. Additionally, we will look at what we can do to ensure quality, looking into unit testing, linting, and formatting.

Let's get started.

React

React (also known as ReactJS) is a JavaScript library developed by Facebook (https://github.com/facebook/react) to create user interfaces for the Web.

React was invented by Jordan Walke, who was working on Facebook Ads at the time. It competes with other web frameworks and libraries such as jQuery, Angular, Vue.js, Svelte, etc.

In the previous version of React 16.x, released in September 2017, the React team added more tools and development support while eliminating bugs. The latest version of React (at the time of writing) is 17, which was released in October 2020.

Note   React 17 is a "stepping stone" release, and the release is primarily focused on making it easier to upgrade React to future versions as well as adding better compatibility with browsers. React team's support shows that the library has great momentum and is not going away any time soon.

Why React?

Did you know?

- React is a favorite among developers. In fact, according to a Stack Overflow survey (`https://insights.stackoverflow.com/survey/2020`), React is the most loved web framework and has been for two consecutive years.

- The need for React developers has ballooned; according to Indeed. com (`https://www.indeed.com/q-React-jobs.html`), there are close to 56,000 open React developer positions.

- The React library is light (around 100KB) and fast.

- React is easy to start using.

React Advantages and Limitations

As I mentioned, when React is compared with other web frameworks such as jQuery, Angular, and Vue.js, the biggest advantage is that React uses the VDOM and can improve performance. Here are few more advantages:

- React can be used as a single-page application (SPA) like with Create-React-App (CRA) or for server-side rendering (SSR) like with Gatsby. js and Next.js.

- React can follow unidirectional data flow as well as data binding.

- React's JSX produces better code readability.

- React was made to integrate with other frameworks easily.

React has a few limitations, listed here:

- On its own, React is just a UI library, not a full-blown framework like Angular.

- Developers are left to decide which libraries to add and which best practices to follow.

- React has a steeper learning curve to master than other tools.

React Template Starter Project

When it comes to creating React applications, there many options to choose from. You can just write the code yourself and then add libraries to help you take care of packaging your code, getting it ready for production (the toolchain), and doing other common tasks that are standard when writing code.

Note   The React *toolchain* is a set of programming tools used to perform the complex development tasks for our final development/deployment product.

Another option to get started is for you to use the many React starter template projects that already take care of the scaffolding and configurations and include libraries to help you get the job done quickly. The most popular template for creating a React app is Create-React-App (`https://github.com/facebook/create-react-app`); the project was created by Facebook and has 85,000 stars on GitHub. CRA is based on a single-page application, so there is no page refresh, and the experience feels like you are inside a mobile app. The pages are meant to be rendered on the client side. This is ideal for small to medium-sized projects.

The other option is SSR, which renders the page on the server so the client (browser) will display the app without doing any work. SSR is good for certain use cases, where there is a lot going on and the user experience would be sluggish if the rendering happened on the client side.

CRA doesn't support SSR out of the box. There are ways to configure and get CRA to work with SSR, but that may be too complex for some developers and involve maintaining the configuration on your own, so it may not be worth the effort.

If you're building something that needs SSR, it's better to just work with different React libraries that are already configured out of the box with SSR such as the Next.js framework, Razzle, or Gatsby (which converts a prerendered website into HTML at build time).

If you prefer SSR with React check out Next.js, Razzle, or Gatsby.

With that being said, with CRA you can do prerendering, which is the closest you can get to SSR, as you will see in later chapters of this book when we optimize our React app.

In this book's examples, we will be using CRA; however, the components we will be building are loosely coupled and can be easily imported into any React project with little or no effort.

Tip   We will be using CRA in this book, and the projects will be easy to follow. However, feel free to use any React template starter project or even create your React project from scratch and handle your own toolchain. In Chapter 10, I will show you how to set up your project with React using SSR with Next.js.

Prerequisites

The libraries we will be installing are submitted to NPM (https://www.npmjs.com/). Node.js is needed to get NPM, and NPM is used to download packages from the NPM repository.

NPM and Node.js go hand in hand. NPM is the JavaScript package manager and is the default package manager for the JavaScript Node.js environment.

Installing Node and NPM on a Mac/PC

If you don't have Node.js installed, you will need to install it. Node.js needs to be at least at version 8.16.0 or 10.16.0. The reason we need that version is we need to use NPX, which is an NPM task runner introduced in 2017 that is used to set up CRA.

Make sure you have it by checking the version, as shown here:

```
$ node -v
```

If it's not installed, you can install it for both Mac and PC from here (Figure 1-1):

```
https://nodejs.org/en/
```

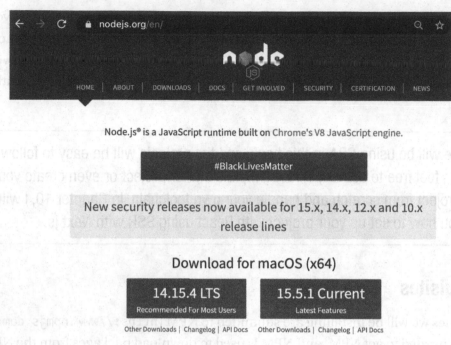

Figure 1-1. *Downloading Node.js on a Mac*

The installer recognizes your platform, so if you are on a PC, it's the same steps.

Once you download the installer, run it; once that's complete, run the node command in Terminal/DOS.

```
$ node -v
```

The command will output the Node.js version number.

Download Libraries: Yarn or NPM

To download packages from the NPM repository, we have two options: Yarn or NPM. NPM comes with Node.js and can be used without installation. However, in this book, we mostly will use another library: Yarn. We will be using Yarn as much as possible for downloading packages instead of NPM.

The reason we will be using Yarn instead of NPM in this book is that Yarn is faster than NPM. Yarn caches the installed packages as well as installs packages simultaneously. We have NPM installed as well because it comes with Node.js.

Install Yarn on a Mac/PC

To install Yarn on a Mac, a good option is brew in Terminal.

$ brew install yarn

Just like with Node.js, running Yarn with the -v flag outputs the version number.

$ yarn -v

On a PC you can download the MSI download file from here:

https://classic.yarnpkg.com/latest.msi

You can find more installation options here:

https://classic.yarnpkg.com/en/docs/install/#mac-stable

Create-React-App MHL Template Project

Equipped with Node.js as well as NPM and Yarn, we are ready to get started. We can use the CRA Must-Have-Libraries (MHL) template project I have created for you at https://github.com/EliEladElrom/cra-template-must-have-libraries.

CRA is opinionated and includes libraries such as Jest, service workers, and ES6. The MHL template project is even more opinionated and includes the following libraries:

- *Type checker*: TypeScript

- *Preprocessors*: Sass/SCSS

- *State management*: Redux Toolkit/Recoil

- *CSS framework*: Material-UI

- *CSS-in-JS modules*: Styled Components

- *Router*: React Router

- *Unit testing*: Jest and Enzyme + Sinon

- *E2E testing*: Jest and Puppeteer

- Folder structure

- Generate templates

- ESLint and Prettier

- *Other useful libraries*: Lodash, Moment, Classnames, Serve, react-snap, React-Helmet, Analyzer Bundle

If you want to understand how these libraries were installed, you can create your own template or modify an existing one. That is beyond the scope of this book; however, you can read this article for a complete step-by-step installation of each library:

https://medium.com/react-courses/setting-up-professional-react-project-with-must-have-reactjs-libraries-2020-9358edf9acb3

Or you can take my course on Udemy:

https://www.udemy.com/course/getting-started-react17-with-must-have-libraries/

Let's begin by creating our react-d3-hello-world "Hello World" project with Yarn with one command, as shown here:

```
$ yarn create react-app react-d3-hello-world --template must-have-libraries
```

Or we can use npx, as shown here:

```
$ npx create-react-app react-d3-hello-world --template must-have-libraries
```

Once the installation of libraries and all the dependencies have completed downloading, you can run the project by starting a local server.

Change the directory to the react-d3-hello-world project and run the start command in Terminal (see Figure 1-2).

```
$ cd react-d3-hello-world
$ yarn start
```

```
Compiled successfully!

You can now view react-d3-hello-world in the browser.

  Local:            http://localhost:3000
  On Your Network:  http://192.168.0.143:3000

Note that the development build is not optimized.
To create a production build, use yarn build.
```

Figure 1-2. *CRA compiled successfully*

You can see this run command in the package.json file. The command points to the react-scripts library and starts the project on a local server on port 3000 as the default (which you can change).

Now navigate to the localhost and view the project, as shown in Figure 1-3.

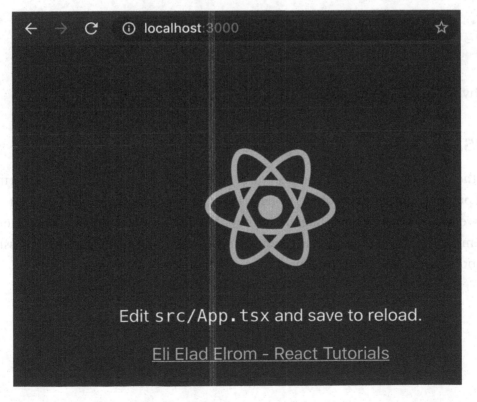

Figure 1-3. *Local server running CRA starter project*

Type Checker: TypeScript

When it comes to writing React code, there are two options to choose from; you can write your code using JavaScript (JS) or TypeScript (TS). TypeScript is a transpiler, meaning ES6 doesn't understand TS, but TS gets compiled down to standard JS, which can be done with Babel.

The CRA MHL project is already set up with TS as a type checker out of the box, so there is nothing you need to do. However, I want to expand a bit on why I picked TS over JS.

Why Should You Integrate TypeScript into Your React Project?

Here are a few interesting facts:

- Did you know that TypeScript is an open source programming language developed and maintained by Microsoft?

- According to Stack Overflow's 2020 survey, the TypeScript programming language is the second most popular, surpassing even Python last year!

Why is TypeScript so popular?

TS vs. JS, What's the Big Deal?

TS, as the name suggests, is all about setting "types." TS is easier to debug and test than JS and prevents potential problems by describing what to expect (you will see that when we test our components later in this book). Using TS, a full blown object-oriented programming (OOP) language and modules brings development to a more professional level and increases our code quality.

If we do a quick TS over JS comparison:

- TypeScript is an OOP; JavaScript is a scripting language.

- TypeScript uses static typing following the ECMAScript specification.

- TypeScript supports modules.

A type system associates a type to each value—by examining the flow of these values, it ensures there are no type errors.

Static typing means that types are checked before runtime (allowing you to track bugs before runtime).

JS includes only the following eight dynamic (at runtime) types: BigInt, Boolean, Integers, Null, Number, Strings, Symbol, Object (objects, functions, and arrays), and Undefined.

Note   All these types are called *primitive types*, except for Object, which is called a *nonprimitive type*. TS adds static types to JavaScript by setting a compiler to type-check the source code to turn it into dynamic code.

React and TypeScript work nicely together, as TypeScript improves the code quality of your app using OOP best practices, so it's worth the learning curve.

The latest version of TS is the version 4 public iteration. To play around with coding in TS, you can run TS code in the TS Playground at https://www.typescriptlang.org/play/ (see Figure 1-4).

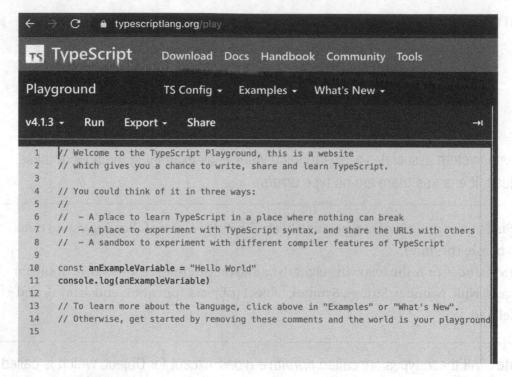

Figure 1-4. TS Playground

The TS Playground site has plenty of examples that can help you better understand TS. I recommend exploring these examples.

Notice the example uses "strict," and in the TS Config menu item, you can set the compiler options. The different compiler options are explained at `https://www.typescriptlang.org/docs/handbook/compiler-options.html`.

It may be antagonizing writing your code with errors and warning popping up left and right at compile time, but it is worth it as it will help you avoid issues later when the compiler can't figure out the types and your app breaks during runtime.

Tip   We would rather our app breaks during compile time than runtime.

I mentioned that TS is an OOP language and follows the ECMAScript specification; however, the specification is a living thing and changes often, so you can specify the ECMAScript (ES) target. See Figure 1-5.

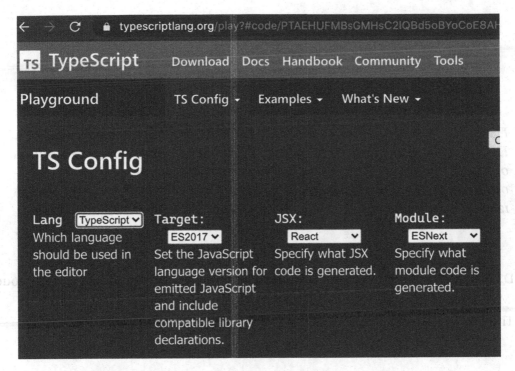

Figure 1-5. *Specify the ECMAScript (ES) target in the TS playground*

A great place to start with TS is to understand its power by looking at the different types available. If you are just getting started with TS, it's beyond the scope of this book to explain the types, but I welcome you to check the following article, which also includes a cheat sheet with plenty of examples:

```
https://medium.com/react-courses/instant-write-reactjs-typescript-
components-complete-beginners-guide-with-a-cheatsheet-e32a76022a44
```

D3

D3 (aka D3js or D3.js) stands for "data-driven documents," and it enables you to create neat data-driven documents (`https://github.com/d3/d3`). It is a chart library that helps bring data to life. It was created by Mike Bostock at the *New York Times* to create interactive web visualizations. It was based on his work during his PhD studies at the Stanford Visualization Group.

- D3 includes a comprehensive library with close to 170 examples. See `https://observablehq.com/@d3/gallery`.

- D3 takes advantage of these base technologies: JavaScript, HTML, CSS3, Canvas, and last but not least SVG.

D3.js is a JavaScript library for manipulating documents based on data. D3 helps you bring data to life using HTML, SVG, and CSS. D3's emphasis on web standards gives you the full capabilities of modern browsers without tying yourself to a proprietary framework, combining powerful visualization components and a data-driven approach to DOM manipulation.

`https://d3js.org/`

D3 is written in JavaScript and focuses on attaching data to Document Object Model (DOM) elements.

The process of typical pure D3 can be split into three efforts.

- *Attach*: Attach data to DOM elements.

- *Display*: Use CSS, HTML, and/or SVG to display data.

- *Interactive*: Make data interactive with the use of D3 data-driven transformations and transitions.

The latest version at the time of writing is v6. Read the changelog (`https://github.com/d3/d3/blob/master/CHANGES.md`) to see what's new in version 6.

D3 has a steep learning curve, and adding React and TypeScript to the mix makes the curve even steeper.

In fact, D3 has more than 30 modules and 1,000 methods! To get a deep understanding of D3, there are few free resources provided by the D3 team.

- `https://observablehq.com/@d3/learn-d3`

- `https://observablehq.com/@observablehq/five-minute-introduction?collection=@observablehq/notebook-fundamentals`

D3 Version >4

As I mentioned, D3 is in its sixth iteration. In D3 version 4 and up, the biggest change is that D3 is modular. Thanks to this modularity, you can import only what is needed instead of bringing in the entire kitchen sink. Here's an example:

```
$yarn add d3-axis d3-interpolate d3-scale d3-selection
```

Keep in mind that with TS, we need to bring in the types as well (yarn @types/ module-name).

Tip   When you look at examples on the Web such as the ones at https:// observablehq.com/@d3/gallery, it's important to check the D3 version used in that example. D3 v4 and up have gone through a major change, and upgrading requires good knowledge of the D3 libraries.

Other Data Viz Libraries

In addition to D3, there are many other React libraries built on top of D3 including ready-to-use components. Here are some of the more popular ones:

- *Recharts*: https://github.com/recharts/recharts

- *Visx*: https://github.com/airbnb/visx (examples: https:// airbnb.io/visx/gallery)

- *Nivo*: https://github.com/plouc/nivo (examples: https:// nivo.rocks/components)

- *React-vi*: https://github.com/uber/react-vis

- *Victory*: https://github.com/FormidableLabs/victory (examples: https://formidable.com/open-source/victory/gallery)

- *Semiotic*: https://github.com/nteract/semiotic (examples: https://semiotic.nteract.io/examples)

- *react-d3-components*: https://github.com/codesuki/react-d3-components (examples: https://github.com/codesuki/react-d3-components#examples)

In Chapter 9, I will show you how to implement some of these popular libraries as well as review the libraries to help you pick one.

Many will argue that the last thing we need is another chart component library, and they are right. If you need ready-to-use charts, there are plenty to choose from.

With that said, creating truly innovative and performant visualizations may be a challenge using a chart library, and you will likely find yourself needing to use D3 or fork an existing chart library and make changes.

In addition to D3 and React libraries, there are other high-level libraries that you can use such as Vega (`https://vega.github.io/vega-lite/`).

Additionally, there are business intelligence (BI) tools such as Tableau or PowerBI that you can use to analyze data as well as integrate that visualization into your React project.

Keep in mind that besides the top libraries I mentioned, GitHub is littered with failed attempts to make the ultimate chart library. You will quickly drown in options, flags, and `props` to satisfy all the use cases.

D3 is the ultimate "chart lib." If you want to do a customized data visualization, take the time to learn D3.

With that being said, there are specific projects that require a quicker release or greater customization such as proof-of-concept (POC) projects. In these cases, knowing what's out there and how to integrate or fork it will come in handy, so I will cover some of these libraries for your reference in Chapter 9.

ReactTransitionGroup Adds-Ons

Besides D3, `ReactCSSTransitionGroup` is one example of a React library that provides a high-level API based on `ReactTransitionGroup`. It is an easy way to perform CSS transitions and animations when a React component enters or leaves the DOM (the library is inspired by Angular's `ng-animate`).

You can use this library as well as others in conjunction with other libraries such as D3; you can learn more about it here: `https://reactjs.org/docs/animation.html`.

React v17 + D3 + TypeScript

We have covered our starter project called `react-d3-hello-world` as well as looked at TypeScript and D3, so we can now put it all together and create our first "Hello World" D3 project.

First, install D3 and all the D3 types (for TS).

```
$ yarn add d3 @types/d3
```

React Function Component with D3

Next, let's create a simple component; we'll call it `HelloD3`. For that we will be using a template that I created using the `generate-react-cli` library (`https://github.com/arminbro/generate-react-cli`) to move the files and create the folder structure.

```
npx generate-react-cli component HelloD3 --type=d3
```

You can see the settings here: `generate-react-cli.json`. Navigate to `src/components`, and you can see that three files were generated for you automatically (see Figure 1-6).

- `HelloD3.scss`

- `HelloD3.test.tsx`

- `HelloD3.tsx`

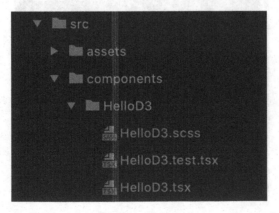

Figure 1-6. *HelloD3 components*

17

App.tsx

Open our app entry point, which is App.tsx, and add the HelloD3 component we created.

```
import React from 'react'
import './App.scss'
import HelloD3 from './components/HelloD3/HelloD3'

function App() {
 return (
  <div className="App">
   <header className="App-header">
    <HelloD3 />
   </header>
  </div>
 )
}

export default App
```

Now, let's look at localhost again: http://localhost:3000/ (see Figure 1-7). You can see a "Hello World" message and two squares.

Figure 1-7. *CRA MHL D3 "Hello World"*

Congratulations, you just created your first project that integrates React with D3.

HelloD3.tsx

Now, let's examine the `HelloD3` component code.

```
// src/components/HelloD3/HelloD3
```

From React we will be using the `useEffect` and `refObject` libraries.

```
import React, { useEffect, RefObject } from 'react'
```

Let's import the style file; we are not using it right now, but it will be ready in case we need to add a style.

```
import './HelloD3.scss'
```

Next, we will import the whole D3 library.

```
import * as d3 from 'd3' // yarn add d3 @types/d3
```

For our component, we will be using a pure function component and set our reference object.

> *Refs provide a way to access* DOM *nodes or React elements created in the render method.*
>
> https://reactjs.org/docs/refs-and-the-dom.html

```
const HelloD3 = () => {
 const ref: RefObject<HTMLDivElement> = React.createRef()
```

Notice that the TS type is set to `HTMLDivElement`. How do I know that? I had to dig into the React code to find out the `ref` object type. This is common practice when using TS, and I find it helpful to dig inside the actual React libraries as it increases my understanding of React.

Next, we will use the `useEffect` hook to call a `draw()` method that we will create once the `useEffect` is called.

> *Hooks are a new addition in React 16.8. They let you use state and other React features without writing a class.*
>
> https://reactjs.org/docs/hooks-effect.html

```
useEffect(() => {
  draw()
})
```

Our `draw()` method consists of "selecting" or choosing the HTML element we will be using. Next, we "append" or in other words add a text element that says "Hello World."

Note   Throughout the book I will often be using the `draw()` function and not listing the `draw()` function as dependent in `useEffect`. The best approach is to memorize the draw object with `useCallback` to ensure there won't be an infinite loop (see `https://reactjs.org/docs/hooks-reference.html#usecallback`). If you are unfamiliar with this method, I will be covering this when I show you how to optimize in Chapter 11 (the `Memorize` function with `useCallback`).

In addition, we select the SVG element we will render in JSX, append a group element and a rectangle element, and transform the width and fill color attributes on the SVG. Our SVG is of size 250×500px.

```
const draw = () => {
  d3.select(ref.current).append('p').text('Hello World')
  d3.select('svg').append('g').attr('transform', 'translate(250, 0)').
  append('rect').attr('width', 500).attr('height', 500).attr('fill', 'tomato')
}

return (
```

On the JSX rendering side, we set our `div` that holds our reference we are using to add the text element.

```
<div className="HelloD3" ref={ref}>
```

Similarly, we set an SVG element with a width and height of 500px, and inside we draw a rectangle that fills that space with green color.

```
<svg width="500" height="500">
  <g transform="translate(0, 0)">
    <rect width="500" height="500" fill="green" />
```

```
      </g>
    </svg>
  </div>
 )
}
```

```
export default HelloD3
```

What's happening here is that we have a rectangle in the size of 500×500px and then D3 overlays another rectangle in the size of 250×500px, which takes half the size of the React JSX rectangle.

This example is simple and doesn't show why we would need D3 as we can just write this text and these rectangle elements in JSX and have our code be more readable.

However, this is a simple minimalist "Hello World," intended to help you understand the working pieces, and later in this chapter, you will see the power of d3.HelloD3.scss.

Our div included a className called HelloD3 that is tied to our HelloD3.scss file.

```
<div className="HelloD3" ref={ref}>
```

Our SCSS file content just holds a placeholder at this time.

```
// src/components/HelloD3/HelloD3.scss
```

```
.HelloD3 {
}
```

Our project comes out of the box with SCSS, and Webpack is already configured with the SCSS loader, so in addition to CSS, you can just use SCSS without configuring anything.

If you haven't used SCSS before, you may be asking, why am I using SCSS and not CSS?

CSS Preprocessors: Sass/SCSS

Cascading Style Sheets (CSS) is a core functionality in HTML, and you need to familiarize yourself with CSS if you are not already. This goes for working with HTML in particular and with React specifically. On large projects, CSS preprocessors are often used to complement CSS and add functionality.

There are four main CSS preprocessors that are often used with React projects: Sass/SCSS, PostCSS, Less, and Stylus.

Note   CSS is used to represent the visual layout of the web page on different devices. CSS preprocessors are often used to enhance CSS functionality.

The quick answer is that Sass/SCSS is better for the majority of today's projects, so that's what we will be using.

Sass/SCSS is the most popular and will probably lead you to the best paying jobs as a developer according to surveys (`https://ashleynolan.co.uk/blog/frontend-tooling-survey-2019-results`). Sass/SCSS is considered a well-known tool. If you want to learn more and see a comparison between the different CSS preprocessors, check out my article on Medium: `http://shorturl.at/dJQT3`.

HelloD3.test.tsx

As I mentioned, you already have a unit testing test file created for you automatically.

```
// src/component/HelloD3/HelloD3.test.tsx

import React from 'react'
import { shallow } from 'enzyme'
import HelloD3 from './HelloD3'

describe('<HelloD3 />', () => {
 let component

 beforeEach(() => {
  component = shallow(<HelloD3 />)
 })

 test('It should mount', () => {
  expect(component.length).toBe(1)
 })
})
```

If you look at the code, you can see that the test file only tests that the component was mounted (added) to our display.

```
expect(component.length).toBe(1)
```

The code is using the Jest and Enzyme libraries. Jest comes out of the box with CRA and Enzyme, and Sinon comes out of the box with MHL, so there's nothing you need to do on your part to get that configured.

Why Jest and Enzyme + Sinon?

Jest and Enzyme + Sinon

Jest is a JavaScript unit testing framework and the standard for React applications. It was built to be used with any JavaScript project, and it comes with CRA out of the box. However, we do need Jest-dom and Enzyme to enhance the capabilities of Jest.

Sinon

Another must-have library that we should be aware of and add to our toolbox is Sinon (https://github.com/sinonjs/sinon).

Jest and Sinon serve the same purpose, but there are times that you may find one framework more natural and easier to work with for the specific test.

I wanted to introduce you to testing as early as possible, as it's an integral part of development and needs to be considered when building interfaces.

```
$ yarn test
```

Now to get the tests running, the package.json file is already configured with a run task.

```
"test": "react-scripts test"
```

When you run the script, you can see that the test passed, as shown in Figure 1-8.

```
PASS   src/App.test.tsx
PASS   src/components/HelloD3/HelloD3.test.tsx
PASS   src/AppRouter.test.tsx


Test Suites: 3 passed, 3 total
Tests:       3 passed, 3 total
Snapshots:   0 total
Time:        6.891s, estimated 14s
Ran all test suites related to changed files.


Watch Usage
 › Press a to run all tests.
 › Press f to run only failed tests.
 › Press q to quit watch mode.
 › Press p to filter by a filename regex pattern.
 › Press t to filter by a test name regex pattern.
 › Press Enter to trigger a test run.
```

Figure 1-8. *The unit testing tests passed*

As you make changes to your component, make sure to update the unit testing file as well as test different portions of the component functionality.

I want to point out that your project also comes with end-to-end (e2e) testing out of the box.

```
"test:e2e": "jest -c e2e/jest.config.js",
"test:e2e-alone": "node e2e/puppeteer_standalone.js",
"test:e2e-watch": "jest -c e2e/jest.config.js --watch"
```

As I mentioned earlier, if you want to understand how these libraries were installed, you can create your own template or modify one. That is beyond the scope of this book; however, you can read this article for the step-by-step installation process of each library:

https://medium.com/react-courses/setting-up-professional-react-project-with-must-have-reactjs-libraries-2020-9358edf9acb3

Or you can take my course on Udemy, which includes a 40-page ebook to help you understand all the moving pieces and how they were installed and configured:

https://www.udemy.com/course/getting-started-react17-with-must-have-libraries/

React Class Component with D3

In the previous section, we created a function component. If we want to create a React class component that integrates D3, the process is similar. We can use the template I set up for you as a starting point:

```
$ npx generate-react-cli component HelloD3Class --type=d3class
```

Just like with the React function component, the d3class creates three files.

- HelloD3Class.scss

- HelloD3Class.test.tsx

- HelloD3Class.tsx

HelloD3Class.tsx

Let's review HelloD3Class.tsx.

The difference is that we set the reference object before we set the constructor; then on the constructor level we can initialize the reference object.

Once the component lifecycle event componentDidMount is called, we can append our elements to the DOM.

Take a look:

```
import React, { RefObject } from 'react'
import './HelloD3Class.scss'
import * as d3 from 'd3' // yarn add d3 @types/d3

export default class HelloD3Class extends React.PureComponent<IHelloD3Class
Props, IHelloD3ClassState> {
 ref: RefObject<HTMLDivElement>

 constructor(props: IHelloD3ClassProps) {
  super(props)
  this.state = {
```

```
  // TODO
  }
  this.ref = React.createRef()
}

componentDidMount() {
  d3.select(this.ref.current).append('p').text('Hello World')

  // const svg = d3.select(this.myRef.current).append('svg').attr('width',
      500).attr('height', 500)
  d3.select('svg')
   .append('g')
   .attr('transform', 'translate(250, 0)')
   .append('rect').attr('width', 500)
   .attr('height', 500)
   .attr('fill', 'tomato')
}

render() {
  return (
   <div className="HelloD3Class" ref={this.ref}>
    <svg width="500" height="500">
     <g transform="translate(0, 0)">
      <rect width="500" height="500" fill="green" />
     </g>
    </svg>
   </div>
  )
 }
}

interface IHelloD3ClassProps {
// TODO
}

interface IHelloD3ClassState {
// TODO
}
```

Lint ESLint and Prettier

How neat would it be to have a code review and have someone formatting your code to make sure it's consistent?

> *All code in any code-base should look like a single person typed it, no matter how many people contributed.*
>
> —Rick Waldron

Luckily, this can be done.

Lint is a tool for analyzing your code. It is a static code analysis tool created to identify problematic patterns found in code. Prettier is an opinionated code formatter.

Note   *Linting* is the process of running a program to analyze your code to find potential errors.

Lint tools can analyze your code and warn you of potential errors. For it to work, we need to configure it with specific rules.

It's not wise to get into a debate about whether there should be two spaces in every newline or a tab, single quote, double quotes, etc. The idea is to have somewhat of a style guide and follow the style for consistency. As was nicely said,

> *Arguments over style are pointless. There should be a style guide, and you should follow it.*
>
> —Rebecca Murphey

Airbnb—as part of its style guide—provides an ESLint configuration that anyone can use and become the standard.

ESLint is already installed on CRA MHL template, but it's optimized with a styling guide you don't need to do a thing to enjoy using it.

The project is already set up with ESLint and Prettier for TypeScript using Airbnb's styling guide (which is considered the standard).

However, if you want to understand better, read my article at `https://medium.com/react-courses/react-create-react-app-v3-4-1-a55f3e7a8d6d` to set up your project with ESLint and Prettier for TypeScript using Airbnb's styling guide.

There are three files that were configured for you.

- .eslintrc: ESLint run commands configuration file

- .eslintignore: ESLint ignore files

- .prettierrc: Prettier run commands configuration file

The package.json file's run scripts are already there for you, so we can run the lint and format utilities and even run the app build (the production build we will cover later in this book) with just one command.

```
"scripts": {
  ..
  ..
  ..
  "lint": "eslint --ext .js,.jsx,.ts,.tsx src --color",
  "format": "prettier --write 'src/**/*.{ts,tsx,scss,css,json}'",
  "isready": "npm run format && npm run lint && npm run build"
}
```

We are ready to let lint do its job and change our code, as shown in Figure 1-9.

```
$ yarn run lint
```

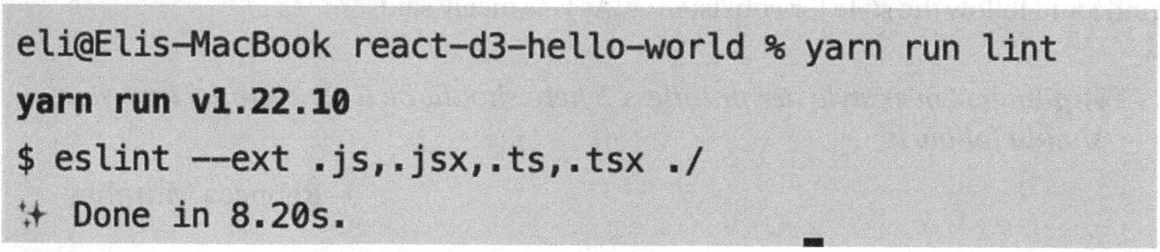

```
eli@Elis-MacBook react-d3-hello-world % yarn run lint
yarn run v1.22.10
$ eslint --ext .js,.jsx,.ts,.tsx ./
✦ Done in 8.20s.
```

Figure 1-9. *Output after running the lint command*

To run the formatter to clean our code, we can use yarn as well, as shown here (see Figure 1-10):

```
$ yarn run format
```

```
eli@Elis-MacBook react-d3-hello-world % yarn run format
yarn run v1.22.10
$ prettier --write 'src/**/*.{ts,tsx,scss,css,json}'
src/App.scss 77ms
src/App.test.tsx 268ms
src/App.tsx 10ms
src/AppRouter.test.tsx 11ms
src/AppRouter.tsx 20ms
src/components/HelloD3/HelloD3.scss 5ms
src/components/HelloD3/HelloD3.test.tsx 10ms
src/components/HelloD3/HelloD3.tsx 24ms
src/index.scss 9ms
src/index.tsx 11ms
src/react-app-env.d.ts 4ms
src/redux/store.ts 10ms
src/serviceWorker.ts 86ms
src/setupTests.ts 13ms
+ Done in 1.26s.
```

Figure 1-10. *Output after running format*

Summary

In this chapter, I introduced you to the tools that we will be using throughout this book.

We talked about React and its advantages and limitations. We set up our starter project using CRA and the MHL template project and looked at TS, SCSS, unit testing, formatting, and linting. I also touched briefly on D3, ReactTransitionGroup add-ons, and other data viz libraries available to use.

We created our first "Hello World" project with React and D3 using TS as a function component as well as a class component, and we ensured its quality with testing, linting, and formatting.

Quality is important generally, and even more so when working with charts and animations as the resource. Low-quality code can cause a degraded user experience as many charts use large data sets (memory usage), as well as lots of CPU power, to render on the client's machine.

In the next chapter, we will continue learning how to create React components that utilize D3 to perform tasks such as drawing graphics, creating animations, and handling user interactions events.

CHAPTER 2

Graphics and Interactions

In this chapter, I will show you what your options are and break the process of creating charts down into smaller chunks so you can understand the process better before diving deeper and creating charts. The process can be broken into three layers: data, view, and user interaction.

At any part of these layers, you can use React, D3, or any other libraries that integrate with React. Having options is great; however, it can also be confusing to decide what to use and when. Understanding your options is important as it helps you make an educated decision.

This chapter is broken down into three main sections.

- Graphics

- User gestures

- Animating

In the first portion of this chapter, I will show you how to create graphics with HTML and SVG elements using both React function components and class components. We will utilize React's JSX as well as D3. We will consume data and draw elements. In the last portion of this section, we will create our first simple chart.

In the second part of this chapter, I will show you how to set mouse events, both in React and in D3.

Lastly, we will learn about animating graphics using React and also how to animate with D3.

By the end of this chapter, you will understand what your options are when it comes to drawing, setting events, and animating graphics. Along the way, I will show you options for setting up function and class components, and we'll talk a bit about component lifecycle hooks. Also, I will give you some tips.

Let's begin.

© Elad Elrom 2021
E. Elrom, *Integrating D3.js with React*, https://doi.org/10.1007/978-1-4842-7052-3_2

Overview of Creating Charts

As I mentioned, to create a data visualization component, the process can be broken down into three main layers: data, view, and user interactions.

Let's take a look at what each layer includes.

The data layer consists of the following tasks:

- Get the data.

- Set the data.

- Process the data.

The view layer consists of the following:

- Integrate with the React lifecycle hooks.

- Draw a chart.

- Style the component.

The user interaction layer consists of the following:

- Add transitions.

- Handle user gestures.

When drawing charts, a good place to start is with the data. You need to see what story the data is telling. Once you understand the story, it's time to select a chart. There are many different ready-made chart libraries you can integrate, and you can also create your custom solution with D3. Your options are limitless. No matter what you decide to use, understanding the basics of how everything works is crucial.

Drawing Graphics

As you probably know, React JSX code may look a lot like HTML, but it is not. It's JavaScript extension (JSX) code.

Note   JSX is a React extension that uses JavaScript tags that mimic HTML code, so the code is mostly similar to HTML, but it is not HTML.

To understand why React is using JSX instead of just pure HTML, we first need to talk about the Document Object Model (DOM). React processes your JSX code in the background before committing these changes into the user's browser to speed up how quickly the user's page loads.

Note   The Document Object Model (DOM) is an in-memory representation of HTML and is tree-structured.

React has made an effort to match HTML, and JSX can recognize tags that are supported in HTML. A good example is SVG. We saw in Chapter 1 how we are able to add SVG tags to our React rendering portion.

> *Scalable Vector Graphics (SVG) is an XML-based markup language for describing two-dimensional-based vector graphics. As such, it's a text-based, open Web standard for describing images that can be rendered cleanly at any size and are designed specifically to work well with other web standards including CSS, DOM, JavaScript, and SMIL. SVG is, essentially, to graphics what HTML is to text.*

<code>https://developer.mozilla.org/en-US/docs/Web/SVG</code>

SVG elements include many different types of graphics, and each element has its own set of attributes from an image to a circle, a line, a text element, a rectangle, a group, and so on. Even the most seasoned HTML developers are unaware of all the SVG elements and properties in the SVG API.

To learn more about SVG, you can see the complete list of available SVG tags here:

`https://developer.mozilla.org/en-US/docs/Web/SVG/Element`

I recommend you bookmark this page and reference it when needed.

SVG vs. HTML

To draw graphics, SVG is the standard. SVG is mature and at the time of writing is at version 2 (since 2016). You can read about version 2 here:

`https://github.com/w3c/svgwg/wiki/SVG-2-new-features`

However, I want to point out there are other ways to draw graphics. For example, we can use the HTML `<canvas>` element via JavaScript. The `<canvas>` element is a container for graphics.

SVG gives better performance with a smaller number of objects or a larger surface. A canvas gives better performance with a smaller surface or a larger number of objects.

A canvas can become blurry, and the device pixel ratio needs to be checked and adjusted. To avoid blurry images with different device pixel ratios, check out the Mozilla documentation here:

`https://developer.mozilla.org/en-US/docs/Web/API/Window/devicePixelRatio`

Here is a quick rundown of the differences between using a canvas and SVG:

- SVG allows styling with CSS; a canvas can only be changed through scripts.

- SVG is vector-based; a canvas is raster-based (a rectangular grid of pixels).

- SVG gives better scalability than a canvas, so once an element needs scaling, SVG is preferred.

- SVG has a performance advantage over a canvas for a larger screen and a low number of objects; however, if you work with a smaller screen size and many objects, a canvas is better.

JSX Canvas

A canvas (`https://www.w3schools.com/html/html5_canvas.asp`) can be used to draw components in HTML. In fact, not only can you use a canvas to draw components, but you can also animate it and manipulate the element attributes. The React JSX version of a canvas is no different.

Let's create an example. We can use the same project we created in Chapter 1 (`react-d3-hello-world`) and add a component that will include a canvas. You can download the final code of all the examples of this chapter from the book's repository.

`https://github.com/Apress/integrating-d3.js-with-react/tree/main/ch02`

JSXCanvas.tsx

We will call the component JSXCanvas. You can create the file on your own, or you can get help from generate-react-cli using the template I set up for you.

```
npx generate-react-cli component JSXCanvas --type=d3
```

In our JSXCanvas component, we will use the canvas JSX component, which matches the HTML canvas. We will change the attributes to change the color of the canvas to be tomato red.

Let's take a look at the code.

```
// src/component/JSXCanvas/JSXCanvas.tsx
```

First, we import the React libraries we will be using and the SCSS file.

```
import React, { RefObject, useEffect, useRef } from 'react'
import './JSXCanvas.scss'
```

We will be using the ref object and useEffect. We first create a reference to our canvas.

When it comes to TypeScript, we need to define the type of objects (when the type is not clearly inferred by the assignment of a value). For a canvas, that would be of type HTMLCanvasElement.

```
const JSXCanvas = () => {

  const canvasRef: RefObject<HTMLCanvasElement> = useRef(null)
```

Once the component is initialized, we can set the useEffect method.

What is useEffect? useEffect is called after the rendering process is completed. useEffect checks dependency values from the last render and will call your effect function if any one of them has changed.

In our case, when that happens, we can draw our canvas. We are working here with the React function component, and setting a draw method is a good way to go instead of just writing the code inside useEffect, because the function can be used by other methods. However, there are cases where writing the actual code inside useEffect would make more sense, as you will see later in this book.

```
useEffect(() => {
  draw()
})
```

Our draw method will use the reference we created to the `<canvas>` element, and then using the canvas context, we can set the canvas attributes such as `width`, `height`, and `color`.

> *The CanvasRenderingContext2D interface, part of the Canvas API, provides the 2D rendering context for the drawing surface of an <canvas> element. It is used for drawing shapes, text, images, and other objects.*
>
> https://developer.mozilla.org/en-US/docs/Web/API/
> CanvasRenderingContext2D

Take a look:

```
const draw = () => {
  const canvas = canvasRef.current
  const context = canvas?.getContext('2d')
  if (context) {
    context.fillStyle = 'tomato'
    context.fillRect(0, 0, context.canvas.width, context.canvas.height)
  }
}
```

Lastly, on the render side, we will set up the JSX canvas with the reference we created.

```
return (
  <>
    <canvas ref={canvasRef} />
  </>
)
}
export default JSXCanvas
```

There is another way to write less code in regard to the reference. Instead of defining the variable and then assigning it in the component, we can do that inline. Let's take a look.

We set the `ref`.

```
ref: SVGCircleElement | undefined
```

Next, we can assign the `ref` inline inside the JSX code.

```
<canvas
  ref={canvasRef} />
  // eslint-disable-next-line no-return-assign
  ref={(ref: SVGCircleElement) => (this.ref = ref)}
/>
```

However, this is not the cleanest code since we are not supposed to return the assignment according to best coding practices; however, that's why I am disabling the ESLint from complaining by adding an `eslint` comment. This approach is not recommended, though, because of the ambiguity of the code; I wanted you to see these options.

App.tsx

Remember to add the component to your `App.tsx` parent component.

```
// src/App.tsx

function App() {
  return (
    <div className="App">
      <header className="App-header">
        <JSXCanvas />
      </header>
    </div>
  )
}
```

To see the graphic, make sure you are still running on port 3000 from Chapter 1.

```
$ yarn start
```

Figure 2-1 shows the final results.

Figure 2-1. *Canvas drawing manipulated to size and color we selected*

What about scaling? Yes, you can use scaling and adjust the canvas based on the screen size to avoid your canvas turning blurry once it's enlarged. To do that, use context.scale.

```
const { devicePixelRatio: ratio = 1 } = window
context.scale(ratio, ratio)
```

However, SVG would give better results if you wanted that crispy print quality on all devices or you needed scaling such as for zooming functionality. I am not going to dive deeper into canvas as I recommend staying with SVG; however, I wanted you to be aware that it's possible, and if you ever have a use case that needs a canvas such as in a case targeting a smaller screen size and many objects, you will have it in your toolbox.

React SVG

To create SVG graphics with React, let's add another component, called HelloSVG.

```
npx generate-react-cli component HelloSVG --type=d3
```

The generate-react-cli template already includes the code we need to write to show an SVG element in React. Take a look:

```
import React from 'react'
import './HelloSVG.scss'

const HelloSVG = () => {

  return (
    <div className="HelloSVG">
      <svg width="500" height="500">
        <g transform="translate(0, 0)">
          <rect width="300" height="300" fill="tomato" />
        </g>
      </svg>
    </div>
  )
}

export default HelloSVG
```

Notice that I am using the transform attribute. The transform shifts the group element to top left corner. You can read more about the transform attribute in the Mozilla documentation.

https://developer.mozilla.org/en-US/docs/Web/SVG/Attribute/transform

Now if we want to change the design properties on our rectangle without using the fill attribute to fill the SVG rectangle with a color. React has a matching attribute for the HTML class (https://developer.mozilla.org/en-US/docs/Web/SVG/Attribute/class): className. We can assign a class name and define that in our SCSS file. That's nothing new, and that's how all React component operate.

```
// HelloSVG.tsx
<rect className="myRect" width="300" height="300" />

// HelloSVG.scss
.myRect {
  fill: #ba2121;
}
```

Lastly, we need to add our component into our enter point `App.tsx`.

```
// src/App.tsx
```

```
<HelloSVG />
```

Figure 2-2 shows our SVG rectangle element.

Figure 2-2. *Drawing a rectangle using SVG*

The `transform` attribute can be used for many things such as rotate, scale, and skews.

For example, if we want to implement the example from the Mozilla docs (`https://developer.mozilla.org/en-US/docs/Web/SVG/Attribute/transform`). The example is using `xlink` to assign an SVG path to an element for reuse in order to create a heart shape and a shadow effect. Unfortunately, you will often see that you cannot just copy and paste most code you will see online (D3 related or not) into React without some level of modification and knowledge of what you are doing.

In our case, the reason that the Mozilla example won't compile is that React SVG doesn't include use `xlink`, so this code will generate an error:

```
<use xlink:href="#heart" fill="none" stroke="white"/>
```

The code will generate the error "Type { xlink: true; } is not assignable to type SVGProps<SVGUseElement>."

The error is caused because the React `SVGUseElement` doesn't include `xlink` in the current version of React (version 17 at the time of writing). However, don't panic, because it's not the end of the world. What we need to do is define the tag, and then we can use it.

```
const useTag = '<use xlink:href="#heart" />'
```

Next, we can set up a group with an SVG path (in our case the shape of a heart), and the transform properties will align the heart to look like a shadow.

```
<g
  fill="grey"
  transform="rotate(-10 50 100)
    translate(-36 45.5)
    skewX(40)
    scale(1 0.5)"
>
  <path id="heart" d="M 10,30 A 20,20 0,0,1 50,30 A 20,20 0,0,1 90,30 Q
  90,60 50,90 Q 10,60 10,30 z" />
</g>
```

Then we can use the `useTag` constant we set up in an SVG tag that will drag the actual heart.

```
<svg dangerouslySetInnerHTML={{__html: useTag }} fill="none" stroke="white" />
```

The assignment to `useTag` is done using `dangerouslySetInnerHTML`.

`dangerouslySetInnerHTML` sounds scary, as the name suggests, you should be careful using it, as malicious code can be injected into that tag. That's why you would need to add the `eslint` comment to prevent ESLint from barking about this message.

```
{/* eslint-disable-next-line react/no-danger */}
```

In our case, we know what we are doing, and we are not passing some runtime string that can cause an injection attack, so we are fine.

Take a look at the entire code block:

```
const HelloSVG = () => {
  const useTag = '<use xlink:href="#heart" />'
  return (
    <div className="HelloSVG">
      <svg width="500" height="500">
        <g transform="translate(0, 0)">
          <rect className="myRect" width="300" height="300" /*
          fill="tomato" */ />
        </g>
        <g
          fill="grey"
          transform="rotate(-10 50 100)
            translate(-36 45.5)
            skewX(40)
            scale(1 0.5)"
        >
          <path id="heart" d="M 10,30 A 20,20 0,0,1 50,30 A 20,20 0,0,1
          90,30 Q 90,60 50,90 Q 10,60 10,30 z" />
        </g>
        {/* eslint-disable-next-line react/no-danger */}
        <svg dangerouslySetInnerHTML={{__html: useTag }} fill="none"
        stroke="white" />
      </svg>
    </div>
  )
}
```

The output creates for us the heart outline and shadow, as shown in Figure 2-3. If I wanted to add an outline to the shadow, that's not a problem. We can put the same SVG code inside the group element. Let's go ahead and try it.

Figure 2-3. *Using SVG with xlink*

Map Data in React Using JSX

To make it more realistic and interesting than just using SVG, we want to now pass data from the parent component using React props and draw the data using the HTML p tag with some straightforward React code. Let me show you how it's done.

HelloJSXData.tsx

Create a new component on your own or with the template and call it HelloJSXData.

```
npx generate-react-cli component HelloJSXData --type=d3
```

Next, import the style SCSS and React.

```
// src/component/HelloJSXData/HelloJSXData.tsx

import React from 'react'
import './HelloJSXData.scss'
```

Next, set the props we will be passing into our child component. I am pointing to an interface that I will define at the bottom of the file.

```
const HelloJSXData = ( props : IHelloJSXDataProps ) => {
```

On the JSX rendering side, I will be mapping the array and passing it from the parent component. Once the data is mapped, we can just display the data on the screen using the p HTML tag. Take a look:

```
return (
  <div className="HelloJSXData">
    {props.data.map((d, index) => (
      <p key={`key-${ d}`}>
        jsx {d}
      </p>
    ))}
  </div>)
}
```

Here is our interface for the props, just passing an array that is made out of strings:

```
interface IHelloJSXDataProps {
  data: string[]
}

export default HelloJSXData
App.tsx
```

As always, remember to add HelloJSXData to the app.

```
// src/app
function App() {
  return (
    <div className="App">
      <header className="App-header">
        <HelloJSXData data={['one', 'two', 'three', 'four']} />
      </header>
    </div>
  )
}
```

See the final results in Figure 2-4.

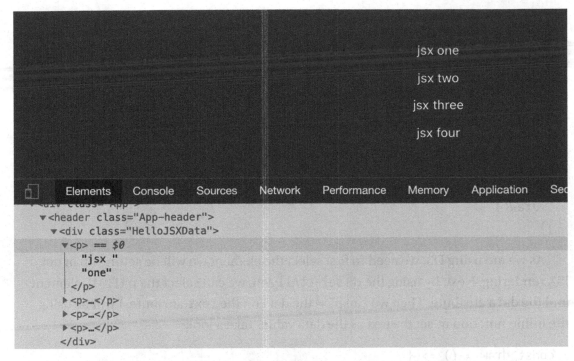

Figure 2-4. *Mapping data example using React code*

I am showing you how to use the p HTML tag to simplify things, but this could be an SVG element such as a circle or a rectangle, as I will be showing in the other examples.

Map Data in React Using D3

The previous example was pure, straightforward React code. In this example, let's add D3 to add a map and draw for us. Let's call the component HelloD3Data.

HelloD3Data.tsx

```
npx generate-react-cli component HelloD3Data --type=d3
```

We will be using D3, so make sure you already have D3 and the types imported, if you haven't done that for this project before.

```
yarn add d3 @types/d3
```

Let's start by defining the import we will be using.

```
// src/component/HelloD3Data/HelloD3Data.tsx

import React, { useEffect } from 'react'
import './HelloD3Data.scss'
import * as d3 from 'd3'
```

Just as before, we will set our props interface to pass the same array of strings.

```
const HelloD3Data = ( props : IHelloD3DataProps ) => {

  useEffect(() => {
    draw()
  })
```

As we are using D3, we need to first select the element we will be setting up in our JSX rendering. Next, by using the d3 selectAll API, we can select the p HTML element and the data attribute. Than we can pass the data on the text attribute. I will be using the inline function to set the text as the data value. Take a look:

```
  const draw = () => {
    d3.select('.HelloD3Data')
      .selectAll('p')
      .data(props.data)
      .enter()
      .append('p')
      .text((d) => `d3 ${ d}`)
  }
```

For our rendering, we'll set a div to be the wrapper for our p tags.

```
  return <div className="HelloD3Data" />
}

interface IHelloD3DataProps {
  data: string[]
}

export default HelloD3Data
```

Lastly, let's set the parent component.

```
// src/app
<HelloD3Data data={['one', 'two', 'three', 'four']} />
```

You can see the results in Figure 2-5.

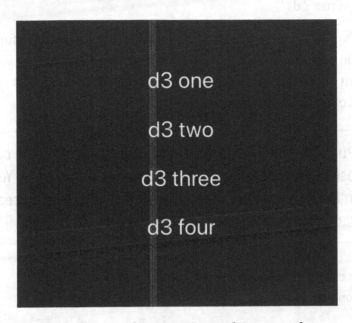

Figure 2-5. *Mapping data example using D3 and React code*

As you can see, when comparing the two examples of iterating through data between React and D3, D3 doesn't look as intuitive as React. Our example is simple in nature, but when there is a need for lots of calculation and a large data set, D3 will start to shine.

Simple Bar Chart with D3

So far, we have worked with simple examples and manipulated HTML elements such as <canvas>, p tags, and div. Additionally, we have worked with SVG and D3.

Now we are ready to create our first data visualization chart with D3 and React. Our example is similar to what we did in the previous example. We take data, and using the data attribute in D3, we will iterate through our data and use the rectangle SVG element to draw bars just as we used the p HTML tag. Take a look:

47

```
// src/component/SimpleChart/SimpleChart.tsx

import React, { RefObject } from 'react'
import './SimpleChart.scss'
import * as d3 from 'd3'
```

This time let's create our chart with a class component instead of a function component so you can see the difference.

I want to point out that it's preferred to extend React PureComponent when you don't need the shouldComponentUpdate life cycle event.

Tip   React.PureComponent gives a performance boost in some cases in exchange for losing the shouldComponentUpdate lifecycle hook. You can read about it more in the React docs (https://reactjs.org/docs/react-api.html#reactpurecomponent).

```
export default class Component extends
React.PureComponent<ISimpleChartProps, ISimpleChartState> {
```

I will hold a reference to the div I will use to wrap the chart and hold the data in a data array of type numbers.

```
  ref: RefObject<HTMLDivElement>
```

```
  data: number[]
```

In the class constructor, I am setting the interface, creating the reference, and setting the data.

Notice that I don't have a need for the state, but I'm setting it up anyway in case I need it in the future. This is a good habit.

```
  constructor(props: ISimpleChartProps) {
    super(props)
    this.state = {
      // TODO
    }
```

```
  this.ref = React.createRef()
  this.data = [100, 200, 300, 400, 500]
}
```

As you recall from previous examples of function components, we called the draw function. In the React class component, we can call the draw method during the componentDidMount lifecycle hook.

Tip   The componentDidMount() lifecycle hook is part of the mounting phase and can be overridden with class components. Any actions defined within a componentDidMount() lifecycle hook are called only once when the component is first mounted.

```
componentDidMount() {
  this.drawChart()
}
```

On the drawChart method, I will take help from D3. I first select the reference, then add an SVG element using the append, and finally set our width and height.

Since I am setting the data attribute, D3 will automatically iterate through the data to draw all of our rectangle. This is the same as we did in the previous example with the p tag, but here we are using a rectangle tag instead of the HTML p tag. Take a look:

```
drawChart() {
  const size = 500
  const svg = d3.select(this.ref.current)
  .append('svg')
  .attr('width', size)
  .attr('height', size)

  const rectWidth = 95
  SVG
    .selectAll('rect')
    .data(this.data)
    .enter()
    .append('rect')
    .attr('x', (d, i) => 5 + i * (rectWidth + 5))
```

```
      .attr('y', (d) => size - d)
      .attr('width', rectWidth)
      .attr('height', (d) => d)
      .attr('fill', 'tomato')
  }
}
```

For rendering, I am setting the div wrapper we will be using. Notice that I don't really need the reference since I can select the element using className. In this example, this is a matter of preference for you to decide what is more intuitive.

```
  render() {
    return <div className="SimpleChart" ref={this.ref} />
  }
}
```

Tip   We are using the D3 select on the element class name in some examples while using a reference in other examples. Using a class name as a reference works fine in our examples; however, there are cases where we want React to control our component, and that's where setting a reference is better as React knows about changes in the element. Such a case would be on a list: array. map((item: object) => (<ListItem item={item} />))}. React iterates through a list, and if we use a map to render the list and that component is not using reference, the calculations can be off.

Lastly, just as I have done before, I am defining the props and state, which I don't need in this example, but I am setting them up in this example, because they may be needed in the future.

```
interface ISimpleChartProps {
  // TODO
}

interface ISimpleChartState {
  // TODO
}
```
App.tsx

Add the `<SimpleChart />` component to `App.tsx`, just as we did in the previous example. You can see the final results in Figure 2-6.

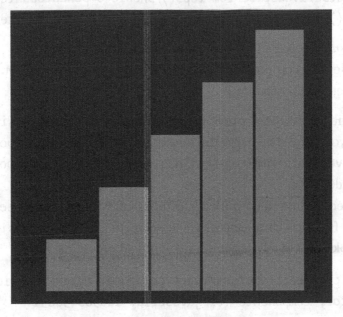

Figure 2-6. *Simple bar chart using React and D3*

Congratulations, you just created your first chart—a bar chart!

React Component Lifecycle Hooks

When it comes to React, you really want to familiarize yourself with React's version 16.9 and up lifecycle hooks as they have changed since version 16.9. Having a solid understanding of React's lifecycle hooks can help ensure changes to the DOM are made only when needed to tie in better with React's VDOM paradigm and make sure your component is optimized.

Each component in React has a lifecycle that you can monitor and manipulate during its three main lifecycle phases.

- *Mounting phase*: The component is created to start its unidirectional data flow journey and make its way to the DOM. It uses `constructor()`, and the following methods: static `getDerivedStateFromProps()`, `render()`, and `componentDidMount()`.

- *Updating phase*: The component is added to the DOM, updates can be rerendered on a prop or state change. The events are: static getDerivedStateFromProps(), shouldComponentUpdate(), render(), getSnapshotBeforeUpdate(), componentDidUpdate().

- *Unmounting phase*: This is the final phase of a component's life cycle. The component is destroyed and removed from DOM. componentWillUnmount().

In React 17, the access to the previous methods such as componentWillMount was deprecated, and you should be using the new hooks to access the component lifecycle. It includes getDerivedStateFromProps, getSnapshotBeforeUpdate, componentDidMount, and componentDidUpdate.

You might need to dust off your lifecycle hooks knowledge or just see all the different types of class and function components you can create with React. This is beyond the scope for this book, but I highly recommend you read my article here:

https://medium.com/react-courses/react-component-types-functional-class-and-exotic-factory-components-for-javascript-1a098a49a831

User Gestures

User interactions with graphics are not different from user interactions with any of the React components. React JSX aligns itself to HTML and SVG when it comes to mouse events.

However, you still have options for how to tap into these events.

You can use the JSX events or use D3. When to use a tool depends on what you are building. If you use D3 to create the graphics, you will need to also use the D3 events; however, if you use JSX to create your graphics, you can use either JSX or D3. The choice is yours.

For these reasons, I will show you both approaches. Let's take a look.

React Mouse Events

Let's create a class component and call it `CircleWithEvents`.

```
// src/component/CircleWithEvents/CircleWithEvents.tsx
```

```
import * as React from 'react'
import './CircleWithEvents.scss'
```

```
export default class CircleWithEvents extends React.PureComponent<ICircle
WithEventsProps> {

  componentDidMount() {
    // TODO
  }
```

Next, set up the event handlers. I am just setting up an alert to show the event getting dispatched. The code is commented out for you to play around with.

```
onMouseOverHandler(event: React.MouseEvent<SVGCircleElement, MouseEvent>) {
    // alert('onMouseOverHandler')
  }

onMouseOutHandler() {
    // alert('onMouseOutHandler')
  }
```

Notice that I am using `React.MouseEvent` instead of the standard HTML's `MouseEvent`.

Tip   In React, events are the triggered reactions to specific actions like mouse hover, mouse click, keypress, etc. Handling events in React is similar to handling events in DOM elements. But there are some syntactical differences.

SyntheticEvent, a cross-browser wrapper around the browser's native event. It has the same interface as the browser's native event, including stopPropagation() and preventDefault(), except the events work identically across all browsers.

```
                        https://reactjs.org/docs/events.html
```

Events are named using camel case instead of just using the lowercase. Here are two examples: `React.KeyboardEvent` and `React.MouseEvent`.

Events are passed as functions instead of strings. If you follow the code, you can see that React events extend `UIEvents`, which extends `SyntheticEvent`.

React uses its own event system. That's why we can't typically use `MouseEvent` from the standard DOM.

We need to use React's events; otherwise, we get an error, or we just won't be able to access methods. Generally speaking, most events are mapped with the same name.

Luckily, React's typings give you the proper equivalent of each event you might be familiar with from standard DOM.

We can either use `React.MouseEvent` or import the `MouseEvent` typing from the React module.

On the rendering side, I will be setting an empty wrapper tag as in , an SVG group, a circle inside with a radius (r) of 100 pixels, and the mouse events.

```
render() {
  return (
  <>
      <svg width="500" height="500">
        <g>
          <circle
            className="circle"
            transform="translate(150 150)"
            r="100"
            onMouseOver={(event) => {
              event.stopPropagation()
              this.onMouseOverHandler(event)
            }}
            onMouseOut={(event) => {
              event.stopPropagation()
              this.onMouseOutHandler()
            }}
```

For the click event, let's do something different. I will be using the inline function (arrow function aka *fat function*) to display my alert on the mouse click event.

```
                onClick={(event) => {
                  event.stopPropagation()
                  // eslint-disable-next-line no-alert
                  alert('onClick')
                }}
              />
            </g>
          </svg>
        </>
      )
    }
  }
interface ICircleWithEventsProps {
  // TODO
}
```

Notice that my SVG circle included a `className` attribute called `circle`, where I will set a few CSS properties such as the display of the cursor pointer, the width and height of the circle, and a gray fill color. These properties can be set on the component itself, but the code is cleaner this way.

```
// src/component/CircleWithEvents/CircleWithEvents.scss

.circle {
  cursor: pointer;
  width: 150px;
  height: 150px;
  fill: #6666;
}
App.tsx
```

Lastly, as always, remember to add the component to `App.tsx`. Go ahead and click the circle; don't be shy.

```
// src/App.tsx

import CircleWithEvents from './components/CircleWithEvents/CircleWithEvents'

<CircleWithEvents />
```

See the final results in Figure 2-7.

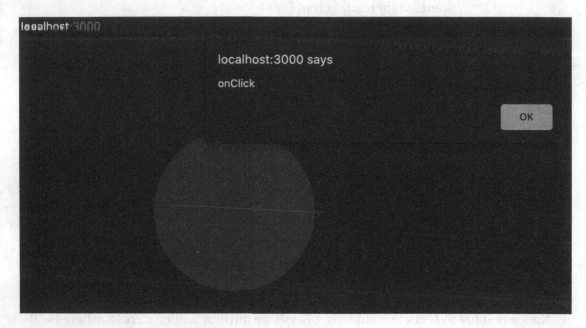

Figure 2-7. *Circle SVG with mouse events*

D3 Mouse Events

In the next example, I am going to replicate the same functionality from the previous example, setting a circle with mouse events; however, this time, I will be using D3 instead of React JSX. Let's take a look.

Set the `imports` and `class` components.

```
// src/component/CircleWithEvents/CircleWithD3Events.tsx

import * as React from 'react'
import './CircleWithEvents.scss'
import * as d3 from 'd3'

export default class CircleWithD3Events extends React.PureComponent<ICircle
WithD3EventsProps> {
```

I will be calling my `draw()` method once the `componentDidMount` event is called.

```
componentDidMount() {
  this.draw()
}
```

Next, I will be setting up the same event handlers I have from the previous example.

```
onMouseOverHandler(event: React.MouseEvent<SVGCircleElement, MouseEvent>) {
  // alert('onMouseOverHandler')
}

onMouseOutHandler() {
  // alert('onMouseOutHandler')
}
```

My `draw()` method will select my SVG wrapper element and then append a group element and a circle element and set the events using the `.on` method on D3.

I am even attaching the same class circle in this example.

Note   React JSX calls the class attribute `className`, and in D3 the attribute matches HTML SVG, so it would be `class`.

```
draw = () => {
  d3.select('svg')
    .append('g')
    .append('circle')
    .attr('transform', 'translate(150, 150)')
    .attr('r', 100)
    .attr('class', 'circle')
    .on('click', () => {
      alert('onClick')
    })
    .on('mouseover', (event) => {
      this.onMouseOverHandler(event)
    })
```

```
      .on('mouseout', (event) => {
        this.onMouseOutHandler()
      })
    }
```

As you would expect, here is my SVG wrapper on the rendering side:

```
render() {
  return (
  <>
      <svg id="svg" width="500" height="500" />
  </>
  )
}
}
interface ICircleWithD3EventsProps {
  // TODO
}
App.tsx
```

Add our component App.tsx, and you will see the same results as in Figure 2-7.

```
// src/App.tsx

import CircleWithD3Events from './components/CircleWithEvents/
CircleWithD3Events'

<CircleWithEvents />
```

As you can see, for most people, React JSX is more intuitive and easier to read; however, if you need to write D3 code, you need to use the D3 event, and it will be straightforward once you understand what you are doing.

Knowing both options gives you flexibility and more control over your code. When we want d3 to be in charge of the DOM for our component, it's better to use React elements and tie as much as possible to React. In cases that we need to take over the task of handling the DOM, having d3 can help us.

Animating Graphics

In this section, I will cover another part of the interaction layer: creating animations. We may want to create a transition when we change the data or show a change of data over time, and we can do that in a more elegant way with animations, or *transitions*.

React offers many ways to create transitions. Here are some examples:

- *CSS transitions*: We can use plain old CSS using CSS transitions either as part of the style sheet or dynamically using `style={{someCSSPrope rtyExample: 50}}`.

- *CSS-in-JS modules*: If you use libraries such as CSS-in-JS modules, you can set transitions in an intuitive way.

- *D3 transition*: D3 also offers transitions using the Transition API.

While we develop charts, we will be using transitions, and just as we saw with events, it's good to know our options.

I will show you both CSS-in-JS modules and D3.

Animating with React

CSS-in-JS modules are a popular option for styling React applications, because they integrate closely with React components and have features that allow you to change properties passed from the parent component or tie properties from the state.

Indeed, the CRA MHL library project is set up with Material-UI and Styled Components out of the box, so you don't need to install anything; we can just start using both Material-UI and Styled Components.

For example, we can change our style based on React `props`. Also, by default, most of these systems scope all styles to the respective component being styled.

There are many options to pick from when it comes to CSS-in-JS modules such as Styled Components, Emotion, and Styled-jsx.

I picked Styled Components because it goes hand in hand with Material-UI; you can read more about it (if you are unfamiliar) at `https://styled-components.com`.

But wait, why do we need Styled Components? Doesn't Material-UI have a styled import similar to Styled Components already?

Yes, it is true that Material-UI is a great component library that emulates Google's Material Design and has a built-in styling mechanism. So why is it not enough? The quick answer is that the Material-UI CSS-in-JS solution doesn't feel as powerful as Styled Components. Material-UI was designed to be used from the get-go with its own styling solution, CSS-in-JS. But sometimes you want other features that are not available in Material-UI style, or you are like me and just like Styled Components better.

Fortunately, Material-UI did make it simple to use other styling solutions.

Styled Components is another great library used to style React components. That's done by defining React "styled" components without CSS classes. Styled Components is best used when you want to write regular CSS, pass functions, and props. You may ask, why not just use Styled Components then?

There aren't many mature libraries out there that are at the Material-UI level at the time of writing, certainly not at Material-UI maturity levels.

We can leverage the advantages of both Material-UI and Styled Components together.

Using Styled Components will give you the following abilities:

- Render CSS conditionally using props

- SCSS support

- Template literal syntax for CSS

And much more.

For one of the charts we will be using later in this book, we will need a pulsating circle. The pulsating circle can be used to highlight something on a chart.

PulsatingCircle.tsx

To create that pulsating circle component using the Styled Components library, let's create a new function component and call it PulsatingCircle.tsx.

```
// src/component/PulsatingCircle/PulsatingCircle.tsx
```

```
import React from 'react'
```

We import keyframes and styled from Styled Components.

```
import styled, { keyframes } from 'styled-components'
```

Now, look at the power of writing dynamic code that can be updated by passing params. Let's define a function that will take two colors.

```
const circlePulse = (colorOne: string, colorTwo: string) => keyframes`
0% {
  fill:${colorOne};
  stroke-width:20px
}
50% {
  fill:${colorTwo};
  stroke-width:2px
}
100%{
  fill:${colorOne};
  stroke-width:20px
}
`
```

Now using animation, we can create an infinite four-second linear loop to form that pulsating effect.

```
const StyledInnerCircle = styled.circle`
  animation: ${() => circlePulse('rgb(245,197,170)', 'rgba(242, 121, 53,
  1)')} infinite 4s linear;
`
```

```
export default function PulsatingCircle(props: IPulsatingCircle) {
```

On the rendering side, we can just use StyledInnerCircle, which we created as a JSX component.

Notice that I am assigning the x, y from the props. The parent component can pass these.

```
  return (
  <>
    <StyledInnerCircle cx={props.cx} cy={props.cy} r="8"
    stroke="limegreen" stroke-width="5" />
  </>
  )
}
```

On our `props` interface side, we can pass the location of our custom component.

```
interface IPulsatingCircle {
  cx: number   cy: number
}
```

Add our component to `App.tsx`.

```
// src/app.tsx

<svg width={400} height={400} viewBox="0 0 800 450">
  <g>
    <PulsatingCircle cy={100} cx={100} />
  </g>
</svg>
```

You now have a pulsating animation circle, as shown in Figure 2-8.

Figure 2-8. *Pulsating circle using React Styled Components*

Animating with D3

In terms of animating with D3, the process follows an animation sequencing. If you
are familiar with any animation software, you will find D3 more intuitive since you
understand the concepts of animation. For others, this can be confusing.

PulsatingCircleD3.tsx

As an example, let's create another pulsating circle, but this time let's use D3.
Import and set a draw method.

```
import React, { useEffect } from 'react'
import * as d3 from 'd3'
```

```
const PulsatingCircleD3 = () /* props */ => {
  useEffect(() => {
    drawPulsatingCircle()
  })
  const drawPulsatingCircle = () => {
```

To keep a loop, I will be creating a function called repeat(). That function will select the circlSVGvg element (I am creating the circle in JSX; by now you know what to do if you want this to be 100 percent pure D3).

Next, I will be setting a transition.

During the first 300 ms, I first set the attributes of the stroke to 0 and then set the duration and change the stroke opacity from 0 to 0.5.

Next, I set another stroke to change and use the D3 ease to create sinus ease (yes the same sinus circle we used in math class) in the animation.

Lastly, the function calls itself to loop using a recursive function (a function that calls itself).

```
    (function repeat() {
      d3.selectAll('.circle')
        .transition()
        .duration(300)
        .attr('stroke-width', 0)
        .attr('stroke-opacity', 0)
        .transition()
        .duration(300)
        .attr('stroke-width', 0)
        .attr('stroke-opacity', 0.5)
        .transition()
        .duration(1000)
        .attr('stroke-width', 25)
        .attr('stroke-opacity', 0)
        .ease(d3.easeSin)
        .on('end', repeat)
    })()
  }
```

In the JSX, I am creating our circle with a radius of 8 pixels and a location of 50, 50 for the x, y, as shown in Figure 2-9.

```
return (
<>
    <svg>
      <circle className="circle" cx="50" cy="50" stroke="orange"
      fill="orange" r="8" />
    </svg>
</>
)
}
export default PulsatingCircleD3
```

Figure 2-9. *Pulsating circle using D3*

You can see that the idea is to sequence the animation. I am sure some will find this more complicated, while others will find it easier than the previous example.

Summary

This chapter broke down the pieces of what you need to know in order to start creating charts with React and D3. The chapter was split into three main sections.

- Graphics

- User gestures

- Animating

In the first section, I showed you how to create graphics with HTML and SVG elements using React function and class components.

We used both React JSX and D3. We consumed data and drew elements. We even created our first chart, a bar chart.

In the second section, you learned about setting events with D3 and React and about animating graphics using React and D3.

As you can see, when it comes to drawing, consuming data, animating, and even interacting with options, you can use React, D3, or other libraries. That's what makes D3 with React unique. These sets of options really come in handy when it's time to integrate your charts into existing code, to test it, and to work with different member teams that hold different skill sets; it even makes your code more readable.

In the next chapter, we will start creating simple charts such as line, area, and bar charts as well as consume data and animate and interact with these charts.

CHAPTER 3

Basic Charts: Part 1

In the previous chapter, I covered what was possible with D3 and React. We created function and class components, and we even created a simple bar chart. In this chapter, I will be covering how to create simple charts with React and D3 using TypeScript as a type checker. I will be showing you how to create the following simple charts with the emphasis of getting D3 to do most of the work. I will be showing you how to create the following charts:

- Line chart
- Area chart
- Bar chart

Let's begin.

Setup

Just as in the previous chapters, I will be using CRA with the MHL template to create our starter project.

```
$ yarn create react-app basic-charts --template must-have-libraries
```

```
$ cd basic-charts
$ yarn add d3 @types/d3
$ yarn start
```

Open the start page.

```
$ open http://localhost:3000
```

You can download the entire code of this chapter from here:

https://github.com/Apress/integrating-d3.js-with-react/tree/main/ch03

© Elad Elrom 2021
E. Elrom, *Integrating D3.js with React*, https://doi.org/10.1007/978-1-4842-7052-3_3

Line Chart

The first chart I will show you is a line chart. A line chart shows graphically quantitative data and is considered as one of the most basic types of charts. The line chart consists of three drawing elements: the x-axis, the y-axis, and a line.

Fortunately, D3 has methods to help you through the entire process of creating a line chart.

line.csv

A good place to start is the data. For the line chart, the data I will be using is straight from Yahoo Financing. I will be pulling historic data for the Boeing stock, with a ticker notation of BA: `https://finance.yahoo.com/quote/BA/history`. Once you get to the page, you will see an option to download the data.

In the downloaded CSV file (see Figure 3-1), I am keeping the Date column and the Open price and deleting the other columns.

	1	2	3	4	5	6	7
1	Date	Open	High	Low	Close	Adj Close	Volume
2	1/31/20	321.75	321.929993	316.98999	318.269989	316.387573	4999600
3	2/3/20	318.75	320.73999	314.880005	316	314.131012	4847700
4	2/4/20	318.279999	319.480011	315.029999	317.940002	316.05954	3779800
5	2/5/20	320.5	329.679993	319.230011	329.549988	327.600861	6071800
6	2/6/20	330.910004	343.440002	325.660004	341.429993	339.410614	12845500
7	2/7/20	340.369995	340.73999	335.690002	336.75	334.758301	5337800
8	2/10/20	337.220001	345.940002	336.320007	344.670013	342.63147	5876400
9	2/11/20	347.640015	348.070007	342.100006	344.420013	342.382935	5311500
10	2/12/20	346.420013	349.950012	345.850006	347.450012	345.39502	4421500
11	2/13/20	344.320007	347.890015	342.630005	342.820007	342.820007	3783100
12	2/14/20	342.299988	344.5	338	340.48999	340.48999	4199800

Figure 3-1. *CSV file of historical stock prices for BA, opened in Microsoft Excel*

Next, I will be reformatting the date to a format of %Y-%m-%d for easier reading (see Figure 3-2).

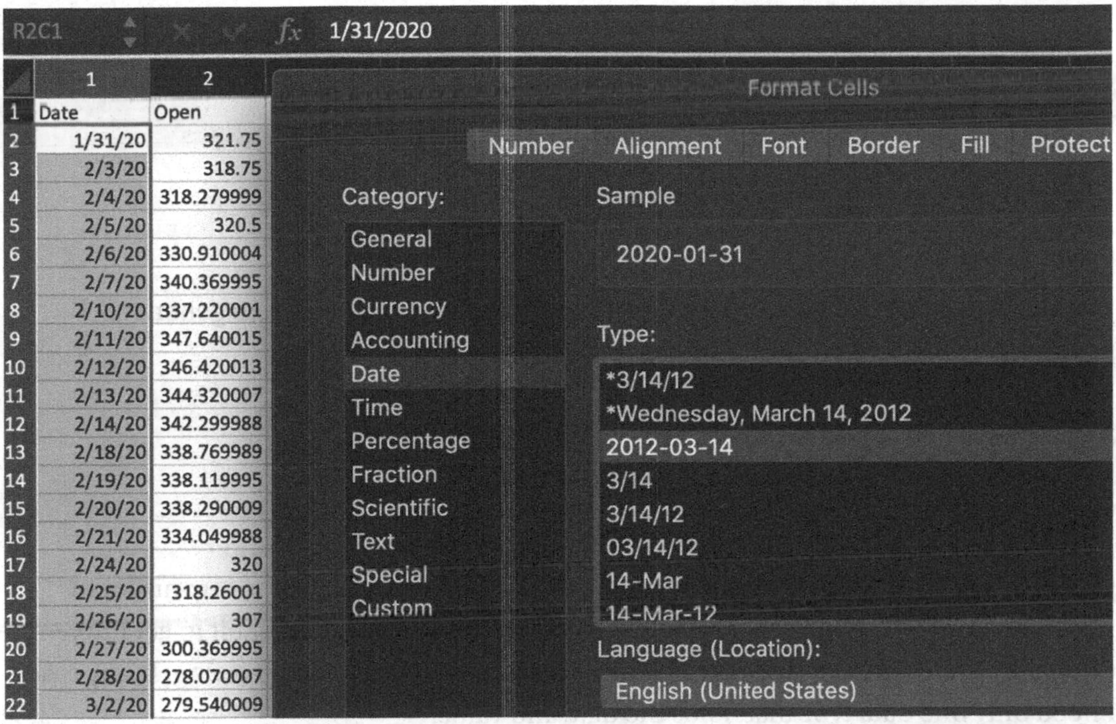

Figure 3-2. *Formatting date of CSV file that contains BA historical stock prices*

I am taking the price history of BA and then converting the CSV to two fields: data and value.

Lastly, I am renaming the Date and Open columns to date and value.

I am saving the file in the public/data folder: public/data/line.csv.

```
date,value
2020-01-27,321.75
2020-02-03,318.75
2020-02-10,337.220001
2020-02-17,338.769989
2020-02-24,320
..
..
..
```

Besides the data file, I will be creating a few more files.

- `BasicLineChart.scss`: SCSS style file

- `BasicLineChart.test.tsx`: Jest/Enzyme test file

- `BasicLineChart.tsx`: Component

- `types.ts`: TS types

As always, you can create these files yourself or get a little help from `generate-react-cli`.

```
$ npx generate-react-cli component BasicLineChart --type=d3
```

types.ts

Creating a types file is a common practice to keep the TypeScript types organized. In my chart, I only need the date and value I created, but this is a good habit to get into, especially for a complex chart as the number of types needed keeps growing. In my case, I need only one data type that holds the date and value.

```
//  src/component/BasicLineChart/types.ts

export namespace Types {
  export type Data = {
    date: string
    value: number
  }
}
```

BasicLineChart.tsx

The function component `BasicLineChart` does the heavy lifting, and it will draw the axis and line chart.

I will be importing React, SCSS, D3, and the types file. The structure is the same as we had in the previous chapter.

I have broken down the function component to a `draw()` function that gets called and a JSX placeholder. The `draw()` function gets called by the `useEffect` hook, just as we did in the previous chapter. Take a look:

```
// src/component/BasicLineChart/BasicLineChart.tsx

import React, { useEffect } from 'react'
import './BasicLineChart.scss'
import * as d3 from 'd3'
import { Types } from './types'

const BasicLineChart = (props: IBasicLineChartProps) => {
  useEffect(() => {
    draw()
  })

  const draw = () => {
```

First, I will set the dimensions and margins of the chart. I will be passing these from the parent component via props.

```
const width = props.width - props.left - props.right
const height = props.height - props.top - props.bottom
```

Next, I will append an SVG object to the wrapper div I am setting in the JSX render section and assign attributes. I am also going to append a group element, just like we did in the previous chapter.

```
const svg = d3
  .select('.basicLineChart')
  .append('svg')
  .attr('width', width + props.left + props.right)
  .attr('height', height + props.top + props.bottom)
  .append('g')
  .attr('transform', `translate(${props.left},${props.top})`)
```

I can use D3 not just to draw the axis and the line but also to retrieve the CSV data. Take a look at the dsv API (https://github.com/d3/d3-dsv). Once the data is retrieved, I am casting the object as my Types.Data and then using d3.timeParse to convert the string into D3 Date object. The dsv API will iterate through the list one by one, and I will return an object that consists of the Date parsed as d3 and value.

```
d3.dsv(',', '/Data/line.csv', (d) => {
  const res = (d as unknown) as Types.Data
  const date = d3.timeParse('%Y-%m-%d')(res.date)
  return {
    date,
    value: res.value,
  }
}
```

Once the dsv method is complete, and I have the object formatted with a date in the D3 Date format and the value. Next is to add the x-axis, which will be a date for the domain. This sets the scale's domain to the specified array's domain values, in our case the date.

```
}).then((data) => {
  const x = d3
    .scaleTime()
    .domain(
      d3.extent(data, (d) => {
        return d.date
      }) as [Date, Date]
    )
    .range([0, width])
```

Notice   I am using d3.extent and casting my domain as [Date, Date]. d3. extent returns the min and max simultaneously. I also change the range from zero to the width of the chart.

Without casting d3.extent as [Date, Date], I will be getting the mean ESLint error message shown in Figure 3-3. You can see from the message that it expects a [Date, Date].

TS2345: Argument of type '[undefined, undefined] | [Date, Date]' is not assignable to parameter of type 'Iterable<number | Date | { valueOf(): number; }>'.

```
  d3.extent(data,   accessor: (d  :{date: Date | null, value: number} ) => {
    return d.date
  }) //
)
.range(       TS2345: Argument of type '[undefined, undefined] | [Date, Date]' is not assignable to
              parameter of type 'Iterable<number | Date | { valueOf(): number; }>'.
                Type '[undefined, undefined]' is not assignable to type 'Iterable<number | Date | {
              valueOf(): number; }>'.
svg.appen        The types returned by '[Symbol.iterator]().next(...)' are incompatible between these types.
                  Type 'IteratorResult<undefined, any>' is not assignable to type 'IteratorResult<number |
              Date | { valueOf(): number; }, any>'.
                  Type 'IteratorYieldResult<undefined>' is not assignable to type 'IteratorResult<number
              | Date | { valueOf(): number; }, any>'.
onst y =           Type 'IteratorYieldResult<undefined>' is not assignable to type
.scaleL   'IteratorYieldResult<number | Date | { valueOf(): number; }>'.
                    Type 'undefined' is not assignable to type 'number | Date | { valueOf(): number; }'.
              Suppress with @ts-ignore  ⌥⇧↵    More actions...  ⌥↵
```

Figure 3-3. *ESLint error message due to incompatible types*

Lastly, I will append a group, set the group to the bottom left position using translate, and call d3.axisBottom(x) to attach my x-axis.

```
svg.append('g').attr('transform', `translate(0, ${height})`).
call(d3.axisBottom(x))
```

Note   The call method is a common way for D3 to return a reference to itself in the form of a selection.

What's happening here is that svg.append('g') appends an SVG group element to the SVG and returns a reference to itself in the form of a selection.

When we call on a selection, we are calling the function axisBottom on the elements of the selection g. We are running the axisBottom function on the newly created and appended group, g.

For the y-axis, the process is similar, except I am setting a value instead of a date. I am using Math (https://developer.mozilla.org/en-US/docs/Web/JavaScript/Reference/Global_Objects/Math/max) to get the max value possible.

```
Math.max(...data.map((dt) => ((dt as unknown) as Types.Data).value), 0)
```

This will ensure that my chart is set to behave based on the max value; otherwise, the height is going to be out of alignment and show the first value, while other values may spill.

```
const y = d3
  .scaleLinear()
  .domain([
    0,
    d3.max(data, (d) => {
      return Math.max(...data.map((dt) => ((dt as unknown) as Types.
      Data).value), 0)
    }),
  ] as number[])
  .range([height, 0])
svg.append('g').call(d3.axisLeft(y))
```

For the domain, I need to make sure the object is casting as the number[ ] to avoid yet another incompatible type message in ESLint.

TS2345: Argument of type '(number | undefined)[]' is not assignable to parameter of type 'Iterable<NumberValue>'. The types returned by '[Symbol. iterator]().next(...)' are incompatible between these types.

Lastly, I need to add the line I want to draw. To do that, I can append an SVG path element and use the datum with my data so it will iterate through my data object to draw each line. I am using the fill I will be passing from the props and a stroke width of 1.6.

```
svg
  .append('path')
  .datum(data)
  .attr('fill', 'none')
  .attr('stroke', props.fill)
  .attr('stroke-width', 1.5)
  .attr(
    'd',
    // @ts-ignore
    d3
      .line()
      .x((d) => {
        return x(((d as unknown) as { date: number }).date)
      })
```

```
        .y((d) => {
          return y(((d as unknown) as Types.Data).value)
        })
      )
    })
  }
```

On the rendering side, I set a wrapper div with a className value of basicLineChart.

```
  return <div className="basicLineChart" />
}
```

For the interface I will be passing properties from the parent component so I can align the component and set a fill color so it will be easy to reuse my component.

```
interface IBasicLineChartProps {
  width: number
  height: number
  top: number
  right: number
  bottom: number
  left: number
  fill: string
}
```

```
export default BasicLineChart
```

Notice that these D3 scale methods really helped a lot; they were able to do the calculations and transform our data into the values needed to draw the chart.

If I need to add a pulsating dot or anything on the basic line chart, what I can do is reuse these x-axis and y-axis values, for example y(300).

When does this come in handy? Let's say I want to draw another line at the end of the chart. I can store the last position of the x, y and then use the y-axis and x-axis to calculate any price I want.

```
svg
 .append('line')
 .style('stroke', 'red')
 .style('stroke-width', 1)
```

```
.attr('x1', lastX)
.attr('y1', lastY)
.attr('x2', lastX + x2)
// y Axis is what turn the value to the value needed
// on the chart
.attr('y2', yAxis(300))
```

BasicLineChart.scss

As for my SCSS file, I could set attributes of my drawing elements here, but I really don't need anything set as I am passing my fill color and other attributes using props. With that said, it's a good habit to have my SCSS ready for future usage.

```
.basicLineChart {
}
```

BasicLineChart.test.tsx

For testing, I am using Jest and Enzyme to ensure that the component mounts and uses the props I set.

If you are new to testing of React with Jest and Enzyme, check out my article at https://medium.com/react-courses/unit-testing-react-typescript-app-with-jest-jest-dom-enzyme-11f52487aa18. For more details, read my React Apress book: https://www.apress.com/gp/book/9781484266953.

```
// src/component/BasicLineChart/BasicLineChart.test.tsx

import React from 'react'
import { shallow } from 'enzyme'
import BasicLineChart from './BasicLineChart'

describe('<BasicLineChart />', () => {
  let component

  beforeEach(() => {
    component = shallow(<BasicLineChart top={10} right={50} bottom={50}
    left={50} width={460} height={400} fill="tomato" />)
  })
```

```
test('It should mount', () => {
  expect(component.length).toBe(1)
})
})
```

App.tsx

Finally, I can add simple BasicLineChart with the props I set.

```
// src/App.tsx

import React from 'react'
import './App.scss'

import BasicBarChart from './components/BasicBarChart/BasicBarChart'

function App() {
  return (
    <div className="App">
      <header className="App-header">
        <BasicBarChart top={10} right={50} bottom={50} left={50}
        width={900} height={400} fill="tomato" />
      </header>
    </div>
  )
}

export default App
```

For the final result, see Figure 3-4.

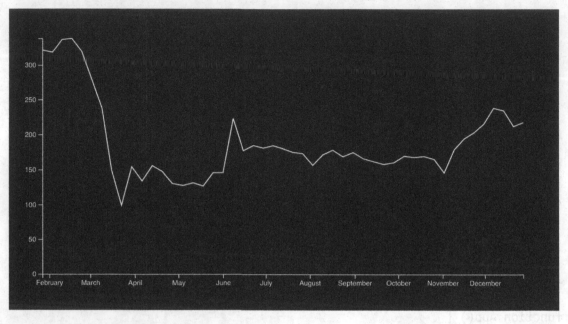

Figure 3-4. *Line chart of BA stock price*

Now that I have my chart ready, I am going to run the format, lint, and test tasks that I set in the `package.json` run scripts to ensure quality.

```
$ yarn format
$ yarn lint
$ yarn test
```

If you open `package.json` and look under the `scripts` tag, you can see these tasks are being set there.

```
"scripts": {
  "format": "prettier --write 'src/**/*.{ts,tsx,scss,css,json}'",
  "lint": "eslint --ext .js,.jsx,.ts,.tsx ./",
  "test": "react-scripts test",
  ..
  ..
}
```

I am not getting into details on how the format, lint, and test got set, but as I pointed out before, you can learn more about these in my React and Libraries book, available at `https://www.apress.com/gp/book/9781484266953`.

If you don't set the test suites, it's fine and won't affect any of the functionality; however, it is just good practice to write your component with full testing coverage.

Area Chart

The area chart shows graphically quantitative data and is similar to the line chart.

The difference is that the area between the axis and the line is emphasized with color.

In terms of coding, it is similar to the line chart we just did in the previous example; the only difference is that the area is colored

area.csv

As for the data, I will be using the S&P 500 ticker and format the data just as I did in the line chart (`https://finance.yahoo.com/quote/%5EGSPC/history`).

I will be saving the results at `public/data/area.csv`.

```
date,value
2020-01-27,3282.330078
2020-02-03,3235.659912
2020-02-10,3318.280029
..
..
```

BasicAreaChart.tsx

My main component, `BasicAreaChart.tsx`, is similar to `BasicLineChart.tsx`. Take a look:

```
// src/component/BasicAreaChart/BasicAreaChart.tsx

import React, { useEffect } from 'react'
import './BasicAreaChart.scss'
import * as d3 from 'd3'
import { Types } from './types'
```

```
const BasicAreaChart = (props: IBasicAreaChartProps) => {
  useEffect(() => {
    draw()
  })
```

```
  const draw = () => {
```

I set the dimensions and margins.

```
    const width = props.width - props.left - props.right
    const height = props.height - props.top - props.bottom
```

Next, I append the svg object to the basicAreaChart JSX div I will be setting on the rendering side.

```
    const svg = d3
      .select('.basicAreaChart')
      .append('svg')
      .attr('width', width + props.left + props.right)
      .attr('height', height + props.top + props.bottom)
      .append('g')
      .attr('transform', `translate(${props.left},${props.top})`)
```

```
    d3.dsv(',', '/Data/area.csv', (d) => {
      const res = (d as unknown) as Types.data
      const date = d3.timeParse('%Y-%m-%d')(res.date)
      return {
        date,
        value: res.value,
      }
    }).then(function results(data) {
```

Now I can set the date format as the x-axis.

```
      const x = d3
        .scaleTime()
        .domain(
          d3.extent(data, (d) => {
            return d.date
```

```
    }) as [Date, Date]
  )
    .range([0, width])

svg.append('g').attr('transform', `translate(0, ${height})`).call(d3.
axisBottom(x))
```

I can also set the y-axis as the value.

```
const y = d3
  .scaleLinear()
  // @ts-ignore
  .domain([
    0,
    d3.max(data, (d) => {
      return +d.value
    }),
  ] as number[])
  .range([height, 0])
svg.append('g').call(d3.axisLeft(y))
```

For the line of the chart, I will be using the path, just as in `BasicLineChart.tsx`.

```
svg
  .append('path')
  .datum(data)
  .attr('fill', props.fill)
  .attr('stroke', 'white')
  .attr('stroke-width', 1.5)
```

The big difference in the area chart is that I am now using the D3 area and curve APIs.

```
d3
.area()
.curve(d3.curveLinear)
```

This code is in addition to the path line since I need to fill the area with color.
We do that by setting the x, y0, and y1 values.

```
* @param x Sets the x accessor - in our case a date
* @param y0 Sets the y0 accessor - in our case it's zero since we start
  from the bottom.
* @param y1 Sets the y1 accessor - in our case it's the value of the stock.
```

Take a look:

```
    .attr(
      'd',
      // @ts-ignore
      d3
        .area()
        .curve(d3.curveLinear)
        .x((d) => {
          return x(((d as unknown) as { date: number }).date)
        })
        .y0(y(0))
        .y1((d) => {
          return y(((d as unknown) as Types.data).value)
        })
    )
  })
}
```

On the rendering side, I am adding the div wrapper.

```
  return <div className="basicAreaChart" />
}
```

The interface is the same as the line chart.

```
interface IBasicAreaChartProps {
  width: number
  height: number
  top: number
  right: number
  bottom: number
```

```
    left: number
    fill: string
}

export default BasicAreaChart
```

Next, set up the `types.ts`, `scss`, and `BasicAreaChart.test.tsx` files. They have the same code as in the line example, so I am not showing them to you here. Make sure they are set up in the `BasicAreaChart` folder (see Figure 3-5).

Figure 3-5. *BasicAreaChart files structure*

App.tsx

Lastly, we need to set up `App.tsx` to include our `BasicAreaChart` and pass the `props`.

```
// src/App.tsx

import React from 'react'
import './App.scss'

import BasicAreaChart from './components/BasicAreaChart/BasicAreaChart'

function App() {
  return (
    <div className="App">
      <header className="App-header">
        <BasicAreaChart top={10} right={50} bottom={50} left={50}
        width={1000} height={400} fill="tomato" />
```

```
      </header>
    </div>
  )
}

export default App
```

And *voilà*! See Figure 3-6.

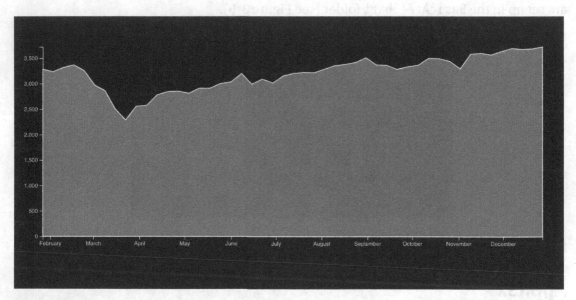

Figure 3-6. *BasicAreaChart complete*

As you saw, both the line and area charts were similar. Once we understand the processes of retrieving and formatting the data, creating our axis for both x and y, and drawing our chart, it starts to get easier each time you draw a chart.

Bar Chart

The last chart I will be creating in this chapter is another commonly used type of graph, a bar chart.

Bar charts are used to display and compare numbers, or frequency, or another measure. Bar charts are popular because of how simple they are to create, and they are easy to interpret.

I already showed you how to create a simple bar chart in Chapter 2; however, the bar chart didn't have an x,y axis, and the data wasn't loaded from an external file.

In this example, for the data, I will be using the Stack Overflow survey data that shows the popularity of React and other frameworks: `https://insights.stackoverflow.com/survey/2020`. This chart helps you choose a web framework.

bar.csv

For the data, I created a CSV file called `public/data/bar.csv` with the values I copied from the Stack Overflow survey. Take a look:

```
framework,value
jQuery,43.3
React.js,35.9
Angular,25.1
ASP.NET,21.9
Express,21.2
.NET Core,19.1
..
..
```

BasicBarChart.tsx

In terms of structure, I will keep the structure similar to the line and area charts I created previously.

```
// src/component/BasicBarChart/BasicBarChart.tsx

import React, { useEffect } from 'react'
import './BasicBarChart.scss'
import * as d3 from 'd3'
import { Types } from './types'

const BasicBarChart = (props: IBasicBarChartProps) => {
  useEffect(() => {
    draw()
  })

  const draw = () => {
```

As before, we set the dimensions and margins.

```
const width = props.width - props.left - props.right
const height = props.height - props.top - props.bottom
```

To draw the x,y ranges, I will be getting some help from D3 and setting them up based on the properties passed through props from the parent component.

```
const x = d3.scaleBand().range([0, width]).padding(0.1)
const y = d3.scaleLinear().range([height, 0])
```

Next, I will append the SVG object to my div wrapper called basicBarChart that I will add at render time, and I will add a group and set my SVG width and height attributes.

```
const svg = d3
  .select('.basicBarChart')
  .append('svg')
  .attr('width', width + props.left + props.right)
  .attr('height', height + props.top + props.bottom)
  .append('g')
  .attr('transform', `translate(${props.left},${props.top})`)

d3.dsv(',', '/Data/bar.csv', (d) => {
  return (d as unknown) as Types.Data
```

Once the data object is ready, I can scale the range of the Data in the domains.

```
}).then((data) => {
  x.domain(
    data.map((d) => {
      return d.framework
    })
  )
  y.domain([
    0,
    d3.max(data, (d) => {
```

I will set the max value of y using the same Math function I used in the inline chart and cast my domain as number[] to avoid ESLint barking at me.

```
    return Math.max(...data.map((dt) => (dt as Types.Data).value), 0)
  }),
] as number[])
```

To draw the actual bars, I will use `selectAll` and the `data` attribute so that D3 will iterate through my data and append the rectangles for the bar chart.

```
svg
  .selectAll('.bar')
  .data(data)
  .enter()
  .append('rect')
  .attr('fill', props.fill)
  .attr('class', 'bar')
  .attr('x', (d) => {
    return x(d.framework) || 0
  })
```

Notice that on the return I am using "or zero": || 0. The reason is that we don't know for sure that there are values, and the data can be undefined (number | undefined). That's why TS needs that "or zero"—it's to avoid getting an ESLint overload error message.

```
TS2769: No overload matches this call. Overload 1 of 4, '(name: string,
value: null): Selection<SVGRectElement, Data, SVGGElement, unknown>', gave
the following error. Argument of type '(this: SVGRectElement, d: Data) =>
number | undefined' is not assignable to parameter of type 'null'.
```

For the width, I am using `x.bandwidth`, which returns the width of each bin (rectangle) that makes our bar chart. For the height → that will be the height of the bounds of the chart less the value to create the bin height value.

```
  .attr('width', x.bandwidth())
  .attr('y', (d) => {
    return y(d.value)
  })
  .attr('height', (d) => {
    return height - y(d.value)
  })
```

Next, I will be adding the x-axis and y-axis.

```
svg.append('g').attr('transform', `translate(0,${height})`).call(d3.
axisBottom(x))

svg.append('g').call(d3.axisLeft(y))
})
}
```

Now I render my div wrapper called basicBarChart.

```
return <div className="basicBarChart" />
}
```

Lastly, I set up my interface.

```
interface IBasicBarChartProps {
  width: number
  height: number
  top: number
  right: number
  bottom: number
  left: number
  fill: string
}

export default BasicBarChart
```

Set up types.ts, scss, and BasicAreaChart.test.tsx just as we have done in the other examples.

types.ts

For the type I am setting two variables: framework and value (of type string and number).

```
// src/component/BasicBarChart/types.ts

export namespace Types {
  export type Data = {
```

```
    framework: string
    value: number
  }
}
```

BasicBarChart.scss

For the SCSS, I could set the fill of each bar there, but since I am setting it in the props, that would be an overlap. I just wanted to show you that if you need to, setting attributes for the D3 elements we created in SCSS is more than acceptable and easy to read and make changes, especially when you work in a team with a designer.

```scss
.basicBarChart {
}

.bar {
  fill: tomato;
}
```

App.tsx

As for App.tsx, you already know what to do, so go ahead and add the component.

```tsx
// src/App.tsx

import React from 'react'
import './App.scss'

import BasicBarChart from './components/BasicBarChart/BasicBarChart'

function App() {
  return (
    <div className="App">
      <header className="App-header">
        <BasicBarChart top={10} right={50} bottom={50} left={50}
        width={900} height={400} fill="tomato" />
      </header>
```

```
    </div>
  )
}
```

```
export default App
```

Voilà again! See Figure 3-7.

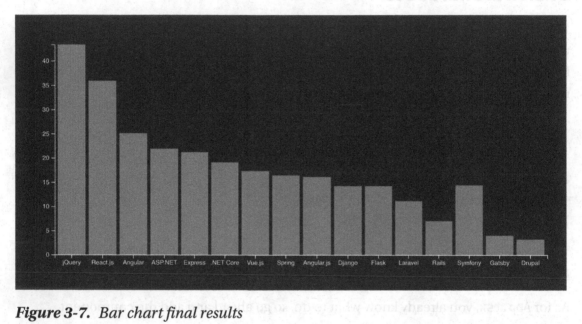

Figure 3-7. *Bar chart final results*

Looking at the chart, you can see that the chart tells a story. At first glance, the 2020 Stack Overflow results appear that React has bypassed Angular by almost 11 percent.

As you can see from the chart (Figure 3-8), jQuery shows up as the king, but React.js is gaining momentum and ready to take over.

Figure 3-8. *https://insights.stackoverflow.com/survey/2020#community*

However, that is not the case.

The survey includes React.js and Gatsby separately, although they are both based on React, and there is also a split between Angular and Angular.js.

In reality, if we add these results together, it is almost an exact split between Angular at 41.2 percent, React at 39.9 percent, and jQuery at 43.3 percent.

The true results are more of an even split between React, Angular, and jQuery. If I were to adjust my data file accordingly, I would have this:

```
framework,value
jQuery,43.3
Angular + Angular.js,41.2
React.js + Gatsby,39.9
```

Once I plug in the new data, I am going to get a whole different story; see Figure 3-9.

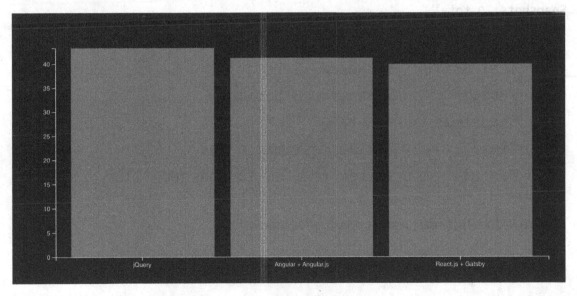

Figure 3-9. *React versus Angular versus jQuery 2020*

If you interested in seeing a comparison between using React and Angular, check out my article on Medium at https://medium.com/react-courses/angular-9-vs-react-16-a-2020-showdown-2b0b8aa6c8e9.

The 2021 Stack Overflow results have not been published at the time of writing this book, but it would be interesting to see how these values change over time. Now that you are equipped with this chart, you can plug in the new data.

Now that I have all the three charts ready, I am going to run the format, lint, and test tasks one last time to ensure quality.

```
$ yarn format
$ yarn lint
$ yarn test
```

Go ahead and compare your results with mine (see Figure 3-10).

```
✦  Done in 1.48s.$ eslint --ext .js,.jsx,.ts,.tsx ./
✦  Done in 9.88s.Test Suites: 5 passed, 5 total
Tests: 5 passed, 5 total
Snapshots: 0 total
```

```
Test Suites: 5 passed, 5 total
Tests:       5 passed, 5 total
Snapshots:   0 total
Time:        7.432s, estimated 10s
Ran all test suites related to changed files.
```

Figure 3-10. *Test suite results passing for all charts*

Summary

In this chapter, I showed you how to create popular and basic charts with React, TS, and D3. We created the following three types of charts:

- Line chart

- Area chart

- Bar chart

I showed you how to utilize D3 for the fullest not just for drawing but even to retrieve data, and I showed you how to avoid common ESLint error messages due to the TS requirement to have the types. I also gave you some tips in terms of how to organize your composition and run a quality check with the format, lint, and test run scripts.

Check my d3 and React interactive course to see other ways you can implement all the examples in this chapter with different approaches. The interactive course covers more topics for this section, such as, taking more control over the DOM, color spaces, interactivity, design, as well as expanding on what's in this chapter. The course compliment this chapter and book neatly; `https://elielrom.com/BuildSiteCourse`

The next chapter is going to be a continuation of creating basic charts, and we will be creating three more basic charts.

- Pie chart

- Scatter plot

- Histogram chart

CHAPTER 4

Basic Charts: Part 2

As you have already seen, D3 is the standard for creating charts, so if you are serious about creating and customizing charts, you can't escape learning about D3. React is made to integrate with other libraries such as D3; however, adding TypeScript to the mix does require special attention.

In the previous chapters, I showed you how to create popular and basic types of charts with React, TS, and D3. Additionally, if you took my React + d3 interactive course (`https://elielrom.com/BuildSiteCourse`) you seen other ways you can implement all the examples in the previous chapter with different approaches such as applying memorizing callbacks, handling resizing, more interactions, and handling the DOM. That combo of React + d3 + TS needs some special attention versus using just JS, and the basic charts in this chapter and the previous one reflect things that I have found to work the best.

In this chapter, I will be covering how to create more simple charts with React and D3 using TypeScript as a type checker.

I will be showing you how to create the following simple charts with the emphasis of getting D3 to do most of the work:

- Pie chart
- Scatter chart
- Histogram chart

Let's begin.

Pie Chart

A pie chart is one of the most basic and popular types of chart. The type of chart is a circular, statistical graphic. A pie chart represents numbers by using slices to represent a proportion of the whole.

© Elad Elrom 2021
E. Elrom, *Integrating D3.js with React*, https://doi.org/10.1007/978-1-4842-7052-3_4

pie.csv

The data metrics of my chart is just random numbers that total 100 percent.

```
name,value
a,25
b,3
c,45
d,7
e,20
```

Besides the data file, I will be creating a few more files, just as I did in the previous chapter.

- BasicPieChart.tsx: Main component

- BasicPieChart.test.tsx: Jest and Enzyme testing

- BasicPieChart.scss: The SCSS preprocessors

- types.ts: A file to hold the types I will be using

Once again, as in Part I, you can create these files yourself or get some help from generate-react-cli.

```
$ npx generate-react-cli component BasicPieChart --type=d3
```

types.ts

My type consists of the same columns as the data file such as name and value.

```
// src/component/BasicPieChart/types.tsexport namespace Types {
  export type Data = {
    name: string
    value: number
  }
}
```

BasicPieChart.tsx

For the BasicPieChart, the process is similar to the chart we built in Part I, using useEffect to draw the method, load the data, and draw the chart. Take a look:

```
// src/component/BasicPieChart/BasicPieChart.tsx

import React, { useEffect } from 'react'
import './BasicPieChart.scss'
import * as d3 from 'd3'
```

D3 is built in a modular way, so I need PieArcDatum (https://github.com/d3/d3-shape). The PieArcDatum generic refers to the data type of an element in the input array passed into the Pie generator. I will be using PieArcDatum to better cast my object. Make sure you add the module, as shown here:

```
yarn add d3-shape
```

Take a look:

```
import { PieArcDatum } from 'd3-shape'
import { Types } from './types'
const BasicPieChart = (props: IBasicPieChartProps) => {
  useEffect(() => {
    draw()
  })
```

For the draw() method, I will be setting up the width, height, and radius of the pie.

```
const draw = () => {
  const width = props.width - props.left - props.right
  const height = props.height - props.top - props.bottom
  const radius = Math.min(width, height) / 2
```

Next, I select the basicPieChart div I will be rendering and add a group called svg with a transform attribute.

```
const svg = d3
  .select('.basicPieChart')
  .append('svg')
```

```
    .attr('width', width)
    .attr('height', height)
    .append('g')
    .attr('transform', `translate(${width / 2},${height / 2})`)
```

I will upload the CSV pie.csv data file.

```
d3.dsv(',', '/Data/pie.csv', (d) => {
  const res = (d as unknown) as Types.Data
  return {
    name: res.name,
    value: res.value,
  }
}).then((data) => {
```

Once my data object is ready, the next step is to set up the color scale. I will be using d3.scaleOrdinal(), and for the domain, I can set each name to have its own unique color.

D3 makes things easy, as there are a set of predefined categorized color schemes, so I can use d3.schemeCategory10 or any other (https://github.com/d3/d3-scale-chromatic) color categories.

```
const color = d3
      .scaleOrdinal()
      .domain(
        (d3.extent(data, (d) => {
          return d.name
        }) as unknown) as string
      )
      .range(d3.schemeCategory10)
```

Notice that although I am using d3.schemeCategory10, I could create my own color scheme that can be passed as props or defined in my data file.

```
.range(['#000000', '#000000', '#000000', '#000000', '#000000'])
```

The next step is to iterate through my data and create the pie. I could turn my data into key-value pairs and then pass it to a path element, like so:

```
const map = d3.map(data, (d) => {
  return { 'key': d.name, value: d.value }
})
```

But there is a better way. I can set the pie with my data type, use the generic PieArcDatum with my data type, and generate the path for the radius. Then I plug in my data to create a pie data that I can use to iterate through the results.

```
const pie = d3
  .pie<Types.Data>()
  .sort(null)
  .value((record) => record.value)

const path = d3.arc<PieArcDatum<Types.Data>>().innerRadius(0).
outerRadius(radius)

const pieData = pie(data)
```

Now all I need to do is generate the arch SVGs for each pie data and use the color I created for each name.

```
const arch = svg
  .selectAll('.arc')
  .data(pieData)
  .enter()
  .append('g')
  .attr('class', 'arc')
  .attr('fill', (d) => {
    return color(d.data.name) as string
  })

  arch.append('path').attr('d', path)
  })
}
```

For the rendering side, I need a wrapping div.

```
return <div className="basicPieChart" />
}
```

For my `props` interface, I am placing the alignment elements that I will be passing from my parent component.

```
interface IBasicPieChartProps {
  width: number
  height: number
  top: number
  right: number
  bottom: number
  left: number
}

export default BasicPieChart
```

BasicPieChart.test.tsx

For testing, I am using Jest and Enzyme to ensure that the component mounts and am using the props I set.

```
// src/component/BasicPieChart/BasicPieChart.test.tsx

import React from 'react'
import { shallow } from 'enzyme'
import BasicPieChart from './BasicPieChart'

describe('<BasicPieChart />', () => {
  let component

  beforeEach(() => {
    component = shallow(<BasicPieChart width={900} height={400} top={10}
    right={50} bottom={50} left={50} />)
  })

  test('It should mount', () => {
    expect(component.length).toBe(1)
  })
})
```

App.tsx

Lastly, my parent component App.tsx needs to include my BasicPieChart with the alignment props.

```
// src/App.tsx

import React from 'react'
import './App.scss'

import BasicPieChart from './components/BasicPieChart/BasicPieChart'

function App() {
  return (
    <div className="App">
      <header className="App-header">
        <BasicPieChart width={400} height={400} top={10} right={10}
        bottom={10} left={10} />
      </header>
    </div>
  )
}

export default App
```

BasicPieChart.scss

For the SCSS file, I defined a placeholder. I don't need any SCSS yet, but it's good practice to create a SCSS file.

```
.basicPieChart {
}
```

Look again at localhost port 3000: http://localhost:3000/. You can compare your results with mine, shown in Figure 4-1.

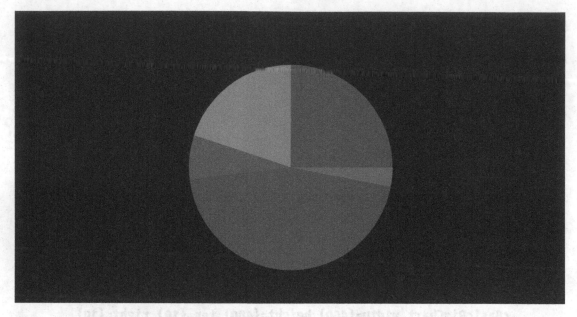

Figure 4-1. *React and D3 pie chart*

As always, you can download the complete code of this chapter from here:

https://github.com/Apress/integrating-d3.js-with-react/tree/main/ch03

To see this basic pie chart with better integration with React and interactions of resizing and switching metrics check my React + d3 interactive course: https://elielrom.com/BuildSiteCourse.

BasicDonutChart.tsx

To create a small donut chart, the process is almost identical. I will use `PieArcDatum` to draw arcs for the inner and outer circles in order to create a donut. The change is simple. Just update `'innerRadius'` property when we create the arc; `innerRadius(10)`.

In the following example, I can change the code and use the `props` to pass the data from the parent component instead of loading it inside my component. I am also going to write the code so the component can be used to change the data, if needed. Let's take a look.

First import the library using `yarn add d3-shape`.

Take a look at the `BasicDonutChart.tsx` code:

```
import React, { RefObject, useEffect, useState } from 'react'
import * as d3 from 'd3'
```

```
import { PieArcDatum } from 'd3-shape'
import { Types } from './types'

const BasicDonutChart = (props: IBasicDonutChartProps) => {
 const ref: RefObject<HTMLDivElement> = React.createRef()
 const [data, setData] = useState<Types.Data[]>([])
```

Inside of useEffect, I will be checking the data. This is needed to ensure that I am changing the pie only once new data is being updated. That can happen when you have new data, for instance.

What I am doing is storing the data on a React state object and then comparing the state data with the props data to see if there is a change using JSON.stringify. If there is a change, I will store the new data inside the state.

```
useEffect(() => {
  if (JSON.stringify(props.data) !== JSON.stringify(data)) {
    setData(props.data)

    const { width } = props
    const { height } = props

    const svg = d3
      .select(ref.current)
      .append('svg')
      .attr('width', width)
      .attr('height', height)
      .append('g')
      .attr('transform', `translate(${width / 2}, ${height / 2.5})`)

    const color = ['#068606', '#C1C0C0']

    const donut = d3
      .pie<Types.Data>()
      .sort(null)
      .value((record) => record.value)

    const path = d3.arc<PieArcDatum<Types.Data>>().innerRadius(10).
    outerRadius(20)

    const donutData = donut(props.data)
```

```
    const arch = svg
      .selectAll('.arc')
      .data(donutData)
      .enter()
      .append('g')
      .attr('class', 'arc')
      .attr('fill', (d, i) => {
        return color[i] as string
      })

    arch.append('path').attr('d', path)
  }
}, [data, props, props.data, props.height, props.width, ref])
```

I need to specify the variable I am using inside useEffect.

```
return <div className="basicDonutChart" ref={ref} />
}

interface IBasicDonutChartProps {
 data: Types.Data[]
 width: number
 height: number
}

export default BasicDonutChart
```

Notice that in my example I am using a reference instead of D3 select. That way I can include my pie as a list item renderer, in case I need to use this component inside a list.

App.tsx

To implement this, you can set the chart in a parent component and pass the data in App.tsx.

```
<BasicDonutChart
 data={[
   { name: 'Yes', value: 80 },
   { name: 'No', value: 20 },
 ]}
```

```
width={50}
height={50}
/>
```

Take a look at Figure 4-2.

Figure 4-2. *Basic donut pie chart*

As for the data, in the previous examples, I showed you how the actual chart component retrieves the data.

This made our code easy to read and loosely coupled, which is a great design to keep the charts simple and the data in one place; however, to prepare you for the next chapter of dealing with a state management, here I extracted the data to the parent component App.tsx.

The reason we would want to extract the data from the chart component is for cases where the data is shared between multiple components. In this case, we want to load the data once and share it with multiple components. A good example is using the same data to draw different charts types.

Scatter Chart

A scatter chart (aka a *scatter plot chart* or a *scatter graph*) represents values with dots. Scatter charts are a great way to observe relationships between variables.

scatter.csv

An interesting way to use a scatter chart is to look at diamond prices in relationship to diamond sizes. I found the data posted on GitHub (https://github.com/sakshi296/ P1-1-Predicting-Diamond-Prices). Once I download the chart, I can open it in Excel or any other program to revise it, as shown in Figure 4-3.

R6C10								

	1	2	3	4	5	6	7	8
1		carat	cut	cut_ord	color	clarity	clarity_ord	price
2	1	0.51	Premium	4	F	VS1	4	1749
3	2	2.25	Fair	1	G	I1	1	7069
4	3	0.7	Very Good	3	E	VS2	5	2757
5	4	0.47	Good	2	F	VS1	4	1243
6	5	0.3	Ideal	5	G	VVS1	7	789
7	6	0.33	Ideal	5	D	SI1	3	728
8	7	2.01	Very Good	3	G	SI1	3	18398
9	8	0.51	Ideal	5	F	VVS2	6	2203
10	9	1.7	Premium	4	D	SI1	3	15100
11	10	0.53	Premium	4	D	VS2	5	1857
12	11	0.39	Premium	4	H	SI1	3	834
13	12	1.5	Very Good	3	H	SI1	3	7708
14	13	1	Premium	4	E	VS2	5	6272
15	14	1.29	Ideal	5	J	VS1	4	5676
16	15	2.01	Good	2	D	SI2	2	16776
17	16	1.13	Ideal	5	G	VS1	4	7404
18	17	0.7	Ideal	5	I	SI2	2	1702
19	18	0.38	Very Good	3	I	VS1	4	606
20	19	1.17	Ideal	5	H	SI2	2	5423
21	20	1.51	Premium	4	F	SI1	3	8033

Figure 4-3. *Diamond prices per carat CSV data*

I will be deleting all the columns I don't need and keeping the price and carat metrics (see Figure 4-4).

	1	2	3	4
1	price	carat		
2	1749	0.51		
3	7069	2.25		
4	2757	0.7		
5	1243	0.47		
6	789	0.3		
7	728	0.33		
8	18398	2.01		
9	2203	0.51		
10	15100	1.7		
11	1857	0.53		
12	834	0.39		
13	7708	1.5		
14	6272	1		
15	5676	1.29		
16	16776	2.01		

Figure 4-4. *Diamond prices per carat cleaned*

Our data set is small and has a little footprint, but cleaning up your data and setting up your data set to only consume what you need is a good practice to optimize your data and increase performance. In Chapter 10, I will dive deeper into the best practices of optimizing your charts.

I will be saving my file as scatter.csv in public/data/scatter.csv.

```
price,carat
1749,0.51
7069,2.25
2757,0.7
1243,0.47
789,0.3
728,0.33
...
...
```

types.ts

For my TypeScript data I will set the same names as my CSV columns: price and carat metrics.

```
// src/component/BasicScatterChart/types.ts
```

```typescript
export namespace Types {
  export type Data = {
    price: number
    carat: number
  }
}
```

BasicScatterChart.tsx

Now I am ready to start plotting my chart.

```
// src/component/BasicScatterChart/BasicScatterChart.tsx
```

```typescript
import React, { useEffect } from 'react'
import './BasicScatterChart.scss'
import * as d3 from 'd3'
import { Types } from './types'

const BasicScatterChart = (props: IBasicScatterChartProps) => {
  useEffect(() => {
    draw()
  })  const draw = () => {
    const width = props.width - props.left - props.right
    const height = props.height - props.top - props.bottom

    const svg = d3
      .select('.basicScatterChart')
      .append('svg')
      .attr('width', width + props.left + props.right)
      .attr('height', height + props.top + props.bottom)
      .append('g')
      .attr('transform', `translate(${props.left},${props.top})`)
```

```
d3.dsv(',', '/Data/diamonds.csv', (d) => {
  return {
    price: d.price,
    carat: d.carat,
  }
}).then((data) => {
```

Once the data is ready, I will create the x-axis and y-axis peripherals. The first step is to find out what the highest values are for the price and carat, which I can then set as my axis max values.

```
const maxPrice = Math.max(...data.map((dt) => (dt as unknown as Types.
Data).price), 0)
const maxCarat = Math.max(...data.map((dt) => (dt as unknown as Types.
Data).carat), 0)
```

Next, I can use d3.scaleLinear to set my x-axis and y-axis.

```
const x = d3.scaleLinear().domain([0, 18000]).range([0, width])
svg.append('g').attr('transform', `translate(0,${height})`).call(d3.
axisBottom(x))

const y = d3.scaleLinear().domain([0, 4.5]).range([height, 0])
svg.append('g').call(d3.axisLeft(y))
```

The last part is to plot the dots by using a circle SVG element with a fill color that I will be passing from the parent component. I am setting my radius at 1px since I have so many results, but you could try it with even smaller results.

```
svg
  .append('g')
  .selectAll('dot')
  .data(data)
  .enter()
  .append('circle')
  .attr('cx', (d) => {
    return x(((d as unknown) as Types.Data).price)
  })
```

```
        .attr('cy', (d) => {
          return y(((d as unknown) as Types.Data).carat)
        })
        .attr('r', 0.8)
        .style('fill', props.fill)
    })
  }

  return <div className="basicScatterChart" />
}

interface IBasicScatterChartProps {
  width: number
  height: number
  top: number
  right: number
  bottom: number
  left: number
  fill: string
}

export default BasicScatterChart
```

App.tsx

Add the BasicScatterChart component to my App.tsx.

```
// src/App.tsx
```

**import BasicScatterChart from './components/BasicScatterChart/
BasicScatterChart'**

**<BasicScatterChart width={800} height={400} top={10} right={50} bottom={50}
left={50} fill="tomato" />**

Lastly, if you did not do this before, create BasicScatterChart.scss and
BasicScatterChart.test.tsx.

- `BasicScatterChart.scss`: This is just a placeholder for SCSS.

- `BasicScatterChart.test.tsx`: This is the same as `BasicPieChart.test.tsx`.

Now, we see the diamond per carat historic prices, as shown in Figure 4-5.

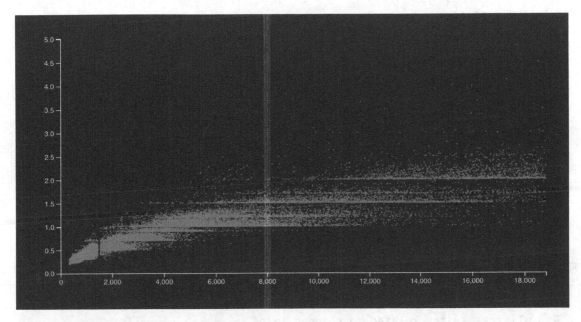

Figure 4-5. *React and D3 scatter chart*

The chart can show me the price range at a glance, and I can see what to expect in terms of carat size and price for each diamond. If I want to improve the chart, I could insert other fields such as the diamond color's grade metrics and give these different colors on the chart. I could change the chart per year and filter the data.

Now that I have all the three charts ready, I am going to run the format, lint, and test tasks one last time to ensure quality.

```
$ yarn format
$ yarn lint
$ yarn test
```

Compare your results with mine.

```
✦ Done in 1.97s.
$ yarn lint
yarn run v1.22.10
$ eslint – ext .js,.jsx,.ts,.tsx ./
✦ Done in 10.14s.
Test Suites: 7 passed, 7 total
Tests: 7 passed, 7 total
Snapshots: 0 total
Time: 9.476s
```

See Figure 4-6.

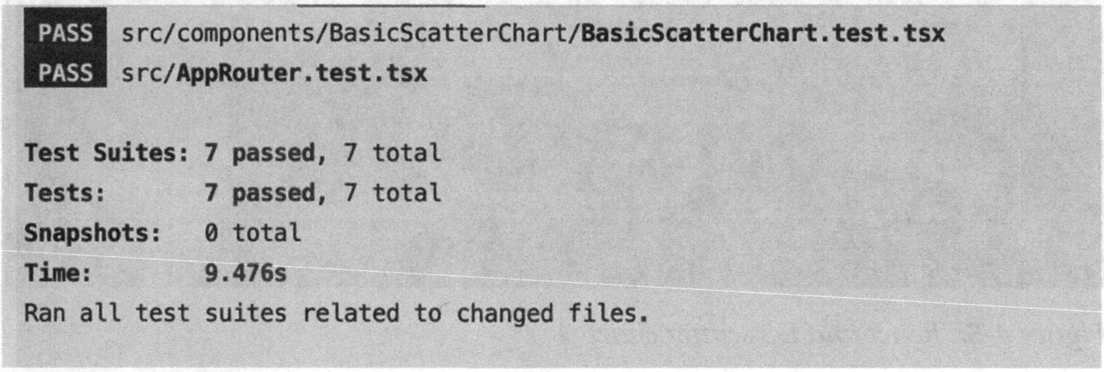

```
PASS   src/components/BasicScatterChart/BasicScatterChart.test.tsx
PASS   src/AppRouter.test.tsx


Test Suites: 7 passed, 7 total
Tests:       7 passed, 7 total
Snapshots:   0 total
Time:        9.476s
Ran all test suites related to changed files.
```

Figure 4-6. *Test results for basic chart components*

In 'my d3 and React interactive course you will learn how to include interactive means lines and set resizing, as well as set the component so react control the DOM better, see https://elielrom.com/BuildSiteCourse.

Setting interactive mean lines that move on mouse move events can help the user read the results better and quickly figure price prediction per carat.

Histogram Chart

The charts we have created so far were relatively simple.

In the donut pie chart, we did check if the data had changed, and we stored the new data set in the function component state, but we haven't implemented any changes in the chart.

My intention was to just show you how to integrate D3 into a React component that uses TypeScript as the type checker and uses D3 as much as possible.

The last chart in this chapter we will be creating is a basic histogram chart that is going to include input from the user, interactions, and animation. We will use the class component this time, so you can see how to use the hooks built into the React class component to tie together the animations and changes.

A histogram is a bar chart that made out of price and time metrics. Histogram is a common way to show how often values fall into ranges.

The histogram chart groups numeric data into bins. Then bins can be displayed as segmented columns.

We will be building a chart that reviews the price of Ethereum coins over time, so you can see at what price the coin is sold at over time in an easy, intuitive way.

types.ts

For the TypeScript types, I am creating two types. The first type is for the data (Data), and that object holds the price of the coin. The second type that I will be using (BarsNode) is to deal with bars, as well as to redraw these bars. Take a look:

```
//src/component/Histogram/types.ts

export namespace Types {
  export type Data = {
    price: number
  }
  export type BarsNode = {
    x0: number
    x1: number
    length: number
  }
}
```

Next, for the actual histogram chart component, I am creating three files again. There is nothing new here:

- Histogram.tsx: Custom component

- Histogram.scss: Style

- Histogram.test.tsx: Jest test

Histogram.tsx

In the Histogram component, I will be setting up a slider. The user input will determine how many bars to display. Once the user inputs a selection using the slider, I can redraw the chart. For the slider I will be using the Material-UI slide component, so in addition to all the usual imports, let's import the slider. Additionally, I will be using the Typography module from Material-UI for the tile of my chart.

```
// src/component/Histogram/Histogram.tsx

import React from 'react'
import './Histogram.scss'
import * as d3 from 'd3'
import Slider from '@material-ui/core/Slider'
import { Typography } from '@material-ui/core'
import { Types } from './types'
```

For the class signature, I will be using a class pure component (React.PureComponent) versus React.Component since I don't need to use shouldComponentUpdate event lifecycle.

My props and state props interfaces will include properties to adjust the chart.

```
export default class Histogram extends React.PureComponent<IHistogramProps,
IHistogramState> {
  constructor(props: IHistogramProps) {
    super(props)
```

My state will consist of how many ticks (bars) I the user want to draw; the starting state is 10.

```
    this.state = {
      numberOfTicks: 10,
    }
  }
}
```

Next, we need to redraw the chart once the user makes changes to the slider. To do that, we are using the Material-UI slider change event; however, because of the way the React virtual DOM works, that doesn't guarantee our chart will get updated. The best approach is to use componentDidUpdate in addition to componentDidMount, which gets called on initial rendering.

```
componentDidMount() {
  this.draw()
}

componentDidUpdate(prevProps: IHistogramProps, prevState: IHistogramState) {
  this.draw()
}
```

Now we could also use getDerivedStateFromProps instead of componentDidUpdate, but that method may be called multiple times for a single update, so we would need to place a validator to check whether the state was updated.

componentDidUpdate gets invoked immediately after updating occurs. This method is not called for the initial render.

It's essential to avoid any side effects, so you should use componentDidUpdate, which executes only once after the component updates.

Once the slider changes, we need to update our state with the new values of the number of ticks we want to display, which happens in the handleChange method. The event is of type React.ChangeEvent. I can also pass the new value that was a result of the update.

```
handleChange = (event: React.ChangeEvent<{}>, newValue: number |
number[]) => {
```

Once that event is called, I can set the state to numberOfTicks. I will bind numberOfTicks, so the update will happen.

```
  const value = newValue as number
  this.setState((prevState: IHistogramState) => {
    return {
      ...prevState,
      numberOfTicks: value,
    }
  })
}
```

The heavy lifting is done in the draw method. I could split this code more into an helper class, but the example is not too complex.

I am using d3.selectAll to set histogramChart to the wrapper element.

```
draw = () => {
  const histogramChart = d3.selectAll('.histogramChart')
```

Next, I will be clearing the x and y from the chart as they may change. This is not needed on the first draw but for the redraw. To do that, I use remove. The remove will delete all the groups elements under my main wrapper.

```
d3.selectAll('.histogramChart').selectAll('g').remove()
```

Once the bars are removed, I will create a new group SVG element for the x-axis and y-axis to be added to the histogramChart group element.

```
const xAxisGroupNode = histogramChart.append('g')
const yAxisGroupNode = histogramChart.append('g')
```

Next, let's initialize and scale the x-axis. I am baking in the values, but they could be set dynamically.

```
const xAxis = d3.scaleLinear().domain([75, 650]).range([0, this.props.
width])
```

Then, I can draw the x-axis.

```
xAxisGroupNode.attr('transform', `translate(0,${this.props.height})`).
call(d3.axisBottom(xAxis))
```

It's the same with the y-axis: initialize, scale, and then draw.

```
const yAxis = d3.scaleLinear().range([this.props.height, 0])
```

I can utilize d3.bin (https://github.com/d3/d3-array), which groups data points into buckets. We can set up the data, the domain, and the parameters for the histogram. My domain data is between 0–750, so I am baking it in.

```
const histogram = d3
  .bin()
  .value((d) => {
    return ((d as unknown) as Types.Data).price
  })
  .domain([0, 750])
  .thresholds(xAxis.ticks(this.state.numberOfTicks))
```

Next, apply this function to the data to get the bins:

```
const bins = histogram(this.props.data as Array<never>)
```

The y-axis will update the values once we set the domain and draw the chart.

```
const yAxisMaxValues = d3.max(bins, (d) => {
  return d.length
}) as number
yAxis.domain([0, yAxisMaxValues])
```

Next, draw the y-axis.

```
yAxisGroupNode.transition().duration(750).call(d3.axisLeft(yAxis))
```

For the bar nodes, we join rectangles with bin data and deal with the bars as well as new ones that we are redrawing.

```
const barsNode = histogramChart.selectAll<SVGRectElement,
number[]>('rect').data(bins)

const { height } = this.props

barsNode
  .enter()
  .append('rect')
  .merge(barsNode) // get existing elements
  .transition() // apply changes
  .duration(750)
  .attr('transform',  (d) => {
    // @ts-ignore
    return `translate(${xAxis(d.x0)},${yAxis(d.length)})`
  })
  .attr('width', (d) => {
    return xAxis((d as Types.BarsNode).x1) - xAxis((d as Types.
    BarsNode).x0) - 1
  })
```

```
    .attr('height', (d) => {
      return height - yAxis(d.length)
    })
    .style('fill', this.props.fill)
```

Lastly, if there are extra bars because of the changes, we need to remove them.

```
  barsNode.exit().remove()
}
```

The jsx is straightforward.

However, this time I am adding a title and labels using the Material-UI typography component to include our text labels and SVG to hold the <g> elements and a Material-UI slider.

I am also utilizing the props set by the parent component to align the chart neatly.

```
render() {
  const { width, height, margin } = this.props
  return (
    <div className="histogram">
      <Typography id="discrete-slider" gutterBottom>
      2020 Eth Price days/price Histogram Chart
      </Typography>
      <svg height={height + margin.top + margin.bottom} width={width +
      margin.left + margin.right}>
        <text x={margin.left - 35} y={margin.top - 10} fontSize={10}>
          Days
        </text>
        <text x={width + margin.left + 20} y={height + margin.top + 16}
        fontSize={10}>
          Price
        </text>
        <g className="histogramChart" transform={`translate(${margin.
        left},${margin.top})`} />
      </svg>
      <div className="sliderDiv">
        <Typography id="discrete-slider" gutterBottom>
        Number of ticks:
```

```
        </Typography>
        <Slider
          defaultValue={this.state.numberOfTicks}
          getAriaValueText={(value: number) => {
            return `${value} ticks`
          }}
          valueLabelDisplay="auto"
          min={10}
          max={85}
          onChange={this.handleChange}
        />
      </div>
    </div>
  )
}
}
```

The interface will hold the data and the alignment attributes.

```
interface IHistogramProps {
  data: Types.Data[]
  margin: {
    top: number
    right: number
    bottom: number
    left: number
  }
  width: number
  height: number
  fill: string
}
```

The state holds the number of ticks to be displayed.

```
interface IHistogramState {
  numberOfTicks: number
}
```

Histogram.scss

In my SCSS, I will set up some padding for the div as well as set properties for the slider and SVG text color.

```scss
.histogram {
  padding-top: 50px;
}
.sliderDiv {
  width: 400px;
  padding-left: 50px;
  padding-top: 20px;
}
svg text {
  fill: white;
}
```

App.tsx

Lastly, I am including the histogram component in App.tsx.

In the pie donut you saw, the data was passed through the props from the parent component.

As I mentioned, we want to extract the data from the chart component for cases where the data is shared between multiple components.

In the chart here, I am using d3.dsv. However, I am passing the data to the child component histogram from App.tsx. Take a look:

```tsx
import React, { useEffect } from 'react'
import './App.scss'
import * as d3 from 'd3'
import Histogram from './components/Histogram/Histogram'
import { Types } from './components/Histogram/types'

function App() {
```

I am using the function state so once the data is updated, it will reflect automatically on the Histogram component. My data type is of type number[], since I will be setting an array with price metric. For the initial value, I can use ([{ 'price': 0 }]).

```
const [data, setData] = React.useState([{ 'price': 0 }] as Types.Data[])
useEffect(() => {
```

useEffect will be called multiple times, on every rendering, so I want to limit loading the data only once.

To do that, I can check whether the data has just the initial value I set or not. Since I set the initial value with an array and one result, there are more results than that (`data.length <= 1`), and I can retrieve the data.

```
if (data.length <= 1) {
  d3.dsv(',', '/data/historicalPrice.csv', (d) => {
    return {
      price: d.open as unknown as number
    }
  }).then((d) => {
```

I am using the React set state machanism to set the data.

```
    setData(d)
  })
  }
})
return (
  <div className="App">
    <header className="App-header">
```

On the rendering, I set the Histogram component with the props.

```
    <Histogram data={data} margin={{ top: 20, right: 45, bottom: 20,
    left: 50 }} width={400} height={400} fill="tomato" />
    </header>
  </div>
)
}
```

```
export default App
```

As we did before, use the format, lint, and test functionality to ensure the quality.

```
$ yarn format & yarn lint & yarn test
```

Figure 4-7 shows the final result.

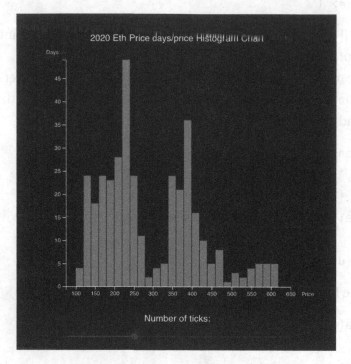

Figure 4-7. *Histogram diagram showing prices of Ethereum coin grouped*

Looking at the chart, it seems that during 2020 most of the time the price of Ethereum was either about $225 (for about 50 days) or $400 (for about 37 days).

That's the power of charts. With one look at a chart, I can get the story.

Note I am using charts that are based on investment vehicles in this chapter, but I am not recommending investing in any of the stocks or coins shown in this book.

You can download the complete code for the Histogram component from here:

```
https://github.com/Apress/integrating-d3.js-with-react/tree/main/ch04-05/
histogram-d3-ts
```

Summary

This chapter was a continuation of the previous chapter, and in this chapter, I covered how to create some simple charts with React and D3 using TypeScript as a type checker.

I showed you how to create the following simple charts using React function and class components with the emphasis of getting D3 to do most of the work:

- Pie chart

- Scatter chart

Also, I showed you how to create histogram charts by integrating D3 and React as well as adding more React libraries into the mix.

We used other React libraries such as Material-UI and retrieved the data from a parent component so the data could be shared between multiple components.

In my d3 and React interactive course you can see other ways you can implement all the examples in this chapter with different approaches. The interactive course covers more topics for this section, such as, taking more control over the DOM, interactivity, design, as well as expanding on what's in this chapter. The course compliment this chapter and book neatly; `https://elielrom.com/BuildSiteCourse`.

In the next chapter, we will integrate React state management into mix so we can share our data across our app and even with multiple components that do not originate from the same parent component.

CHAPTER 5

Integrating State Management

In the previous chapter, I showed you how to create simple charts using React function and class components and D3. In the last example, we created a histogram by integrating D3 and React as well as adding other React libraries into the mix such as Material-UI and Jest.

In the histogram, we retrieved the data from the `App.tsx` parent component so the data could be shared between multiple components.

In this chapter, we will take this chart a step further. We will integrate React state management into the mix so we can share our data across our app and even over multiple components that do not originate from the same parent component. This will be done using state management.

In this chapter, you will learn about the state management architecture introduced by Facebook called Flux, and then you will learn about the new experimental state management architecture from Facebook called Recoil that is poised to take over. In the process, I will show you how to add structure to your chart that can help you build more complex charts, and we will even be integrating a table list component that will use the same data.

State Management

One change in the data by itself sounds insignificant and easy enough for your component to implement and manage. So why do we need a state management library to achieve this task?

In layman's terms, *state management* helps organize data and user interaction of your app until the user's session ends. It also helps ensure your code doesn't get messy as more features are added.

© Elad Elrom 2021
E. Elrom, *Integrating D3.js with React*, https://doi.org/10.1007/978-1-4842-7052-3_5

It makes life easier with testing, and it ensures the code is not dependent on a specific development technique and can scale up.

Note   State management is a method of maintaining the state of our app until our user's session ends.

If you look at the charts we created in the previous chapters, we don't have a problem and don't need a design pattern to help us manage our data movement. In fact, implementing an architecture to control our data movement can be seen as overkill for such simple functionality. The state we used is holding the data once it's received, and it all works just fine.

However, as our code grows and our app becomes larger, with multiple developers and designers, we need some sort of architecture in place to help handle the data movement, as well as enforce best practices to help manage our code so that it doesn't break with every change.

In fact, Facebook encountered these challenges and looked for ways to solve these problems.

Flux

The Facebook team first tried a few tools that already existed. They first implemented the Model-View-Controller (MVC) pattern; however, they found the architecture pattern causing issues as more and more features were added, and a portion of the code was harder to maintain as the code broke constantly.

The React team's challenges with using the MVC pattern for separating concerns and managing the state for the front end ended up with the creation of Flux.

It's important to know that Flux state management is being phased out, and the project is in maintenance mode. There are many more sophisticated alternatives available.

What Does MVC Solve?

In a complex app, the MVC pattern is a common practice to separate concerns.

- *Model*: The model is the data that is used in the app.

- *View*: The view is the front-end presentation layer.

- *Controller*: This is the glue that binds the model and the view.

The Facebook team explained that when the developers tried using MVC, they experienced issues with the data flow that can cause a loop, which can crash an app as it will become a memory leak (cascading effects by nested updates) and keep re-updating the rendering endlessly.

These challenges were solved by the Facebook team coming with an architecture they called Flux and then more recently with an experimental library called Recoil.

Note   Flux is an application architecture for building user interfaces. See `https://facebook.github.io/flux/`.

"Flux is the application architecture that Facebook uses for building client-side web applications. It complements React's composable view components by utilizing a unidirectional data flow. It's more of a pattern rather than a formal framework."

`https://facebook.github.io/flux/docs/in-depth-overview`

From my personal experience, having worked with many MVC-based applications small and large, I have to somewhat disagree with the Facebook team. Some of these projects were very complex enterprise-level applications built on MVC, and by enforcing good habits, MVC-based apps can work seamlessly. With that being said, there is a lot of boilerplate code involved in many of the MVC framework implementations out there, and a code review is often necessary to enforce good habits and to maintain a separation of concerns.

Facebook's Flux architecture does simplify the process of separating concerns and is a fresh and welcomed alternative to state management, while keeping less boilerplate code and our components loosely coupled. You can learn more about Flux here:

`https://github.com/facebook/flux`
`https://facebook.github.io/flux/`

127

Flux is being phased out, but there are several other state management libraries.

- *Redux*: http://redux.js.org/

- *MobX*: https://mobx.js.org/

- *Recoil*: https://recoiljs.org/

Recoil

Redux (and the Redux Toolkit) is the most popular state management library at the time of writing. If you want to learn more about Redux, I recommend you purchase my *React and Libraries* book at https://www.apress.com/gp/book/9781484266953 or read my article at https://medium.com/react-courses/instance-learn-react-redux-4-redux-toolkit-in-minutes-a-2020-reactjs-16-tutorial-9adaec6f2836.

Unlike Redux or the Redux Toolkit, with Recoil there is no need to deal with setting up complex middleware, connecting your components, or using anything else to get the React components to play along nicely with each other.

Did you know?   The Recoil library is still at the experimental stage, but it has already gained some extraordinary popularity, passing even Redux. The Recoil library has close to 10,000 stars on GitHub, passing the Redux Toolkit's 4,100 stars!

It is my opinion and many others that Recoil will become the standard for state management in React and is a much better investment of your time learning than continuing developing utilizing the Redux Toolkit for the middleware.

However, keep in mind that it is still good to know the Redux Toolkit as you may be involved in a project that uses Redux. Additionally, Recoil is still experimental as of the writing of this book, so it's not for the faint of heart.

To learn about Recoil, we will be refactoring our Histogram component we created in the previous chapter.

Recoil is Facebook's life-changing state management experiment that is sweeping the React developer's community. The Recoil team puts it nicely:

> *"Recoil works and thinks like React. Add some to your app and get a fast and flexible shared state."*

Recoil was developed and published at a time when there are many state management libraries out there, so you may be asking why we need yet another state management to share our app state. Can sharing state across multiple components and setting up middleware can be done better and easier with Recoil? The quick answer is yes!

If all you need to do is store value globally, any library you choose will work; however, things start to get complicated when you start doing more complex stuff such as asynchronous calls or try to get your client in sync with your server state or reverse user interactions.

Ideally, we want our React components to be as pure as possible, and the data management needs to be done to flow through the React hooks with no side effects. We also want the "real" DOM to be changed as little as possible for performance.

Keeping components loosely coupled is always a good place to be as a developer, so having a library that integrates well with React is a great addition to the React library as it puts React up there with other top JavaScript frameworks such as Angular.

Having a solid-state management library will help React applications serve enterprise-level complex applications as well as handle complex operations on both the front and middle tiers. Recoil simplifies state management, and we only need to create two ingredients: atoms and selectors (`https://recoiljs.org/docs/introduction/core-concepts/`).

Atoms are objects. They are units of state that components can subscribe to. Recoil lets us create a data-flow graph that flows from these atoms (shared state) to the components.

Selectors are pure functions that allow you to transform the state either synchronously or asynchronously.

Keep in mind that you don't have to create atoms and selectors. You can just use selectors without any atoms as well as create atoms without selectors.

To show how to get started with Recoil, I will break down the process into two steps.

- *Step 1*: Implementing Recoil

- *Step 2*: Refactoring the view layer

To get started, we would normally first need to install Recoil (`yarn add recoil`). At the time of writing, Recoil is at version 0.1.2, but that will change by the time you read this chapter. However, our CRA MHL template already includes both Recoil and Redux, so Recoil is already set up without any installation on your part.

Historical Price State

Let's get started.

historicalPriceObject.ts: Set Up Our Data Type

In our histogram, we create `types.ts`. The class holds the types we are using in our chart. This type of architecture is great, because it allows us to copy our component and reuse it anywhere we want, keeping our code loosely coupled.

However, Recoil is going to need a definition as well. I could just import the types class, but that would create a composition between our state and our chart.

This would not be ideal if I had multiple charts using the same data, because we would need to import the types.

Note My decision is to create a model class that I can use to initialize my object as well as have an interface for the price object. This design is not mandatory; it depends on what you need. If you can remove code and everything works and is simple to understand, go ahead and remove code. I am just getting you started here.

Take a look:

```
// src/model/historicalPriceObject.ts

export interface historicalPriceObject {
  price: number
}

export const initHistoricalPrice = (): historicalPriceObject => ({
  price: 0,
})
```

> **Note** As they say, there are many ways to skin a cat. There are pros and cons for each approach; you need to be the judge of whether this works for you.

index.ts: Easy Access

Next, set up an index file for easy access to our type.

```
// src/model/index.ts
export * from './historicalPriceObject'
```

historicalPriceAtoms.ts: Shared State

Now that I have my model object, I can create my Recoil atom.

As I mentioned, Recoil atoms are objects. They are units of state that components can subscribe to. Recoil lets us create a data-flow graph that flows from these atoms (shared state) to the components. I can have my model used in my Atom, as shown in the following code. We import the atom from the Recoil library, as well as the mode initHistoricalPrice we created in the previous step to set up the default value.

```
// src/recoil/atoms/historicalPriceAtoms.ts

import { atom } from 'recoil'
import { initHistoricalPrice } from '../../model'

export const historicalPriceState = atom({
  key: 'historicalPriceState',
  default: initHistoricalPrice(),
})
```

The key in Recoil should be a unique key. A good practice is to give the key the same name as the filename. Since all the atoms can live in the same directory, `src/recoil/atoms/`, we can't have duplicate filenames with the same name, so this will ensure our keys are unique.

historicalPriceSelectors.ts: Transforming Our async State

The second element of Recoil is a selector. Selectors are pure functions that allow you to transform the state either synchronously or asynchronously. In our case, we can use the same d3.dsv code to retrieve the prices from our CSV file.

Just like the Recoil atom, our selector needs a unique key, and I am making an async call and setting a promise as I don't want to stop my code.

Once the data is retrieved, I cast it as my type historicalPriceObject[] and use the promise resolve to return the data.

Take a look:

```
//src/model/historicalPriceSelectors.ts

import { selector } from 'recoil'
import * as d3 from 'd3'

import { historicalPriceObject } from '../../model'

export const getHistoricalPriceData = selector({
  key: 'getHistoricalPriceData',
  get: async () => {
    return getData()
  },
})

const getData = () =>
  new Promise((resolve) =>
    d3
      .dsv(',', '/data/historicalPrice.csv', function results(d) {
        return {
          price: d.open,
        }
      })
      .then(function results(data) {
        resolve((data as unknown) as historicalPriceObject[])
      })
  )
```

Notice that TS doesn't know what type of data we have, so I will be casting my data to `historicalPriceObject`.

```
(data as unknown) as historicalPriceObject[]
```

HistogramWidget: Custom Component

In the previous chapter, we had `App.tsx` as the parent component that retrieved the data and `Histogram.tsx` as the chart component.

What I am going to do is add another component. Let's call it a widget. The widget component can handle the data, set a loader when the data is loading, and handle other potential components that use the same data or different data. Figure 5-1 shows the higher-level diagram of the component.

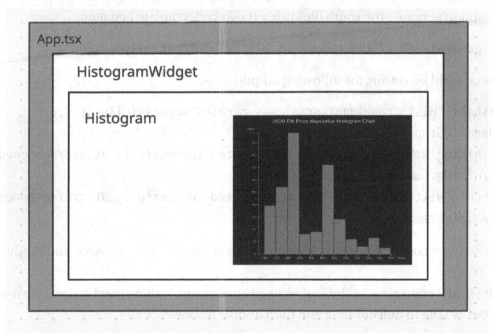

Figure 5-1. *Histogram widget diagram*

This architecture design allows me to be prepared for whatever comes next. For instance, suppose we want to add a list that shows the prices over time or another chart that uses the same data.

Histogram Chart with Recoil

Let's make a histogram with Recoil.

HistogramWidget.tsx: Custom Component

In term of the HistogramWidget component, I will be creating three files.

- Graph.tsx: Component

- Graph.scss: Style

- Graph.test.tsx: Jest testing

CRA MHL has an out-of-the-box library to help create the template, and it's already configured with components that can help get the job faster. Just run the following npx command to generate the graph files using the Recoil template I created..

```
$ npx generate-react-cli component HistogramWidget --type=recoil
```

You should be getting the following output:

```
Stylesheet "HistogramWidget.scss" was created successfully at src/
components/Graph/HistogramWidget.scss
Test "HistogramWidget.test.tsx" was created successfully at src/components/
Graph/HistogramWidget.test.tsx
Component "HistogramWidget.tsx" was created successfully at src/components/
Graph/HistogramWidget.tsx
```

The widget code will retrieve the data we set up in our Recoil selector and render the chart.

The initial code gives us the scaffolding to create our loading mechanism. We use useRecoilValue to pull our data and then update the view.

```
const HistogramWidget= () => {
  const results: useRecoilValue( getMethod )
  useEffect(() => {
    // TODO
  })
  return (
```

```
    {results ? (
      <>Loaded
    ) : (
      <>Loading
    )}

  )
}
export default HistogramWidget
```

Now we plug in the method that will to retrieve the data, getHistoricalPriceData, and the Histogram component we will be creating next with some props to align it. Our HistogramWidget.tsx will look like so.:

```
// src/widgets/HistogramWidget/HistogramWidget.tsx

import React, { useEffect } from 'react'
import './HistogramWidget.scss'
import { useRecoilValue } from 'recoil'
import { getHistoricalPriceData } from '../../recoil/selectors/
historicalPriceSelectors'
import { historicalPriceObject } from '../../model'
import Histogram from '../../components/Histogram/Histogram'

const HistogramWidget = () => {
```

To retrieve the results, we useRecoilValue and call the selector and cast the object.

```
const results: historicalPriceObject = useRecoilValue(getHistoricalPrice
Data) as historicalPriceObject
```

This code is similar to React's useState, and it's very intuitive. That's why Recoil shines.

On the rendering side, I check if there. are results already and either show the histogram component or show a message that says "loading." To do that, I will be using the jsx conditional inline. Take a look:

```
return (
  <>
    {results?.length > 0 ? (
      <>
```

```
      <Histogram data={results} margin={{ top: 20, right: 45, bottom:
      20, left: 50 }} width={400} height={400} fill="tomato" />

    ) : (
      <>Loading!
    )}
  </>
  )
}
export default HistogramWidget
```

The data is binding on the `Histogram` component, and since my two objects `Types.Data[]` and `historicalPriceObject[]` are the same, TypeScript won't complain.

Here I am just using a loading message, but this could be any component, animation, or image.

HistogramWidget.scss

I don't need any SCSS style, so just keep `HistogramWidget.scss`. as a placeholder.

```
.histogramWidget {
}
```

Graph.test.tsx

Our Jest test is a bit different using Recoil. It's good practice to have full coverage.

I am keeping my test simple, just checking that the component was mounted. To do that, I need to wrap my recoil in the `<RecoilRoot>` tag.

```
// src/component/HistogramWidget/HistogramWidget.test.tsx

import React from 'react'
import { shallow } from 'enzyme'
import { RecoilRoot } from 'recoil'
import Graph from './Graph'

describe('<HistogramWidget />', () => {
  let component
```

```
  beforeEach(() => {
    component = shallow(
      <RecoilRoot>
        <HistogramWidget />
      </RecoilRoot>
    )
  })

  test('It should mount', () => {
    expect(component.length).toBe(1)
  })
})
```

App.tsx

Lastly, everything is ready. I can remove the useEffect code that retrieves the data and just place my widget.

```
// src/App.tsx

import React from 'react'
import './App.scss'
import HistogramWidget from './components/HistogramWidget/HistogramWidget'

function App() {
  return (
    <div className="App">
      <header className="App-header">
        <HistogramWidget />
      </header>
    </div>
  )
}

export default App
```

See Figure 5-2.

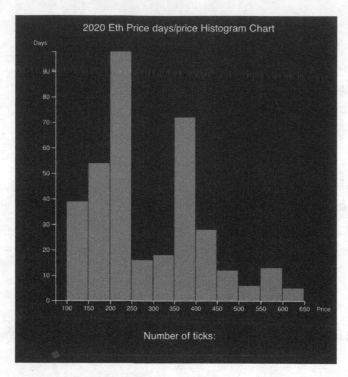

Figure 5-2. Histogram chart with Recoil

Price Table List Component

In this section of this chapter, I will show you how we can now include another component that can share the same data as our histogram chart.

We will create a table list that displays the days and prices next to our chart.

The component will be using Material-UI. I set up a starter component for you, or you can start from scratch.

```
$ npx generate-react-cli component PriceTableList --type=materialui
```

types.ts

For the data type, I am creating another types.ts just for my PriceTableList.tsx component.

This could look like overkill as now I have two types in each component that are the same. However, it's important to me that I be able to borrow these components in future projects, and writing a few lines of code is a small price to pay.

```
// src/component/PriceTableList/types.ts

export namespace Types {
  export type Data = {
    price: number
  }
}
```

PriceTableList.tsx

The PriceTableList.tsx component will be using makeStyle to create our styles for the root container and the table component.

We will be using the TableBody, TableCell, TableContainer, TableRow, and Paper components from Material-UI, so they need to be imported.

To better understand Material-UI tables, take a look at the Material-UI documentation:

https://material-ui.com/components/tables/

Here is the code:

```
// src/components/PriceTableList/PriceTableList.tsx

import React from 'react'
import { makeStyles } from '@material-ui/core/styles'
import Table from '@material-ui/core/Table'
import TableBody from '@material-ui/core/TableBody'
import TableCell from '@material-ui/core/TableCell'
import TableContainer from '@material-ui/core/TableContainer'
import TableHead from '@material-ui/core/TableHead'
import TableRow from '@material-ui/core/TableRow'
import Paper from '@material-ui/core/Paper'
import { Types } from './types'
import './PriceTableList.scss'
```

Using makeStyles from Material-UI, you can set up a style for each component. For me I want the container wrapper to have a max height of 400px as the list and table are long. I can also set the style here.

```
const useStyles = makeStyles({
  root: {
    maxHeight: 400,
  },
  table: {
    minWidth: 650
  },
})
```

My function component will include the IPriceTableListProps prop interface that will include both the data and a color for the table text.

```
const PriceTableList = (props: IPriceTableListProps) => {
```

We set the const to use the style.

```
const classes = useStyles()
```

On the rendering, I create the TableContainer and the table utilizing the Material-UI style I set up.

```
return (
  <TableContainer className={classes.root} component={Paper}>
    <Table className={classes.table} aria-label="simple table">
      <TableHead>
        <TableRow>
```

For the table header and rows, I am using a custom style that I will create in the SCSS file to set the background as well as the text color I am passing from the parent component.

```
            <TableCell className="priceTableListTableCellHead" style={{
            color: props.textColor }}>
              Day
            </TableCell>
            <TableCell className="priceTableListTableCellHead" style={{
            color: props.textColor }}>
              Price
            </TableCell>
```

```
    </TableRow>
  </TableHead>
  <TableBody>
```

To iterate through the data, I can use the map method and pass the value of the price as well as create an index to set the day number.

```
{props.data.map((d: Types.Data, index: number) => (
  <TableRow key={d.price}>
    <TableCell className="priceTableListTableCell" style={{
    color: props.textColor }} component="th" scope="row">
      {index + 1}
    </TableCell>
    <TableCell className="priceTableListTableCell" style={{
    color: props.textColor }} component="th" scope="row">
```

To display the price, I can format the text by adding a dollar sign and converting the variable into a string to be parsed as a float , and I set a fix of 2 (to leave only two digits).

```
      ${parseFloat((d.price as unknown) as string).toFixed(2)}
    </TableCell>
  </TableRow>
))}
    </TableBody>
  </Table>
</TableContainer>
  )
}

export default PriceTableList
```

The interface holds the data type and text color.

```
interface IPriceTableListProps {
  data: Types.Data
  textColor: string
}
```

PriceTableList.scss

For the SCSS file, I am setting two different background colors in shades of gray for the header and actual rows.

```
.priceTableListTableCellHead {
  background-color: #343434;
}

.priceTableListTableCell {
  background-color: #515151;
}
```

That's it, I am ready to integrate the `PriceTableList.tsx` component into the parent component `HistogramWidget.tsx`.

HistogramWidget.tsx

The changes for the `HistogramWidget.tsx` parent component will be to set my two components side by side using the Material-UI grid and to add my `PriceTableList.tsx` component. Take a look in this file (the changes are highlighted):

```
// src/widgets/HistogramWidget/HistogramWidget.tsx
```

I need to import the grid component and `HistogramWidget.tsx`.

```
import React, { useEffect } from 'react'
import './HistogramWidget.scss'
import { useRecoilValue } from 'recoil'
import Grid from '@material-ui/core/Grid'
import { getHistoricalPriceData } from '../../recoil/selectors/
historicalPriceSelectors'
import { historicalPriceObject } from '../../model'
import Histogram from '../../components/Histogram/Histogram'
import PriceTableList from '../../components/PriceTableList/PriceTableList'
```

```
const HistogramWidget = () => {
  const results: historicalPriceObject = useRecoilValue(getHistoricalPrice
  Data) as historicalPriceObject
  return (

      {results?.length > 0 ? (
```

My grid consists of two columns.

```
        <Grid container spacing={5}>
          <Grid item xs={6}>
            <Histogram data={results} margin={{ top: 20, right:
            45, bottom: 20, left: 50 }} width={400} height={400}
            fill="tomato" />
          </Grid>
```

For the price table list, I am wrapping the component with a div to make sure we can scroll down and the widget is in control of the size of the component.

```
      <Grid item xs={6}>
            <div className="priceTableListDivWrapper">
              <PriceTableList data={results} textColor="white" />
            </div>
          </Grid>
        </Grid>

    ) : (
      Loading!
    )}

  )
}
export default HistogramWidget
```

HistogramWidget.scss

From the widget SCSS, I need to add style for my price table list's `div` wrapper.

```scss
.priceTableListDivWrapper {
  padding-top: 100px;
  width: 500px;
  height: 500px;
}
```

Lastly, just as before, remember to run the `format`, `lint`, and `test` commands to ensure quality.

```
$ yarn format && yarn lint && yarn test
```

Figure 5-3 shows the final result.

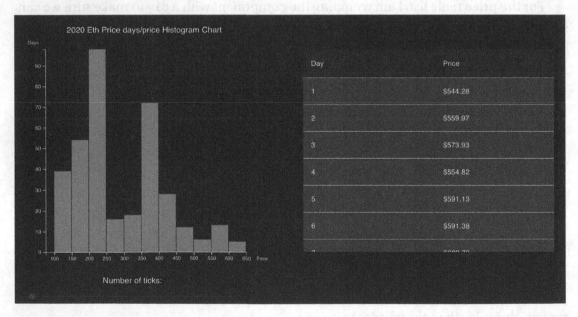

Figure 5-3. *Histogram chart with a list Material-UI component and shared state using Recoil*

Check my d3 and React interactive course to see how you can implement this histogram chart using function components and optimize using hooks: `https://elielrom.com/BuildSiteCourse`.

Summary

In this chapter, I talked about the state management architecture introduced by Facebook called Flux and learned about the new experimental state management from Facebook called Recoil.

We took the histogram we developed in the previous chapter and replaced the React state with Recoil state management. Using Recoil state management, we were able to share our data across our app and with multiple components.

This design takes the best of both worlds, consisting of the module libraries from D3 that help us do storytelling with data visualization charts and of a React SPA paradigm with the help of the virtual DOM to make sure the page gets rendered only once a change is made.

We used the Material-UI table list component to create another component and share the data, and we restructured our component into a widget so we can easily integrate the logic for loading multiple components that share data.

Now that you know how to work with D3, charts, and data management to create custom React components. I encourage you to play around with the examples I gave you, plug in data, change the charts, and create new charts. This will help you gain valuable experience.

The rest of the book focuses on working with more complex charts as well as optimization and publishing techniques.

In the next chapter, we will start working with more complex charts. In the upcoming two chapters, the content is dedicated to creating and working with a common type of chart, a world chart.

CHAPTER 6

World Chart: Part 1

A world map chart is a great way to show items globally. Integrating D3 with React and TS can create readable code that uses the best of all the tools. In this chapter, I will show you how to create a rotating map and assign dots based on coordinates.

Specifically, in this chapter, I will show you how to work with a world map using React, D3, and TS as type checkers. I will break down the process into steps. In each step, I will be adding more functionality until we have the rotating world map with dots that represent coordinates.

I have separated the components into five files so it's easy to see and compare the changes.

- *World map atlas*: WorldMapAtlas.tsx

- *Round world map*: RoundWorldMap.tsx

- *Rotating round world map*: RotatingRoundWorldMap.tsx

- *Rotating round world map with coordinates*:
  RotatingRoundWorldMapWithCoordinates.tsx

- *Refactoring*: WorldMap.tsx

The project can be downloaded from here:

https://github.com/Apress/integrating-d3.js-with-react/tree/main/ch06/
world-map-chart

Setup

The project setup is simple using CRA with the MHL template project.

© Elad Elrom 2021

E. Elrom, *Integrating D3.js with React*, https://doi.org/10.1007/978-1-4842-7052-3_6

```
$ yarn create react-app world-map-chart --template must-have-libraries
$ cd world-map-chart
$ yarn start
$ open http://localhost:3000
```

Install Additional Needed Libraries and Types

There are four additional libraries we going to need to get started.

- d3-geo: We will use d3-geo for geographic projections (drawing the map). See https://github.com/d3/d3-geo.

- topojson-client: This is a client to manipulate TopoJSON. TopoJSON is the library that provides the map of the world, which I can use to draw the map. See https://github.com/topojson/topojson-client.

- geojson: This is a format for encoding geographic data. See https://geojson.org/. TopoJSON files are type "Topology" and follow the TopoJSON specification. GeoJSON will then be used to format the encoding of the geographic data structures. See https://geojson.org/.

- react-uuid: Create a random UUID that we will be using for the list key needed when we map the React component. See https://github.com/uuidjs/uuid.

Go ahead and install these libraries with Yarn:

```
$yarn add d3-geo @types/d3-geo
$yarn add topojson-client @types/topojson-client
$yarn add geojson @types/geojson
$yarn add react-uuid
```

Lastly, download the data of the world atlas. The data is provided from TopoJSON that has prebuilt countries data (https://github.com/topojson/world-atlas). Here is the actual JSON I will be using:

```
https://d3js.org/world-110m.v1.json
```

Place the file in the public folder for easy access: /public/data/world-110m.json.

World Map Atlas

The first map I will be creating is just a flat world atlas type map that will show the world.

WorldMapAtlas.tsx

Create the files yourself or use generate-react-cli.

```
$ npx generate-react-cli component WorldMap --type=d3
```

As I mentioned, I will be creating the components as separate components, so it will be easy to track the work and compare the changes. The first file is WorldMapAtlas.tsx. Here is the complete component code:

```tsx
// src/components/WorldMap/WorldMapAtlas.tsx
import React, { useState, useEffect } from 'react'
import { geoEqualEarth, geoPath } from 'd3-geo'
import { feature } from 'topojson-client'
import { Feature, FeatureCollection, Geometry } from 'geojson'
import './WorldMap.scss'

const uuid = require('react-uuid')

const scale: number = 200
const cx: number = 400
const cy: number = 150

const WorldMapAtlas = () => {
  const [geographies, setGeographies] = useState<[] |
  Array<Feature<Geometry | null>>>([])

  useEffect(() => {
    fetch('/data/world-110m.json').then((response) => {
      if (response.status !== 200) {
        // eslint-disable-next-line no-console
        console.log(`Houston we have a problem: ${response.status}`)
        return
      }
```

```
      response.json().then((worldData) => {
        const mapFeatures: Array<Feature<Geometry | null>> =
        ((feature(worldData, worldData.objects.countries) as unknown) as
        FeatureCollection).features
        setGeographies(mapFeatures)
      })
    })
  }, [])

  const projection = geoEqualEarth().scale(scale).translate([cx, cy]).
  rotate([0, 0])

  return (
    <>
      <svg width={scale * 3} height={scale * 3} viewBox="0 0 800 450">
        <g>
          {(geographies as []).map((d, i) => (
            <path
              key={`path-${uuid()}`}
              d={geoPath().projection(projection)(d) as string}
              fill={`rgba(38,50,56,${(1 / (geographies ? geographies.length
              : 0)) * i})`}
              stroke="aliceblue"
              strokeWidth={0.5}
            />
          ))}
        </g>
      </svg>

    )
}

export default WorldMapAtlas
```

Let's review.

In the first step, we import React and the libraries we installed. I am also creating WorldMap.scss as a style placeholder for future usage.

```
import React, { useState, useEffect } from 'react'
import { geoEqualEarth, geoPath } from 'd3-geo'
import { feature } from 'topojson-client'
import { Feature, FeatureCollection, Geometry } from 'geojson'
import './WorldMap.scss'
```

For the react-uuid library, there is no type for TS, so I will be using require so that ESLint doesn't complain.

```
const uuid = require('react-uuid')
```

Next, we set the attributes such as the map scale and positioning.

```
const scale: number = 200
const cx: number = 400
const cy: number = 150
```

WorldMapAtlas is set as function component. This is a matter of preference, and I could have used a class component.

As for the data of the countries, I am setting the client data as a state. Once the data is loaded, I am converting the JSON into a feature geometry array that I can render.

```
const [geographies, setGeographies] = useState<[] |
Array<Feature<Geometry | null>>>([])
```

In terms of the type, I had to figure the type by drilling into the actual geojson library.

Next, I am loading the data on the useEffect hook. Later in this chapter I will refactor this code and move it to the parent component, but for now I want the code to be as simple as possible. Here is my working map:

```
useEffect(() => {
  fetch('/data/world-110m.json').then((response) => {
    if (response.status !== 200) {
      console.log(`Houston we have a problem: ${response.status}`)
      return
    }
    response.json().then((worldData) => {
```

Notice that I am using the 'fetch', however, another approach is to use d3.json module. D3 already format the object as a JSON so it's less code.

```
useEffect(() => {
  d3.json('/data/world-110m.json').then((d) => { return d }).then(
  (worldData) => {
      // @ts-ignore const mapFeature: Array<Feature<Geometry |
      null>> = (feature(worldData, worldData.objects.countries) as
      FeatureCollection).features setGeographies(mapFeature)
  })
})
```

Once I get a response, I can convert the JSON to a `Geometry` feature array and set it as the function state.

```
    const mapFeatures: Array<Feature<Geometry | null>> =
    ((feature(worldData, worldData.objects.countries) as unknown) as
    FeatureCollection).features
    setGeographies(mapFeatures)
  })
 })
}, [])
```

The projection, in layman's terms, is what I want my actual atlas to look like. There are many options to choose from (see `https://github.com/d3/d3-geo/blob/master/README.md`). Let's go with `geoEqualEarth` as a first try.

```
const projection = geoEqualEarth().scale(scale).translate([cx, cy]).
rotate([0, 0])
```

To render my atlas, I will be first setting an SVG wrapper that holds a group element and then iterates paths using a map through the geographies data I set as the state to draw each country.

```
return (
  <>
    <svg width={scale * 3} height={scale * 3} viewBox="0 0 800 450">
      <g>
```

```
    {(geographies as []).map((d, i) => (
      <path
        key={`path-${uuid()}`}
        d={geoPath().projection(projection)(d) as string}
        fill={`rgba(38,50,56,${(1 / (geographies ? geographies.length
        : 0)) * i})`}
        stroke="aliceblue"
        strokeWidth={0.5}
      />
    ))}
    </g>
  </svg>
  </>
  )
}

export default WorldMapAtlas
```

Notice that I am using key={`path-${uuid()}`}.

Keys are common practice for identifying unique virtual DOM (VDOM) UI elements with their corresponding data. Without doing this step, React VDOM can get confused when there is a need to refresh the DOM. This is best practice. You can use a random number, but be mindful not to use the map index as the key because the map can change and cause the VDOM to reference the wrong item.

> *Keys help React identify which items have changed, are added, or are removed. Keys should be given to the elements inside the array to give the elements a stable identity.*

> https://reactjs.org/docs/lists-and-keys.html

Keys and refs are added as an attribute to a React.createElement() call. They help React optimize the rendering by recycling all the existing elements in the DOM.

App.tsx

Next, let's add our WorldMapAtlas component to App.tsx as a child.

153

Notice that the changes are highlighted in bold.

```
import React from 'react'
import './App.scss'
import WorldMapAtlas from './components/WorldMap/WorldMapAtlas'

function App() {
  return (
    <div className="App">
      <header className="App-header">
        <WorldMapAtlas />
      </header>
    </div>
  )
}

export default App
```

App.scss

For the App.scss style, I am changing the background color to white.

```
.App-header {
  background-color: #ffffff;
  min-height: 100vh;
  display: flex;
  flex-direction: column;
  align-items: center;
  justify-content: center;
  font-size: calc(10px + 2vmin);
  color: white;
}
```

Voilà! See Figure 6-1.

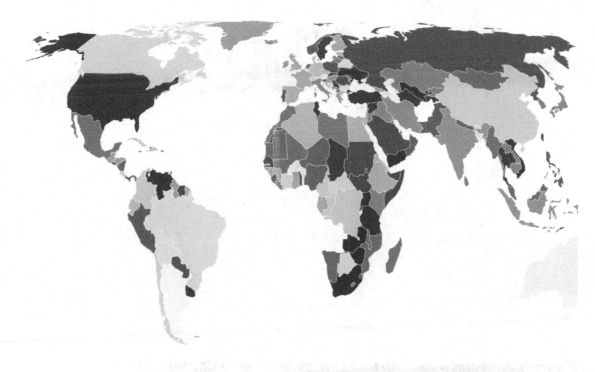

Figure 6-1. *Simple world map atlas*

As I mentioned, for the projections, I used geoEqualEarth; however, I can change the projection easily to other projections. For instance, if I want to change to geoStereographic, my map will change. See Figure 6-2.

Change the projection from this:

```
import { geoEqualEarth, geoPath} from 'd3-geo'

const projection = geoEqualEarth().scale(scale).translate([cx, cy]).
rotate([0, 0])
```

to the following:

```
import { geoPath, geoStereographic } from 'd3-geo'
const projection = geoStereographic().scale(scale).translate([cx, cy]).
rotate([0, 0])
```

Figure 6-2. *World atlas map using the geoStereographic projection*

Another example is the geoConicConformal projection (Figure 6-3).

```
const projection = geoConicConformal().scale(scale).translate([cx, cy]).
rotate([0, 0])
```

Figure 6-3. *World atlas map using geoConicConformal projection*

Round World Map

Now we know how to draw a world map atlas. Next we will see how to create a round world map.

To change the map to be round, all I have to do is use the geoOrthographic projection.

To make the round map look better, I am also going to draw a round light gray background using a SVG circle element.

RoundWorldMap.tsx

Create a new component called RoundWorldMap.tsx; see the changes highlighted here.

```tsx
// src/components/WorldMap/RoundWorldMap.tsx

  const projection = geoOrthographic().scale(scale).translate([cx, cy]).
  rotate([rotation, 0])

  return (
    <svg width={scale * 3} height={scale * 3} viewBox="0 0 800 450">
      <g>
        <circle
          fill="#0098c8"
          cx={cx}
          cy={cy}
          r={scale}
        />
      </g>
      <g>
        {(geographies as []).map((d, i) => (
          <path
            key={`path-${uuid()}`}
            d={geoPath().projection(projection)(d) as string}
            fill={`rgba(38,50,56,${(1 / (geographies ? geographies.length :
            0)) * i})`}
            stroke="aliceblue"
            strokeWidth={0.5}
          />
        ))}
      </g>
    </svg>
  )
}
```

Remember to update `App.tsx`.

```
return (
  <div className="App">
    <header className="App-header">
      <RoundWorldMap />
    </header>
  </div>
)
```

See Figure 6-4.

Figure 6-4. *Round world map atlas*

Rotating Round World Map Chart

Now that we have a round world map atlas, wouldn't it be neat to add animation and interactions? We can rotate the atlas and add a button to start the animation.

AnimationFrame.tsx

To add animations, we can call JavaScript window `requestAnimationFrame` API (https://developer.mozilla.org/en-US/docs/Web/API/window/request AnimationFrame).

The requestAnimationFrame method tells the browser that I want to perform an animation, and the browser will call my callback function so that I can update my animation before the next redraw.

To use requestAnimationFrame, I can just place the following code in my React component:

```
window.requestAnimationFrame(() => {
  // TODO
})
```

However, a better architectural design is to create a hook function component using useRef and wrap my requestAnimationFrame. Take a look:

```
// src/hooks/WindowDimensions.tsx
import { useEffect, useRef } from 'react'

export default (callback: (arg0: ICallback) => void) => {
  const frame = useRef()
  const last = useRef(performance.now())
  const init = useRef(performance.now())

  const animate = () => {
    const now = performance.now()
    const time = (now - init.current) / 1000
    const delta = (now - last.current) / 1000
    callback({ time, delta })
    last.current = now
    ;((frame as unknown) as IFrame).current =
    requestAnimationFrame(animate)
  }

  useEffect(() => {
    ((frame as unknown) as IFrame).current = requestAnimationFrame(animate)
    return () => cancelAnimationFrame((((frame as unknown) as IFrame).
    current)
  })
}
```

```
interface ICallback {
  time: number
  delta: number
}
```

Let's review the code.

I am passing the callback as an argument.

```
export default (callback: (arg0: ICallback) => void) => {
```

Next, I will keep track of the frame using `performance.now()` (https://developer. mozilla.org/en-US/docs/Web/API/Performance/now). That feature brings a timestamp in the one-millisecond resolution that I can use to figure out the time delta in case I need it.

Note   Time deltas are the differences in times.

```
const frame = useRef()
const last = useRef(performance.now())
const init = useRef(performance.now())
```

On every `requestAnimationFrame` call, animate will return the current timestamp.

```
const animate = () => {
  const now = performance.now()
  const time = (now - init.current) / 1000
  const delta = (now - last.current) / 1000
  callback({ time, delta })
  last.current = now;
  (frame as unknown as IFrame).current = requestAnimationFrame(animate)
}
```

I can then use the `useEffect` hook to tie the animate method.

My effects will need to be cleaned up before the component leaves the screen. To do this, the function passed to `useEffect` needs to return a cleanup function. In my case, `cancelAnimationFrame` needs to be called on the `useEffect` return callback. You can learn more about React effects and clean up here: https://reactjs.org/docs/hooks-reference.html.

```
useEffect(() => {
  (frame as unknown as IFrame).current = requestAnimationFrame(animate)
  return () => cancelAnimationFrame((frame as unknown as IFrame).current)
})
}
```

RotatingRoundWorldMap.tsx

Now that we have the AnimationFrame hook ready to be used for our animation, I can add my rotating animation. Additionally, I will be adding a user gesture in the form of an icon button from Material-UI to start the animation.

Copy the RoundWorldMap.tsx file from our previous example and save it as a new file called RotatingRoundWorldMap.tsx. Take a look at these changes from RoundWorldMap.tsx:

```
// src/components/WorldMap/RotatingRoundWorldMap.tsx

import PlayCircleFilledWhiteIcon from '@material-ui/icons/
PlayCircleFilledWhite'
import { Button } from '@material-ui/core'
```

The animation logic checks whether a 360-degree rotation ended to reset the rotation variable on each completion of 360 degrees. The animation checks if the isRotate state is set to true so that my map will only start rotating when I click the start button.

```
AnimationFrame(() => {
  if (isRotate) {
    let newRotation = rotation
    if (rotation >= 360) {
      newRotation = rotation - 360
    }
    setRotation(newRotation + 0.2)
    // console.log(`rotation: ${ rotation}`)
  }
})
```

I am adding a button to start the animation. This is done by setting the isRotate state to true using the fat arrow inline function.

```
  return (
    <>
      <Button
        size="medium"
        color="primary"
        startIcon={<PlayCircleFilledWhiteIcon />}
        onClick={() => {
          setIsRotate(true)
        }}
      />
      <svg width={scale * 3} height={scale * 3} viewBox="0 0 800 450">
        <g>
          <circle
            fill="#0098c8"
            cx={cx}
            cy={cy}
            r={scale}
          />
        </g>
        <g>
          {(geographies as []).map((d, i) => (
            <path
              key={`path-${uuid()}`}
              d={geoPath().projection(projection)(d) as string}
              fill={`rgba(38,50,56,${(1 / (geographies ? geographies.length
              : 0)) * i})`}
              stroke="aliceblue"
              strokeWidth={0.5}
            />
          ))}
        </g>
      </svg>
    </>
  )
}
```

Remember to update `App.tsx` to include the `RotatingRoundWorldMap` component.

```
return (
  <div className="App">
    <header className="App-header">
      <RotatingRoundWorldMap />
    </header>
  </div>
)
```

Figure 6-5 shows the final results.

Figure 6-5. *Rotating round world map atlas*

One more change we need to make is to place the loading of the map data inside of a statement that checks if the data was loaded.

The reason is that since using the animation hook, the useEffect will get called all the time.

Take a look;

```
useEffect(() => { if (geographies.length === 0) {
    // load map
}
```

Rotating Round World Map Chart with Coordinates

In this section, I will show you how to add coordinate dots to our map.

RotatingRoundWorldMapWithCoordinates.tsx

Copy the RotatingRoundWorldMap.tsx file from the previous example and name it
RotatingRoundWorldMapWIthCoordinates.tsx.

Yes, I know it's a long name, but using Shakespeare's method names, it's easy to tell
what this component is doing.

To create the coordinate dots, I will be adding a new data array feed that includes
the coordinates' longitude and latitude. Take a look at the changes from the previous
RotatingRoundWorldMap.tsx component:

```
// src/components/WorldMap/RotatingRoundWorldMapWIthCoordinates.tsx
import React, { useState, useEffect } from 'react'
import { geoOrthographic, geoPath } from 'd3-geo'
import { feature } from 'topojson-client'
import { Feature, FeatureCollection, Geometry } from 'geojson'
import './WorldMap.scss'
import PlayCircleFilledWhiteIcon from '@material-ui/icons/
PlayCircleFilledWhite'
import { Button } from '@material-ui/core'
import AnimationFrame from '../../hooks/AnimationFrame'

const uuid = require('react-uuid')

const data: { name: string; coordinates: [number, number] }[] = [
  { name: '1', coordinates: [-73.9919, 40.7529] },
  { name: '2', coordinates: [-70.0007884457405, 40.75509010847814] },
]
```

```
const scale: number = 200
const cx: number = 400
const cy: number = 150
const initRotation: number = 50

const RotatingRoundWorldMapWithCoordinates = () => {
  const [geographies, setGeographies] = useState<[] |
  Array<Feature<Geometry | null>>>([])
  const [rotation, setRotation] = useState<number>(initRotation)
  const [isRotate, setIsRotate] = useState<Boolean>(false)

  useEffect(() => {
    if (geographies.length === 0) {
        fetch('/data/world-110m.json').then((response) => {
          if (response.status !== 200) {
            // eslint-disable-next-line no-console
            console.log(`Houston we have a problem: ${response.status}`)
            return
          }
          response.json().then((worldData) => {
            const mapFeatures: Array<Feature<Geometry | null>> =
            ((feature(worldData, worldData.objects.countries) as unknown) as
            FeatureCollection).features
            setGeographies(mapFeatures)
          })
        })
    }
  }, [])

  // geoEqualEarth
  // geoOrthographic
  const projection = geoOrthographic().scale(scale).translate([cx, cy]).
  rotate([rotation, 0])
```

```
AnimationFrame(() => {
  if (isRotate) {
    let newRotation = rotation
    if (rotation >= 360) {
      newRotation = rotation - 360
    }
    setRotation(newRotation + 0.2)
    // console.log(`rotation: ${ rotation}`)
  }
})

function returnProjectionValueWhenValid(point: [number, number], index:
number) {
  const retVal: [number, number] | null = projection(point)
  if (retVal?.length) {
    return retVal[index]
  }
  return 0
}

const handleMarkerClick = (i: number) => {
  // eslint-disable-next-line no-alert
  alert(`Marker: ${JSON.stringify(data[i])}`)
}

return (
<>
    <Button
      size="medium"
      color="primary"
      startIcon={<PlayCircleFilledWhiteIcon />}
      onClick={() => {
        setIsRotate(true)
      }}
    />
```

```
        <svg width={scale * 3} height={scale * 3} viewBox="0 0 800 450">
        <g>
          <circle fill="#f2f2f2" cx={cx} cy={cy} r={scale} />
        </g>
        <g>
          {(geographies as []).map((d, i) => (
            <path
              key={`path-${uuid()}`}
              d={geoPath().projection(projection)(d) as string}
              fill={`rgba(38,50,56,${(1 / (geographies ? geographies.length
              : 0)) * i})`}
              stroke="aliceblue"
              strokeWidth={0.5}
            />
          ))}
        </g>
        <g>
          {data.map((d, i) => (
            <circle
              key={`marker-${uuid()}`}
              cx={returnProjectionValueWhenValid(d.coordinates, 0)}
              cy={returnProjectionValueWhenValid(d.coordinates, 1)}
              r={5}
              fill="#E91E63"
              stroke="#FFFFFF"
              onClick={() => handleMarkerClick(i)}
              onMouseEnter={() => setIsRotate(false)}
            />
          ))}
        </g>
      </svg>
    </>
  )
}

export default RotatingRoundWorldMapWithCoordinates
```

Let's review the changes in RotatingRoundWorldMapWIthCoordinates from RoundWorldMapAtlas. I am setting a data object that includes the names and coordinates.

```
const data: { name: string; coordinates: [number, number] }[] = [
  { name: '1', coordinates: [-73.9919, 40.7529] },
  { name: '2', coordinates: [-70.0007884457405, 40.75509010847814] },
]
```

For the initial world map rotation location, I can set that in a constant with where I want the world map to start rotating in degrees.

```
const initRotation: number = 50
```

Next, I am adding a returnProjectionValueWhenValid method to adjust the locations of the dots. That is needed because the world map is animating and the location on the projection map is going to change.

```
function returnProjectionValueWhenValid(point: [number, number], index:
number) {
    const retVal: [number, number] | null = projection(point)
    if (retVal?.length) {
      return retVal[index]
    }
    return 0
}
```

I am going to set a handler once the user clicks the dots. This can be used to open a detailed information window or anything you want to do once the user is clicked.

```
const handleMarkerClick = (i: number) => {
  alert(`Marker: ${ JSON.stringify( data[i])}` )
}
```

On the rendering, I will iterate through the array of coordinates using the array map attribute and set the onClick handler as well as mouse enter event to stop the animation so it's easier to click the marker.

```
    <g>
      {data.map((d, i) => (
        <circle
          key={`marker-${uuid()}`}
          cx={returnProjectionValueWhenValid(d.coordinates, 0)}
          cy={returnProjectionValueWhenValid(d.coordinates, 1)}
          r={5}
          fill="#E91E63"
          stroke="#FFFFFF"
          onClick={() => handleMarkerClick(i)}
          onMouseEnter={() => setIsRotate(false)}
        />
      ))}
    </g>
```

Notice that just like the previous step, every time that I am using the map in React I am adding a unique key to each item.

Lastly, remember to update `App.tsx`.

```
return (
  <div className="App">
    <header className="App-header">
<RotatingRoundRotatingRoundWorldMapWithCoordinatesWIthCoordinates />
    </header>
  </div>
)
```

Figure 6-6 shows the final results.

Figure 6-6. *Rotating the round world map atlas with coordinates*

Refactoring

In the last step for this chapter, I will be doing some neat refactoring effort. I will be doing the following:

- *Props*: Extract the props attributes so the parent component can adjust the attributes and data.

- *Coordinates*: Set the coordinate data as a second data feed in the form of CSV.

- *Loader*: Load the data from the parent component and pass the data to the map chart using asynchronous tasks.

- *Types*: Add the TypeScript types to make the code more readable, avoid errors, and help with testing.

coordinates.csv

It's better to extract the coordinate data to a separate CSV data file. That's not just to clean the code. The data may grow, and I may need to get this data from an external source. I am breaking down the coordinates into latitude and longitude in case I ever need to use that information.

```
id,latitude,longitude
1,-73.9919,40.7529
2,-70.0007884457405,40.75509010847814
```

Place the file here for easy access: `world-map-chart/public/data/coordinates.csv`.

types.tsx

A common practice in TS, as you will seen throughout this book, is to create types for TypeScript. That's not only good practice, but it will clean the code and make it more readable. In my case, there are two types I will be setting for the two data feeds: `CoordinatesData` and `MapObject`.

```
// src/component/BasicScatterChart/types.ts

import { Feature, Geometry } from 'geojson'

export namespace Types {
  export type CoordinatesData = {
    id: number
    latitude: number
    longitude: number
  }

  export type MapObject = {
    mapFeatures: Array<Feature<Geometry | null>>
  }
}
```

When referencing a type, it's common to use a lowercase first letter. We are creating the reference, so either way is fine. In other words, you can decide what you prefer, but just stay consistent. I wanted you to be aware of both options.

```
export type coordinatesData
```

Notice that if you start with a lowercase letter, you will get a lint error since our lint rules are set to complain on any export types that are not starting with uppercase. You can disable that, just for this time or globally.

```
// eslint-disable-next-line @typescript-eslint/naming-convention
export type coordinatesData
```

WorldMap.tsx

For our refactoring effort, copy the `RotatingRoundWorldMapWIthCoordinates.tsx` file from the previous example and name it `WorldMap.tsx`.

Most of the code stays the same.

For the `props` interface, I will be adding the data feeds and the alignment attributes, so I need to add the `props` interface and change the function signature.

Most of the change to `WorldMap.tsx` is just adding these `props` instead of the data. The change is highlighted in bold.

```
// src/components/WorldMap/WorldMap.tsx

import React, { useState } from 'react'
import { geoOrthographic, geoPath } from 'd3-geo'
import './WorldMap.scss'
import PlayCircleFilledWhiteIcon from '@material-ui/icons/
PlayCircleFilledWhite'
import { Button } from '@material-ui/core'
import AnimationFrame from '../../hooks/AnimationFrame'
import { Types } from './types'

const uuid = require('react-uuid')

const WorldMap = (props: IWorldMapProps) => {
  const [rotation, setRotation] = useState<number>(props.initRotation)
  const [isRotate, setIsRotate] = useState<Boolean>(false)

  const projection = geoOrthographic().scale(props.scale).translate([props.
cx, props.cy]).rotate([rotation, 0])
```

```
  AnimationFrame(() => {
    if (isRotate) {
      let newRotation = rotation
      if (rotation >= 360) {
        newRotation = rotation - 360
      }
      setRotation(newRotation + 0.2)
    }
  })

  function returnProjectionValueWhenValid(point: [number, number], index:
  number ) {
    const retVal: [number, number] | null = projection(point)
    if (retVal?.length) {
      return retVal[index]
    }
    return 0
  }

  const handleMarkerClick = (i: number) => {
    alert(`Marker: ${  JSON.stringify( props.coordinatesData[i].id)}` )
  }
  return (
  <>
      <Button
        size="medium"
        color="primary"
        startIcon={<PlayCircleFilledWhiteIcon />}
        onClick={() => {
          setIsRotate(true)
        }}
      />
      <svg width={props.scale * 3} height={props.scale * 3} viewBox="0 0
      800 450">
        <g>
```

```
<circle
  fill="#f2f2f2"
  cx={props.cx}
  cy={props.cy}
  r={props.scale}
/>
</g>
<g>
  {(props.mapData.mapFeatures as ).map((d, i) => (
    <path
      key={`path-${uuid()}`}
      d={geoPath().projection(projection)(d) as string}
      fill={`rgba(30,50,50,${(1 / (props.mapData.mapFeatures ?
      props.mapData.mapFeatures.length : 0)) * i})`}
      stroke="aliceblue"
      strokeWidth={props.rotationSpeed}
    />
  ))}
</g>
<g>
  {props.coordinatesData?.map((d, i) => (
    <circle
      key={`marker-${uuid()}`}
      cx={returnProjectionValueWhenValid([d.latitude,
      d.longitude], 0)}
      cy={returnProjectionValueWhenValid([d.latitude,
      d.longitude], 1)}
      r={5}
      fill="#E91E63"
      stroke="#FFFFFF"
      onClick={() => handleMarkerClick(i)}
      onMouseEnter={() => setIsRotate(false)}
    />
  ))}
```

```
        </g>
      </svg>
  </>
  )
}
```

```
export default WorldMapinterface IWorldMapProps {
  mapData: Types.MapObject
  coordinatesData: Types.CoordinatesData[]
  scale: number
  cx: number
  cy: number
  initRotation: number
  rotationSpeed: number
}
```

As you can see, our code in WorldMap.tsx is now cleaner and more readable compared to the RotatingRoundWorldMapWIthCoordinates.tsx file from the previous example.

App.tsx

For the parent component, I will be extracting the data, placing it inside the effect hook, and using the D3 to load both the JSON and the CSV.

Since I want to load both data sets before I draw the map, a good approach is to use the asynchronous calls to both data sets before passing the data to the chart component.

We can use D3's queue(). See https://github.com/d3/d3-queue. D3's queue() to do asynchronous tasks. Add these D3 modules and TS types.

The first step is to add these libraries to our project;

```
$ yarn add d3-queue d3-request @types/d3-queue @types/d3-request
```

Next, let's refactor our App.tsx.

```
// src/App.tsx

import React, { useEffect, useState } from 'react'
```

```
import './App.scss'
import { queue } from 'd3-queue'
import { csv, json } from 'd3-request'
import { FeatureCollection } from 'geojson'
import { feature } from 'topojson-client'
import WorldMap from './components/WorldMap/WorldMap'
import { Types } from './components/WorldMap/types'

function App() {
  const [mapData, setMapData] = useState<Types.MapObject>({ mapFeatures: [] })
  const [coordinatesData, setCoordinatesData] = useState<Types.
  CoordinatesData[]>([])

  useEffect(() => {
    if (coordinatesData.length === 0) {
      const fileNames = ['./data/world-110m.json', './data/coordinates.csv']
      queue()
        .defer(json, fileNames[0])
        .defer(csv, fileNames[1])
        .await((error, d1, d2: Types.CoordinatesData[]) => {
          if (error) {
            // eslint-disable-next-line no-console
            console.log(`Houston we have a problem:${error}`)
          }
          setMapData({ mapFeatures: ((feature(d1, d1.objects.countries) as
          unknown) as FeatureCollection).features })
          setCoordinatesData(d2)
        })
    }
  })
  return (
    <div className="App">
      <header className="App-header">
        <WorldMap mapData={mapData} coordinatesData={coordinatesData}
        scale={200} cx={400} cy={150} initRotation={50} rotationSpeed={0.5} />
      </header>
```

```
    </div>
  )
}
```

export default App

Let's review the code.

We add imports for geojson and topojson-client since we will be uploading the data here. I am also using d3-request to load the data instead of the fetch I used previously.

```
import { queue } from 'd3-queue'
import { csv, json } from 'd3-request'
import { FeatureCollection } from 'geojson'
import { feature } from 'topojson-client'
import WorldMap from './components/WorldMap/WorldMap'
import { Types } from './components/WorldMap/types'
```

I am setting the data feeds as the state; this will allow me to assign the props and make sure React refreshes the props once the data is loaded.

```
const [mapData, setMapData] = useState<Types.MapObject>({ 'mapFeatures':
[] })
const [coordinatesData, setCoordinatesData] = useState<Types.Coordinates
Data[]>([])
```

The useEffect hook will be doing the heavy lifting. The if statement ensures I am not loading my data multiple times.

The D3 queue will load the two data feeds and set the state.

```
useEffect(() => {
  if ( coordinatesData.length === 0 ) {
    const fileNames = ['./data/world-110m.json', './data/coordinates.csv']
    queue()
      .defer(json, fileNames[0])
      .defer(csv, fileNames[1])
      .await((error, d1, d2: Types.CoordinatesData[]) => {
```

```
    if (error) {
      console.log(`Houston we have a problem:${ error}`)
    }
    setMapData({ mapFeatures: ((feature(d1, d1.objects.countries) as
    unknown) as FeatureCollection).features })
    setCoordinatesData(d2)
  })
}
})
```

Lastly, I need to set the `WorldMap` with the data and attribute `props` to match the props interface we set for the `WorldMap` component.

```
<WorldMap mapData={mapData} coordinatesData={coordinatesData}
scale={200} cx={400} cy={150} initRotation={50} rotationSpeed={0.5} />
```

Nothing really changes, from the user view perspective, once you check port 3000: `http://localhost:3000`. However, my code is more organized and easier to read as well as ready to implement state management such as Recoil or Redux since the data is extracted from the actual component and can be shared with multiple components.

Summary

In this chapter, we created a world map with the help of D3, TopoJSON, and React. The ability to draw maps as a background and add dots, animations, and interaction can help create a compelling chart that can be used for many things to tell your story.

In this chapter, I broke down the steps into five parts and created five components.

- *World map atlas*: `WorldMapAtlas.tsx`

- *Round world map*: `RoundWorldMap.tsx`

- *Rotating round world map* : `RotatingRoundWorldMap.tsx`

- *Rotating round world map with coordinates*: `RotatingRoundWorldMapWithCoordinates.tsx`

- *Refactoring*: `WorldMap.tsx`

As you can see from this chapter, integrating the world map atlas using D3 with the help of topojson and geojson is straightforward.

Having React involved makes adding animations and interaction intuitive. TS helps ensure we understand what we are doing and that we avoid potential errors, and after doing some refactoring, you can see that our component is not just reusable but ready for state management.

In the next chapter, I will show you how to use the map we created here and implement Recoil state management and a list to create a widget that displays a résumé in an interactive way.

CHAPTER 7

World Chart: Part 2

In the previous chapter, we created a world map atlas using React and D3. In this chapter, I will show you how to use the map component we created to share the state across multiple components and interact with the map.

I am often asked by potential clients about my previous work and roles in different companies so they can see if I'm a good fit for their current project. I will be using the map chart to create an interactive résumé to display my previous clients and their locations around the world.

Figure 7-1 shows the final result on my website: `https://elielrom.com/about`.

New York, NY USA
Eli helped HBO with - Improved architecture as well as help with releases - visit them on the web: https://hbogo.com/

Figure 7-1. *Final results of interactive résumé*

This chapter is a continuation of the previous chapter.

181

E. Elrom, *Integrating D3.js with React*, https://doi.org/10.1007/978-1-4842-7052-3_7

In terms of organization, this chapter is broken down into three steps.

- *Step 1*: Setup

- *Step 2*: State management

- *Step 3*: Widget creation

Let's get started.

Setup

To keep everything neat, I will start a new project. The project setup is quick and simple using CRA with the MHL template project, which you should be familiar with by now.

```
$ yarn create react-app world-map-widget --template must-have-libraries
$ cd world-map-widget
$ yarn start
$ open http://localhost:3000
```

Just as we did in the previous chapter, we need to install the additional needed libraries and TS types.

```
$ yarn add d3 @types/d3
$ yarn add d3-geo @types/d3-geo topojson-client @types/topojson-client
$ yarn add @types/geojson geojson
$ yarn add react-uuid
```

In the previous chapter, I worked with `coordinates.csv`, which included `id`, `latitude`, and `longitude`.

Instead of `coordinates.csv`, for the client list I will be creating a new CSV file that will include the client's data feed as CSV and then add additional fields.

Create `/public/data/client-list.csv` with the following fields:

```
id,latitude,longitude,name,logo,description,address,city,state,country,
website
```

For the map data, copy the same `world-110m.json` file from the previous project and place it here: `/public/data/world-110m.json`.

Shared State Management

As you probably recall, in Chapter 5, I showed you how to work with Recoil and share the state. In this chapter, we will do the same thing and expand the topic by actually sharing the data across different components.

I will be creating a model object to hold our types and then create the Recoil selector.

Model Files

There are two data feeds, for the map and client list.

- clientsObject.ts

- mapObject.ts

If you look at the code, you will see that I am initializing the object. That will come in handy later in this chapter when I need to set up some tests and need the default values.

```
// src/model/clientsObject.ts

export interface clientsObject {
  id: number
  latitude: number
  longitude: number
  name: string
  logo: string
  description: string
  address: string
  city: string
  state: string
  country: string
  website: string
}

export const initClientsObject = (): clientsObject => ({
  id: -1,
  latitude: 0,
  longitude: 0,
  name: '',
```

```
  logo: '',
  description: '',
  address: '',
  city: '',
  state: '',
  country: '',
  website: '',
})
```

The map object holds the map feature. This is the same code we had in our previous chapter in `App.tsx`. This time I will move the code out of `App.tsx` and into its own widget component. This process is not new. We did the same thing in Chapter 5.

Our map object will include a method for the object itself as well as a method to initialize and set up the object that holds an array of the countries. Take a look:

```
// src/model/mapObject.ts

import { Feature, Geometry } from 'geojson'

export interface mapObject {
  mapFeatures: Array<Feature<Geometry | null>>
}

export const initMapObject = (): mapObject => ({
  mapFeatures: Array<Feature<null>>(),
})

export const setMapObject = (data: Array<Feature<Geometry | null>>):
mapObject => ({
  mapFeatures: data,
})
```

Atoms

Now that we have our model object set, we can create Recoil's atom and selector. Recoil simplifies state management, so we only need to create two ingredients: atoms and selectors.

For our case, we could use `clientAtom.ts` and `mapAtoms.ts` to set the initial state, but we don't need them. The model we create is enough.

Recoil selectors do not require use to create an atom, and it's nice to be able to skip a step and write less code. The atoms are great for cases such as when we want to get state updates for multiple components or pass state to the selector. In our case, we don't need any of these functionalities, so setting the atoms is overkill and can be skipped.

Selectors

As you probably recall, selectors are pure functions that allow you to transform the state either synchronously or asynchronously.

Our selectors will pull the CSV data for the client list and map. I will be using the D3 dsv API to pull the CSV format inside the selector async call.

```
// src/recoil/selectors/clientsSelectors.ts

import { selector } from 'recoil'
import * as d3 from 'd3'

import { clientsObject } from '../../model'

export const getPreviousClientListData = selector({
  key: 'GetPreviousClientListData',
  get: () => {
    return getData()
  },
})

const getData = async () =>
  new Promise((resolve) =>
    d3
      .dsv(',', '/data/client-list.csv', function results(d) {
        return d
      })
      .then(function results(data) {
        resolve((data as unknown) as clientsObject[])
      })
  )
```

For the map, I will be using the fetch built-in command, similar to what we did in the previous chapter, and pull the data from world-110m.json.

```
// src/recoil/selectors/mapSelectors.ts

import { selector } from 'recoil'
import { Feature, FeatureCollection, Geometry } from 'geojson'
import { feature } from 'topojson-client'
import { setMapObject } from '../../model'

export const getMapData = selector({
  key: 'GetMapData',
  get: async () => {
    return getMapDataFromFile()
  },
})

const getMapDataFromFile = () =>
  new Promise((resolve) =>
    fetch('/data/world-110m.json').then((response) => {
      if (response.status !== 200) {
        console.log(`Houston, we have a problem! ${response.status}`)
        return
      }
      response.json().then((worldData) => {
        const mapFeatures: Array<Feature<Geometry | null>> =
        ((feature(worldData, worldData.objects.countries) as unknown) as
        FeatureCollection).features
        resolve(setMapObject(mapFeatures))
      })
    })
  )
```

If you want to create an atom, you can cast the object I am returning as that type. This step is not required, and the code will work fine without doing that, as you will see.

Widget

In terms of our front-end widget, you can see the wireframe for the front end in Figure 7-2.

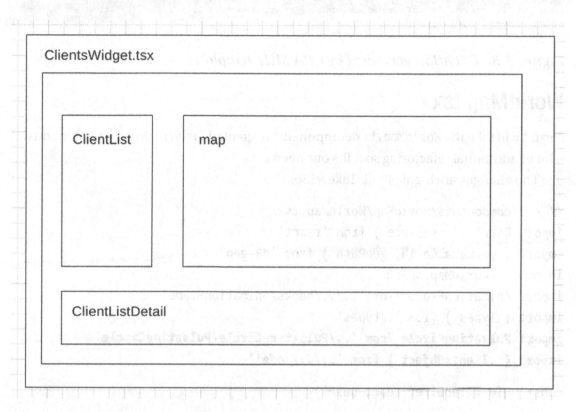

Figure 7-2. *ClientsWidget component and subcomponent high-level wireframe*

To generate these components, Jest tests, and SCSS files, you can use again generate-react-cli with the template I put in CRA/MHL or create on your own.

```
$ npx generate-react-cli component ClientsWidget --type=recoil
$ npx generate-react-cli component WorldMap --type=d3
$ npx generate-react-cli component ClientList --type=recoil
$ npx generate-react-cli component ClientListDetail --type=recoil
```

Each generates three files: Component.tsx, Component.test.tsx, and Component. scss. Take a look at the ClientList output as an example, as shown in Figure 7-3.

```
eli@Elis-MacBook world-chart-ts % npx generate-react-cli component ClientList --type=recoil
npx: installed 72 in 10.362s
Stylesheet "ClientList.scss" was created successfully at src/components/ClientList/ClientList.scss
Test "ClientList.test.tsx" was created successfully at src/components/ClientList/ClientList.test.tsx
Component "ClientList.tsx" was created successfully at src/components/ClientList/ClientList.tsx
eli@Elis-MacBook world-chart-ts %
```

Figure 7-3. *ClientList generated by CRA MHL template*

WorldMap.tsx

Next, I will take the WorldMap.tsx component we created in the previous chapter and do a bit of additional refactoring so it fits our needs.

The changes are highlighted. Take a look:

```
// src/components/WorldMap/WorldMap.tsx
import React, { useState } from 'react'
import { geoEqualEarth, geoPath } from 'd3-geo'
import './WorldMap.scss'
import AnimationFrame from '../../hooks/AnimationFrame'
import { Types } from './types'
import PulsatingCircle from '../PulsatingCircle/PulsatingCircle'
import { clientsObject } from '../../model'

const uuid = require('react-uuid')

const WorldMap = (props: IWorldMapProps) => {
  const [rotation, setRotation] = useState<number>(props.initRotation)
  const [isRotate, setIsRotate] = useState<Boolean>(true)

  const projection = geoEqualEarth().scale(props.scale).translate([props.
  cx, props.cy]).rotate([rotation, 0])

  AnimationFrame(() => {
    if (isRotate) {
      let newRotation = rotation
      if (rotation >= 360) {
        newRotation = rotation - 360
      }
```

188

```
    setRotation(newRotation + 0.2)
  }
})

function returnProjectionValueWhenValid(point: [number, number], index:
number) {
  const retVal: [number, number] | null = projection(point)
  if (retVal?.length) {
    return retVal[index]
  }
  return 0
}

const handleMarkerClick = (index: number) => {
  props.setSelectedItem(props.clientsData[index])
  setIsRotate(false)
}

return (
  <>
    <svg width={props.scale * 3} height={props.scale * 3} viewBox="0 0
    800 450" onMouseMove={() => setIsRotate(false)} onMouseOut={() =>
    setIsRotate(true)}>
      <g>
        {(props.mapData.mapFeatures as []).map((d, i) => (
          <path
            key={`path-${uuid()}`}
            d={geoPath().projection(projection)(d) as string}
            fill={`rgba(30,50,50,${(1 / (props.mapData.mapFeatures ?
            props.mapData.mapFeatures.length : 0)) * i})`}
            stroke="aliceblue"
            strokeWidth={props.rotationSpeed}
          />
        ))}
      </g>
      <g>
        {props.clientsData.map((d, i) => {
```

```
            return props.selectedItem.id !== d.id ? (
              <circle
                style={{ cursor: 'pointer' }}
                key={`marker-${uuid()}`}
                cx={returnProjectionValueWhenValid([d.latitude,
                d.longitude], 0)}
                cy={returnProjectionValueWhenValid([d.latitude,
                d.longitude], 1)}
                r="8"
                fill="rgba(242, 121, 53, 1)"
                stroke="#FFFFFF"
                onClick={() => handleMarkerClick(i)}
              />
            ) : (
              <PulsatingCircle key={`pulsatingCircle-${uuid()}`}
              cx={returnProjectionValueWhenValid([d.latitude, d.longitude],
              0)} cy={returnProjectionValueWhenValid([d.latitude,
              d.longitude], 1)} />
            )
          })}
        </g>
      </svg>
    </>
  )
}

export default WorldMap

interface IWorldMapProps {
  mapData: Types.MapObject
  clientsData: Types.ClientData[]
  setSelectedItem: Function
  selectedItem: clientsObject
  scale: number
  cx: number
  cy: number
```

```
initRotation: number
rotationSpeed: number
}
```

If we look at the code changes from Chapter 6's WorldMap.tsx compared to the latest WorldMap.tsx in this chapter, we can see there are a few changes.

For the function props interface signature, I will be setting the props based on the clientObject and mapObject we created and pass a function we can use to do a callback once the user clicks a selected dot on the map.

```
interface IWorldMapProps {
  mapData: Types.MapObject
  clientsData: Types.ClientData[]
  setSelectedItem: Function
  selectedItem: clientsObject
  scale: number
  cx: number
  cy: number
  initRotation: number
  rotationSpeed: number
}
```

In the render, the big change is that the coordinate dots, which I set up in the previous chapter, are checked if they're the selected.

I am returning either a circle or a PulsatingCircle component for each dot.

```
return (
    <>
      <svg width={props.scale * 3} height={props.scale * 3} viewBox="0 0
      800 450" onMouseMove={() => setIsRotate(false)} onMouseOut={() =>
      setIsRotate(true)}>
        <g>
          {(props.mapData.mapFeatures as []).map((d, i) => (
            <path
              key={`path-${uuid()}`}
              d={geoPath().projection(projection)(d) as string}
              fill={`rgba(30,50,50,${(1 / (props.mapData.mapFeatures ?
              props.mapData.mapFeatures.length : 0)) * i})`}
```

```
                  stroke="aliceblue"
                  strokeWidth={props.rotationSpeed}
              />
          ))}
      </g>
      <g>
```

If a dot is selected, I will be using a custom component that creates a pulsating circle. That's right, I will be using the code we created in Chapter 2 to create an animated pulsating circle. Take a look:

```
          {props.clientsData.map((d, i) => {
            return props.selectedItem.id !== d.id ? (
              <circle
                style={{ cursor: 'pointer' }}
                key={`marker-${uuid()}`}
                cx={returnProjectionValueWhenValid([d.latitude,
                d.longitude], 0)}
                cy={returnProjectionValueWhenValid([d.latitude,
                d.longitude], 1)}
                r="8"
                fill="rgba(242, 121, 53, 1)"
                stroke="#FFFFFF"
                onClick={() => handleMarkerClick(i)}
              />
            ) : (
              <PulsatingCircle key={`pulsatingCircle-${uuid()}`}
              cx={returnProjectionValueWhenValid([d.latitude,
              d.longitude], 0)} cy={returnProjectionValueWhenValid
              ([d.latitude, d.longitude], 1)} />
            )
          })}
        </g>
      </svg>
    </>
  )
}
```

I am using geoEqualEarth, but you can try geoOrthographic or any other D3 geographic projection shape.

Using selectedItem inside the JSX code is crucial because it will ensure the map gets rendered when a new client is selected.

As for the render, I will be using geoEqualEarth for projection and window.requestAnimationFrame to animate; nothing changes here compared to the previous chapter.

```
const projection = geoEqualEarth().scale(props.scale).translate([props.cx,
props.cy]).rotate([rotation, 0])

AnimationFrame(() => {
  if (isRotate) {
    let newRotation = rotation
    if (rotation >= 360) {
      newRotation = rotation - 360
    }
    setRotation(newRotation + 0.2)
  }
})
```

The handleMarkerClick handler passes the client data object back to the parent component ClientsWidget.tsx and stops the rotation of the map.

```
const handleMarkerClick = (index: number) => {
  props.setSelectedItem(props.clientsData[index])
  setIsRotate(false)
}
```

Notice that setSelectedClient is used by ClientList and ClientListDetail to set the selected client. I could have used the Recoil atom state here to avoid prop drilling, however, since it's not drilling through any components that don't need the data. Having one method to handle this is fine and a much safer way to help debug and stay out of trouble.

Avoid prop drilling   In React everything is a component, and the data is passed from the top down (parent to child) via `props`. Let's say you need a prop in a child of a child of a child of a parent component. What do you do? You can pass that prop from one component to another. That technique of deeply nested components using data provided by another component that is much higher in the hierarchy is called *prop drilling*.

The main disadvantage of prop drilling is that components that should not otherwise be aware of the data become unnecessarily complicated and cumbersome. They are also harder to maintain because now we have to add that in our tests (if we can test) as well as try to figure out the parent component that provided the data.

PulsatingCircle.tsx

`PulsatingCircle.tsx` is where React shines. Instead of some D3 complex coding, I can use JSX with the help of Material-UI and Styled Components. I do need to pass `cx` and `cy` so my pulsating circle will move with the rotation map.

```
import React from 'react'
import styled, { keyframes } from 'styled-components'const circlePulse =
(colorOne: string, colorTwo: string) => keyframes`
0% {
  fill:${colorOne};
  stroke-width:20px
}
50% {
  fill:${colorTwo};
  stroke-width:2px
}
100%{
  fill:${colorOne};
  stroke-width:20px
}
`
```

```
const StyledInnerCircle = styled.circle`
  animation: ${() => circlePulse('rgb(245,197,170)', 'rgba(242, 121, 53,
  1)')} infinite 4s linear;
`export default function PulsatingCircle(props: IPulsatingCircle) {
  return (
    <>
      <StyledInnerCircle cx={props.cx} cy={props.cy} r="8"
      stroke="limegreen" stroke-width="5" />
    </>
  )
}interface IPulsatingCircle {
  cx: number
  cy: number
}
```

ClientList.tsx Subcomponent

`ClientList.tsx` is straightforward Material-UI with styles. I am making a list of the logos that represent the companies I worked for and am allowing scrolling and selecting. The item selected is being passed back to the parent component so all the other components can be updated. Take a look at the complete code:

```
// src/component/ClientList/ClientList.tsx
import React from 'react'
import './ClientList.scss'
import { createStyles, makeStyles, Theme } from '@material-ui/core/styles'
import List from '@material-ui/core/List'
import ListItem from '@material-ui/core/ListItem'
import ListItemAvatar from '@material-ui/core/ListItemAvatar'
import { clientsObject } from '../../model'

const useStyles = makeStyles((theme: Theme) =>
  createStyles({
    root: {
      width: '150px',
      maxWidth: 150,
      backgroundColor: theme.palette.background.paper,
```

```
        maxHeight: '340px',
        overflow: 'auto',
        paddingTop: '5px',
        scroll: 'paper',
      },
    })
)

const ClientList = (props: IClientListProps) => {
  const handleClick = (id: number) => {
    // console.log(`id: ${id}`)
    props.setSelectedItem(props.data[id])
  }
  const classes = useStyles()
  return (
    <List dense className={classes.root}>
      {props.data.map((value) => {
        return (
          <ListItem key={value.id} button onClick={() => handleClick(value.
          id - 1)}>
            <ListItemAvatar>
              <img alt={`${value.name} avatar`} src={`/clients-
              logo/${value.logo}`} width="100px" />
            </ListItemAvatar>
          </ListItem>
        )
      })}
    </List>
  )
}

interface IClientListProps {
  data: clientsObject[]
  setSelectedItem: Function
}

export default ClientList
```

Let's review the code.

For the style, I am using a Material-UI theme and style, and I set the component to scrollable so the user can scroll through the list of clients.

```
const useStyles = makeStyles((theme: Theme) =>
  createStyles({
    root: {
      width: '150px',
      maxWidth: 150,
      backgroundColor: theme.palette.background.paper,
      maxHeight: '340px',
      overflow: 'auto',
      paddingTop: '5px',
      scroll: 'paper',
    },
  })
)
```

The function signature IClientListProps includes the setSelectedItem function to pass on a user gesture that indicates an item on the list is selected as well as the data feed of client data.

```
const ClientList = (props: IClientListProps) => {
  const handleClick = (id: number) => {
    props.setSelectedItem(props.data[id])
  }
  const classes = useStyles()
  return (
    <List dense className={classes.root}>
```

I am using the array map attribute to iterate each data and draw a ListItem. The ListItem includes the logo that is mapped to the public/logo folder and the click handler.

```
{props.data.map((value) => {
  return (
    <ListItem key={value.id} button onClick={() => handleClick(value.
    id - 1)}>
```

```
            <ListItemAvatar>
                <img alt={`${value.name} avatar`} src={`/clients-
                logo/${value.logo}`} width="100px" />
            </ListItemAvatar>
        </ListItem>
    )
  })}
  </List>
)
}
```

Lastly, the `IClientListProps` prop interface includes the client data feed and selected item method passed from the `ClientsWidget.tsx` parent component.

```
interface IClientListProps {
  data: clientsObject[]
  setSelectedItem: Function
}
```

ClientListDetail.tsx Subcomponent

For `ClientListDetail`, I am setting the detailed information about the client and my profile avatar picture and contribution to their project. Here is the complete code:

```
// src/component/ClientListDetail/ClientListDetail.tsx
import React from 'react'
import './ClientListDetail.scss'
import { createStyles, makeStyles, Theme } from '@material-ui/core/styles'
import ListItem from '@material-ui/core/ListItem'
import ListItemText from '@material-ui/core/ListItemText'
import { Button, Typography } from '@material-ui/core'
import ChevronLeftIcon from '@material-ui/icons/ChevronLeft'
import ChevronRightIcon from '@material-ui/icons/ChevronRight'
import { clientsObject } from '../../model'
```

```
const useStyles = makeStyles((theme: Theme) =>
  createStyles({
    root: {
      width: '500px',
      backgroundColor: theme.palette.background.paper,
      position: 'absolute',
      top: (props) => `${(props as IClientListDetailProps).paddingTop}px`,
      paddingLeft: '0px',
    },
    inline: {
      display: 'inline',
    },
    button: {
      margin: theme.spacing(0),
    },
  })
)

const profileImage = require('../../assets/about/EliEladElrom.jpg')

const ClientListDetail = (props: IClientListDetailProps) => {
  const classes = useStyles(props)
  const handleNext = () => {
    const index = props.data.indexOf(props.selectedItem)
    let nextItem
    if (index < props.data.length - 1) {
      nextItem = props.data[index + 1]
    } else {
      // eslint-disable-next-line prefer-destructuring
      nextItem = props.data[0]
    }
    props.setSelectedItem(nextItem)
  }
  const handlePrevious = () => {
    const index = props.data.indexOf(props.selectedItem)
    let nextItem
```

```
    if (index > 0) {
      nextItem = props.data[index - 1]
    } else {
      nextItem = props.data[props.data.length - 1]
    }
    props.setSelectedItem(nextItem)
  }
  return (
    <div className={classes.root}>
      <ListItem>
        <Button
          size="medium"
          color="primary"
          className={classes.button}
          startIcon={<ChevronLeftIcon />}
          onClick={() => {
            handlePrevious()
          }}
        />
        <img className="about-image" src={profileImage} alt="Eli Elad Elrom" />
        <ListItemText
          primary={props.selectedItem?.name}
          secondary={
            <>
              <Typography component="span" variant="body2"
              className={classes.inline} color="textPrimary">
                {props.selectedItem?.city}, {props.selectedItem?.state}
                {props.selectedItem?.country}
              </Typography>
              <br />
              Eli helped {props.selectedItem?.name} with - {props.
              selectedItem?.description} - visit them on the web:{' '}
              <a href={props.selectedItem?.website} target="_blank"
              rel="noopener noreferrer">
                {props.selectedItem?.website}
              </a>
```

```
          </>
        }
      />
      <Button
        size="medium"
        color="primary"
        className={classes.button}
        startIcon={<ChevronRightIcon />}
        onClick={() => {
          handleNext()
        }}
      />
    </ListItem>
  </div>
  )
}

interface IClientListDetailProps {
  selectedItem: clientsObject
  setSelectedItem: Function
  data: clientsObject[]
  // eslint-disable-next-line react/no-unused-prop-types
  paddingTop: number
}

export default ClientListDetail
```

Let's review.

I am using the material-ui styles to pass the padding on the top so I can adjust this subcomponent.

```
 import { createStyles, makeStyles, Theme } from '@material-ui/core/styles'
import ListItem from '@material-ui/core/ListItem'
import ListItemText from '@material-ui/core/ListItemText'
import { Button, Typography } from '@material-ui/core'
import ChevronLeftIcon from '@material-ui/icons/ChevronLeft'
import ChevronRightIcon from '@material-ui/icons/ChevronRight'
import { clientsObject } from '../../model'
```

Notice that I am setting padding on the top for the component passed from the parent component through the props. The props are passed to the useStyle method, and they can be used dynamically.

```
const useStyles = makeStyles((theme: Theme) =>
  createStyles({
    root: {
      width: '500px',
      backgroundColor: theme.palette.background.paper,
      position: 'absolute',
      top: (props) => `${(props as IClientListDetailProps).paddingTop}px`,
      paddingLeft: '0px',
    },
    inline: {
      display: 'inline',
    },
    button: {
      margin: theme.spacing(0),
    },
  })
)

const profileImage = require('../../assets/about/EliEladElrom.jpg')
```

The ClientListDetail component includes left and right arrows and methods to handle navigating through the clients using these arrows. Take a look at handleNext and handlePrevious.

For the ClientListDetail component signature, we need the props interface that will include the selected item data as well as the function to set the selected item.

```
const ClientListDetail = (props: IClientListDetailProps) => {
```

The props are passed to the useStyles so they can be used.

```
  const classes = useStyles(props)
  const handleNext = () => {
    const index = props.data.indexOf(props.selectedItem)
    let nextItem
```

```
  if (index < props.data.length - 1) {
    nextItem = props.data[index + 1]
  } else {
    nextItem = props.data[0]
  }
  props.setSelectedItem(nextItem)
}
const handlePrevious = () => {
  const index = props.data.indexOf(props.selectedItem)
  let nextItem
  if (index > 0) {
    nextItem = props.data[index - 1]
  } else {
    nextItem = props.data[props.data.length - 1]
  }
  props.setSelectedItem(nextItem)
}
```

The detail component is wrapped in a ListItem and includes the Material-UI icon buttons, photo, and selected item details.

```
return (
  <div className={classes.root}>
    <ListItem>
      <Button
        size="medium"
        color="primary"
        className={classes.button}
        startIcon={<ChevronLeftIcon />}
        onClick={() => {
          handlePrevious()
        }}
      />
      <img className="about-image" src={profileImage} alt="Eli Elad
      Elrom" />
```

```
      <ListItemText
        primary={props.selectedItem?.name}
        secondary={
          <>
            <Typography component="span" variant="body2"
            className={classes.inline} color="textPrimary">
              {props.selectedItem?.city}, {props.selectedItem?.state}
              {props.selectedItem?.country}
            </Typography>
            <br />
            Eli helped {props.selectedItem?.name} with - {props.
            selectedItem?.description} - visit them on the web:{' '}
            <a href={props.selectedItem?.website} target="_blank"
            rel="noopener noreferrer">
              {props.selectedItem?.website}
            </a>
          </>
        }
      />
      <Button
        size="medium"
        color="primary"
        className={classes.button}
        startIcon={<ChevronRightIcon />}
        onClick={() => {
          handleNext()
        }}
      />
    </ListItem>
  </div>
  )
}
```

The IClientListDetailProps props interface includes the selected item, the
method to set the selected item, the client data feed, and the padding.

```
interface IClientListDetailProps {
  selectedItem: clientsObject
  setSelectedItem: Function
  data: clientsObject
  paddingTop: number
}
```

ClientsWidget Component

The ClientWidget component is the parent component that will fetch the results with the help of Recoil for the map and client list and pass the results down to the subcomponents.

I am using the Material-UI grid component to set a client list and a rotating world map. The grid I am setting will have a container and two columns. Here is the layout to help understand the structure:

```
import Grid from '@material-ui/core/Grid'
<Grid container>
    <Grid item xs={6}>
        ...
    </Grid>
    <Grid item xs={6}>
        ...
    </Grid>
</Grid>
```

Take a look at the ClientsWidget.tsx complete code:

```
// src/widgets/ClientsWidget/ClientsWidget.tsx
import React, { useEffect, useState } from 'react'
import './ClientsWidget.scss'
import { useRecoilValue } from 'recoil'
import { Grid } from '@material-ui/core'
import { getPreviousClientListData } from '../../recoil/selectors/
clientsSelectors'
import { clientsObject, mapObject } from '../../model'
import { getMapData } from '../../recoil/selectors/mapSelectors'
import WorldMap from '../../components/WorldMap/WorldMap'
```

```
import ClientListDetail from '../../components/ClientListDetail/
ClientListDetail'
import ClientList from '../../components/ClientList/ClientList'

const ClientsWidget = () => {
  const clientsData: clientsObject = useRecoilValue(getPreviousClientList
  Data) as clientsObject
  const mapData: mapObject = useRecoilValue(getMapData) as mapObject

  const [selectedItem, setSelectedItem] = useState<clientsObject>(clients
  Data[0])

  useEffect(() => {
    // results
    // console.log(`Result: ${JSON.stringify(clientsData)}`)
    // console.log(`Result: ${JSON.stringify(mapResults)}`)
  })
  return (
    <>
      {clientsData?.length > 0 && mapData.mapFeatures.length > 0 ? (
        <>
          <Grid container>
            <Grid item xs={3}>
              <ClientList data={clientsData} setSelectedItem={setSelected
              Item} />
            </Grid>
            <Grid item xs={8}>
              <WorldMap mapData={mapData} clientsData={clientsData}
              selectedItem={selectedItem} setSelectedItem={setSelect
              edItem} scale={200} cx={0} cy={100} initRotation={100}
              rotationSpeed={0.3} />
            </Grid>
          </Grid>
          <ClientListDetail selectedItem={selectedItem} data={clientsData}
          setSelectedItem={setSelectedItem} paddingTop={400} />
        </>
      ) : (
```

```
      <>Loading!</>
    )}
  </>
  )
}
export default ClientsWidget
```

Let's review.

I am bringing the data feeds from Recoil's selectors.

```
const clientsData: clientsObject[] = useRecoilValue(getPreviousClientList
Data) as clientsObject[]
const mapData: mapObject = useRecoilValue(getMapData) as mapObject
```

For the selected item I am using a state.

```
const [selectedItem, setSelectedItem] = useState<clientsObject>(clients
Data[0])
```

For the JSX rendering, I am checking to make sure the data is uploaded and then include the ClientList, WorldMap, and ClientListDetail subcomponents.

```
return (
  <>
    {clientsData?.length > 0 && mapData.mapFeatures.length > 0 ? (
    <>
      ...
    </>
    ) : (
      <>Loading!</>
    )}
  </>
  )
}
```

App.tsx

As the last step, don't forget to add the widget to the parent component App.tsx.

```
// src/App.tsx

import React from 'react'
import './App.scss'
import ClientsWidget from './widgets/ClientsWidget/ClientsWidget'

function App() {
  return (
    <div className="App">
      <header className="App-header">
        <ClientsWidget />
      </header>
    </div>
  )
}

export default App
```

Quality Check

Now, if you run the format, lint, and test commands, we should get a neat confirmation that we are all good.

```
$ yarn format && yarn lint
```

That will give you the following results:

```
$ eslint --ext .js,.jsx,.ts,.tsx ./
✦  Done in x seconds.
```

WorldMap.test.tsx

For the Jest Enzyme test, I am going to make sure the component is mounted.

You can see from the code that having initClientsObject and initClientsObject comes in handy to set the initial values.

```
// src/component/WorldMap/WorldMap.test.tsx

import React from 'react'
import { shallow } from 'enzyme'
import WorldMap from './WorldMap'
import { initClientsObject, initMapObject } from '../../model'

describe('<WorldMap />', () => {
  let component

  beforeEach(() => {
    component = shallow(<WorldMap mapData={initMapObject()} clien
    tsData={[initClientsObject()]} selectedItem={initClientsObje
    ct()} setSelectedItem={Function} scale={200} cx={0} cy={100}
    initRotation={100} rotationSpeed={0.3} />)
  })

  test('It should mount', () => {
    expect(component.length).toBe(1)
  })
})
```

Runt the test.

```
$ yarn test
```

You can compare your results with mine (see Figure 7-4).

```
PASS  src/AppRouter.test.tsx
PASS  src/components/ClientsWidget/ClientsWidget.test.tsx
PASS  src/components/PulsatingCircle/PulsatingCircle.test.tsx
PASS  src/components/ClientList/ClientList.test.tsx

Test Suites: 7 passed, 7 total
Tests:       7 passed, 7 total
Snapshots:   0 total
Time:        12.401s
Ran all test suites related to changed files.

Watch Usage
 › Press a to run all tests.
 › Press f to run only failed tests.
 › Press q to quit watch mode.
 › Press p to filter by a filename regex pattern.
 › Press t to filter by a test name regex pattern.
 › Press Enter to trigger a test run.
```

Figure 7-4. *world-map-widget test results*

You can download the project from here:

https://github.com/Apress/integrating-d3.js-with-react/tree/main/ch07/
world-map-widget

Summary

In this chapter, I showed you how to use the world map we created in the previous chapter as a foundation to build a working widget to display a client list using D3, React v17, Material-UI, Recoil, and TypeScript.

Using React with D3 is pure goodness. I was able to create components and let React manage the state and the update of the DOM when needed. It required very little D3 code but is useful as JSX can handle most of it, and our front-end code is readable and managed by the VDOM. Recoil helps keep the state and renders only when needed.

As you can see, using D3 with React can help create neat visualization tools to help showcase information more intuitively.

Lastly, I was able to run `format`, `lint`, and `test` to ensure quality.

My hope is that this chapter serves as an inspiration for you to create your own interactive resume to showcase of work, client list, photo album, or anything you want to highlight.

As you saw in this chapter, using this structure of widget, state management, and components, and setting up the types and model for data, helps create code that is readable and testable. You will be able to easily refactor and add features once a change is needed.

In the next chapter, we will be creating a D3 force chart with the help of React components.

CHAPTER 8

Force Charts: Part 1

A force-directed graph is a class of algorithms to lay out data in graphs in an attractive way. Force charts can be used for mechanical spring behavior, network visualization, knowledge representation, etc. Using a combination of React and D3 is great since each library can be used for different things. It gives you the best of all worlds. Adding TypeScript as a type checker to the mix helps ensure the types are well defined and helps you avoid potential bugs. Total goodness!

In this chapter, I will show you how to create a basic force chart, namely, a bubble chart with animation that will force each bubble to the center.

Let's get started.

Bubble Chart

A bubble chart displays multiple circles in a two-dimensional plot (Figure 8-1). The bubble chart is an ideal way to point out specific words that are related to each other.

© Elad Elrom 2021
E. Elrom, *Integrating D3.js with React*, https://doi.org/10.1007/978-1-4842-7052-3_8

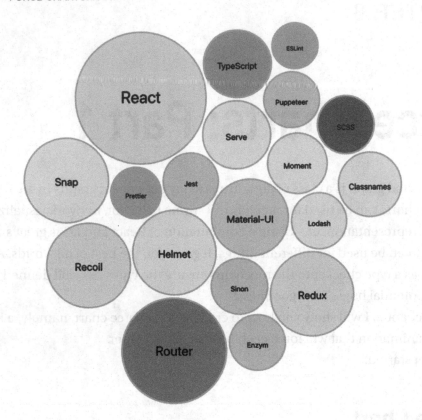

Figure 8-1. Final results of a bubble chart

What We Will Be Building?

In this section of the chapter, I will show you how to create a basic bubble chart with mechanical spring behavior using D3 and React. For the data feed, I will be using popular opinionated React libraries that are must-haves in every developer's toolbox. These libraries are covered in more detail in my *React and Libraries* book: https://www.apress.com/gp/book/9781484266953.

Housekeeping

The technology stack is opinionated and should be familiar to you at this point. Here are the main moving pieces:

- React v17
- TypeScript

- D3 v6

- Other libraries we will be using: Jest and Enzyme, react-uuid

I broke down this chapter down into three steps.

- *Step 1*: Setup

- *Step 2*: Bubble chart creation

- *Step 3*: Redraw

Setup

Set up a new CRA project and name it bubble-chart using the MHL template project, as we did in the previous chapters.

```
$ yarn create react-app bubble-chart --template must-have-libraries
$ cd bubble-chart
$ yarn start // check http://localhost:3000
```

For the force chart, I will be using the d3-force module. Don't forget the types for TS.

```
$ yarn add d3 @types/d3 d3-force @types/d3-force
```

Lastly, I am going to install a library to generate random keys; as you recall, we used this library in previous chapters as well.

```
$ yarn add react-uuid
```

Bubble Chart Components

Our bubble chart components consist of the following:

- BubbleChart.scss

- BubbleChart.test.tsx

- BubbleChart.tsx

- types.tsx

Feel free to create them with the help of generate-react-cli or on your own.

To create the scaffolding using generate-react-cli with my prepopulated templates for the d3 class, use this command:

```
$ npx generate-react-cli component BubbleChart --type=d3class
```

types.ts

To hold the component types I will be using in the bubble chart component, I will be creating a TS types file.

In the type file, I will be holding the data feed as well as the specific data that my force chart needs, which is just the size of each bubble.

Notice that for each bubble I am holding the name, the size, and even the fill color of the bubble. The ForceData object just holds the size of the bubble, which is needed by D3.

```
// src/component/BubbleChart/types.ts
export namespace Types {
  export type Data = {
    id: number
    name: string
    size: number
    fillColor: string
  }

  export type ForceData = {
    size: number
  }
}
```

The bubble component will include both D3 functions as well as React components. Let's take a look at the complete code:

```
// src/BubbleChart/BubbleChart.tsx
import React from 'react'
import * as d3 from 'd3'
import { Simulation, SimulationNodeDatum } from 'd3-force'
import './BubbleChart.scss'
```

```
import { Types } from './types'

const uuid = require('react-uuid')

class BubbleChart extends React.PureComponent<IBubbleChartProps,
IBubbleChartState> {
  public forceData: Types.ForceData[]

  private simulation: Simulation<SimulationNodeDatum, undefined> |
  undefined

  constructor(props: IBubbleChartProps) {
    super(props)
    this.state = {
      data: [],
    }
    this.forceData = this.setForceData(props)
  }

  componentDidMount() {
    this.animateBubbles()
  }

  setForceData = ( props: IBubbleChartProps ) => {
    const d = []
    for (let i= 0; i < props.bubblesData.length; i++) {
      d.push({ 'size': props.bubblesData[i].size })
    }
    return d
  }

  animateBubbles = () => {
    if (this.props.bubblesData.length > 0) {
      this.simulatePositions(this.forceData)
    }
  }

  radiusScale = (value: d3.NumberValue) => {
```

```
    const fx = d3.scaleSqrt().range([1, 50]).domain([this.props.minValue,
    this.props.maxValue])
    return fx(value)
  }

  simulatePositions = (data: Types.ForceData[]) => {
    this.simulation = d3
      .forceSimulation()
      .nodes(data as SimulationNodeDatum[])
      .velocityDecay(0.05)
      .force('x', d3.forceX().strength(0.2))
      .force('y', d3.forceY().strength(0.2))
      .force(
        'collide',
        d3.forceCollide((d: SimulationNodeDatum) => {
          return this.radiusScale((d as Types.ForceData).size) + 2
        })
      )
      .on('tick', () => {
        this.setState({ data })
      })
  }

  renderBubbles = (data: []) => {
    return data.map((item: { v: number; x: number; y: number }, index) => {
      const { props } = this
      const fontSize = this.radiusScale((item as unknown as Types.
      ForceData).size) / 4
      const content = props.bubblesData.length > index ? props.
      bubblesData[index].name : ''
      const strokeColor = props.bubblesData.length > index ? 'darkgrey' :
      this.props.backgroundColor
      return (
        <g key={`g-${uuid()}`} transform={`translate(${props.width / 2 +
        item.x - 70}, ${props.height / 2 + item.y})`}>
          <circle
```

```
            style={{ cursor: 'pointer' }}
            onClick={() => {
              this.props.selectedCircle(content)
            }}
            id="circleSvg"
            r={this.radiusScale((item as unknown as Types.ForceData).size)}
            fill={props.bubblesData[index].fillColor}
            stroke={strokeColor}
            strokeWidth="2"
          />
          <text
            onClick={() => {
              this.props.selectedCircle(content)
            }}
            dy="6"
            className="bubbleText"
            fill={this.props.textFillColor}
            textAnchor="middle"
            fontSize={`${fontSize}px`}
            fontWeight="normal"
          >
            {content}
          </text>
        </g>
      )
    })
  }

  render() {
    return (
      <div>
        <div id="chart" style={{ background: this.props.backgroundColor,
        cursor: 'pointer' }}>
          <svg width={this.props.width} height={this.props.height}>
            {this.renderBubbles(this.state.data as [])}
          </svg>
```

```
        </div>
      </div>
    )
  }
}

interface IBubbleChartProps {
  bubblesData: Types.Data[]
  width: number
  height: number
  backgroundColor: string
  textFillColor: string
  minValue: number
  maxValue: number
  selectedCircle: (content: string) => void
}

interface IBubbleChartState {
  data: Types.ForceData[]
}

export default BubbleChart
```

Let's review the code. The import statements include d3-force, the style file, and the TS types.

```
// src/BubbleChart/BubbleChart.tsx

import React from 'react'
import * as d3 from 'd3'
import { Simulation, SimulationNodeDatum } from 'd3-force'
import './BubbleChart.scss'
import { Types } from './types'

const uuid = require('react-uuid')
```

For the class signature, I am setting props and state interfaces as well as an object for the bubble data object that includes all the properties I need.

```
interface IBubbleChartProps {
  bubblesData: Types.Data[]
  width: number
  height: number
  backgroundColor: string
  textFillColor: string
  minValue: number
  maxValue: number
  selectedCircle: (content: string) => void
}

interface IBubbleChartState {
  data: Types.ForceData[]
}
```

In the previous two chapters, we used a function component. This time, I want to show you that you can do the same thing with the class component. As for the class signature, it's better to use PureComponent and include the props and state instead of React.Component.

```
class BubbleChart extends React.PureComponent<IBubbleChartProps,
IBubbleChartState> {
```

I will be cloning my data because I am feeding D3. D3 takes the data and extends it by adding properties. React props and state variables should not be extended to include other fields that D3 may need, one approach is to clone the data.

```
public forceData: Types.ForceData[]
```

When it comes to the force animation simulation of the bubbles, I am setting that as a private member that I can access within my component.

If you wondered how I know the simulation TS type, I had to drill into the D3 code to find the type. That complexity is worth the effort, because I get type checking throughout my code. It's not a big price to pay.

```
private simulation: Simulation<SimulationNodeDatum, undefined> | undefined
```

My constructor will set up the props and state as well as the method that will create my state variable.

The reason I am setting up a state variable instead of using the data object from the props is that the data variable that the chart bubble needs includes other properties such as the x,y location, so it's better to create a second object instead of trying to set that up on the prop data. forceData will hold the size of each bubble that I can use to generate the bubble. The setForceData method will iterate through the prop data to extract the size of each bubble.

```
constructor(props: IBubbleChartProps) {
  super(props)
  this.state = {
    data: [],
  }
  this.forceData = this.setForceData(props)
}
```

Once the component mounts (componentDidMount), I will animate the bubbles using the D3 force by calling animateBubbles.

The setForceData method I set up is for cloning the size field I need for D3.

```
componentDidMount() {
  this.animateBubbles()
}setForceData = ( props: IBubbleChartProps ) => {
  const d = []
  for (let i= 0; i < props.bubblesData.length; i++) {
    d.push({ 'size': props.bubblesData[i].size })
  }
  return d
}

animateBubbles = () => {
  if (this.props.bubblesData.length > 0) {
    this.simulatePositions(this.forceData)
  }
}
```

The radiusScale function will take d3.scaleSqrt and reduce the scale based on the min and max props we will be providing.

If you need to, you can include logic to handle different use cases for the bubble sizes. That will make the code more complicated, so we're not going to do that here.

```
radiusScale = (value: d3.NumberValue) => {
  const fx = d3.scaleSqrt().range([1, 50]).domain([this.props.minValue,
  this.props.maxValue])
  return fx(value)
}
```

The simulatePosition method is what doing the heavy lifting. The D3 force module does the velocity calculation; see https://github.com/d3/d3-force.

I can adjust the force using the strength method. Once the changes take effect, I can tie that to the component state. Take a look:

```
simulatePositions = (data: Types.ForceData[]) => {
  this.simulation = d3
    .forceSimulation()
    .nodes(data as SimulationNodeDatum[])
    .velocityDecay(0.05)
    .force('x', d3.forceX().strength(0.2))
    .force('y', d3.forceY().strength(0.2))
    .force(
      'collide',
      d3.forceCollide((d: SimulationNodeDatum) => {
        return this.radiusScale((d as Types.ForceData).size) + 2
      })
    )
    .on('tick', () => {
      this.setState({ data })
    })
}
```

Note   These strength, velocity, and collide settings can be moved as props. Small changes will make big changes in animation and visuals.

To render the bubbles, I could use D3, but React is really much better suited for the job because of the VDOM, and the code will be easier to read.

Note   As in previous chapters, I am giving each group's SVG a key using the uuid library. You could generate random a key on your own, but that's my favorite way to generate a key.

I am doing that using the map to iterate through the results and then rendering the results. I am generating both the bubble and the text. These results are clickable and will give the user the name of the bubble that the user clicked. The function renderBubbles returns the JSX code and can be used inside our class return method.

```
renderBubbles = (data: []) => {
  return data.map((item: { v: number; x: number; y: number }, index) => {
    const { props } = this
    const fontSize = this.radiusScale((item as unknown as Types.ForceData).
    size) / 4
    const content = props.bubblesData.length > index ? props.
    bubblesData[index].name : ''
    const strokeColor = props.bubblesData.length > index ? 'darkgrey' :
    this.props.backgroundColor
    return (
      <g key={`g-${uuid()}`} transform={`translate(${props.width / 2 +
      item.x - 70}, ${props.height / 2 + item.y})`}>
        <circle
          style={{ cursor: 'pointer' }}
          onClick={() => {
            this.props.selectedCircle(content)
          }}
          id="circleSvg"
          r={this.radiusScale((item as unknown as Types.ForceData).size)}
          fill={props.bubblesData[index].fillColor}
          stroke={strokeColor}
          strokeWidth="2"
        />
```

```
    <text
      onClick={() => {
        this.props.selectedCircle(content)
      }}
      dy="6"
      className="bubbleText"
      fill={this.props.textFillColor}
      textAnchor="middle"
      fontSize={`${fontSize}px`}
      fontWeight="normal"
    >
      {content}
    </text>
  </g>
)
})
}
```

In the render method, we set a div and svg wrapper and include the renderBubbles method that will return the bubble content. Notice that since we allow the user to click each circle and get the results, we set the cursor as a pointer for the whole div.

```
render() {
  return (
    <div>
      <div id="chart" style={{ background: this.props.backgroundColor,
      cursor: 'pointer' }}>
        <svg width={this.props.width} height={this.props.height}>
          {this.renderBubbles(this.state.data as [])}
        </svg>
      </div>
    </div>
  )
}
}
```

BubbleChart.scss

For the bubble chart's SCSS style file, I am setting up the text inside each bubble with a dark gray color shadow so it's easier to read the text label.

```
.bubbleText {
  text-shadow: 1px 0 0 darkslategrey, 0 1px 0 darkslategrey, -1px 0 0
  darkslategrey, 0 -1px 0 darkslategrey;
}
```

App.tsx

To implement this file, I will be including the bubble chart component inside the App.tsx file.

I am setting up the data as an array. The type of the array will be the type I defined in the bubble component and will hold the name of the bubble, the size of the bubble, and the fill color.

This could be easily extracted as a CSV or JSON file, and the data can be shared across multiple components using Recoil if needed. Just as we did in previous chapters, we are actually going to do that in the next section of this chapter when we create the second force graph.

As for BubbleChart, I will pass the visual setting I set in the bubble component. Take a look:

```
// src/App.tsx

import React from 'react'
import './App.scss'
import BubbleChart from './components/BubbleChart/BubbleChart'
import { Types } from './components/BubbleChart/types'

function App() {

  const d: Types.Data[] = [
    { id: 1, name: 'React', size: 350, fillColor: '#D3D3D3' },
    { id: 2, name: 'TypeScript', size: 100, fillColor: '#9d9a9f' },
    { id: 3, name: 'SCSS', size: 75, fillColor: '#605f62' },
    { id: 4, name: 'Recoil', size: 150, fillColor: '#D3D3D3' },
```

```
        { id: 5, name: 'Redux', size: 150, fillColor: '#D3D3D3' },
        { id: 6, name: 'Material-UI', size: 125, fillColor: '#c6c5c6' },
        { id: 7, name: 'Router', size: 230, fillColor: '#808080' },
        { id: 8, name: 'Jest', size: 70, fillColor: '#C0C0C0' },
        { id: 9, name: 'Enzym', size: 70, fillColor: '#C0C0C0' },
        { id: 10, name: 'Sinon', size: 70, fillColor: '#C0C0C0' },
        { id: 11, name: 'Puppeteer', size: 70, fillColor: '#C0C0C0' },
        { id: 12, name: 'ESLint', size: 50, fillColor: '#A9A9A9' },
        { id: 13, name: 'Prettier', size: 60, fillColor: '#A9A9A9' },
        { id: 14, name: 'Lodash', size: 70, fillColor: '#DCDCDC' },
        { id: 15, name: 'Moment', size: 80, fillColor: '#DCDCDC' },
        { id: 16, name: 'Classnames', size: 90, fillColor: '#DCDCDC' },
        { id: 17, name: 'Serve', size: 100, fillColor: '#DCDCDC' },
        { id: 18, name: 'Snap', size: 150, fillColor: '#DCDCDC' },
        { id: 19, name: 'Helmet', size: 150, fillColor: '#DCDCDC' },
    ]

    const [data, setData] = React.useState<Types.Data[]>(d.slice(1, 10))

    const selectedKeyHandler = (key: string) => {
      alert(key)
    }

    return (
      <div className="App">
        <header className="App-header">
          <BubbleChart bubblesData={data} width={800} height={600}
          textFillColor="drakgrey" backgroundColor="#ffffff" minValue={1}
          maxValue={150} selectedCircle={selectedKeyHandler} />
        </header>
      </div>
    )
}

export default App
```

Notice that we have a function that the BubbleChart can call to pass the circle selectedKeyHandler, and we will call an alert.

App.scss

For the app style, everything stays the same; I am just changing the background color from the default dark color to white, so the chart shows up better in the printed version of this book.

```scss
.App-header {
  background-color: #ffffff;
  min-height: 100vh;
  display: flex;
  flex-direction: column;
  align-items: center;
  justify-content: center;
  font-size: calc(10px + 2vmin);
  color: white;
}
```

Quality Check

Now we run `format`, `lint`, and `test`. We should get a neat confirmation that everything is all good. This is standard practice for me to ensure the code's quality, just like we did in previous chapters.

```
$ yarn format && yarn lint
```

For the test file, the test template file created everything for us; we just need to implement the component `props`.

```
// src/component/BubbleChart/BubbleChart.test.tsx

      <BubbleChart bubblesData={[]} width={800} height={600}
      textFillColor="drakgrey" backgroundColor="#ffffff" minValue={1}
      maxValue={150} selectedCircle={Function} />
    </RecoilRoot>
```

We can now run the test.

```
$ yarn test
```

If you look at the current state of our component (Figure 8-2), you can see the bubbles are rendering and each bubble is clickable and will give you an alert once the library name is clicked. However, the bubbles are covering each other and are not animating at this point.

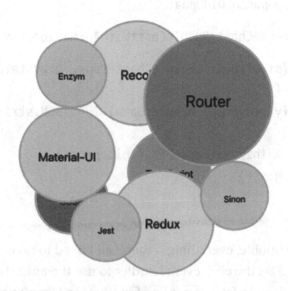

Figure 8-2. *BubbleChart without animation*

Redraw and Animate

Now that we have our bubble chart working, the next step is to add code so we can redraw our bubble chart successfully and provide animations and display them better. We need to be able to redraw in cases where the data changes.

To make these changes, copy the BubbleChart.tsx component, create a new file, and call it BubbleChartWithAnimation.tsx.

BubbleChartWithAnimation.tsx

To animate and enable the changing of the data, we can tap into the React componentDidUpdate class component lifecycle. Once the component updates based on a data change, we can update the bubble chart with the new set of data. To check whether the data changed, we can use JSON.stringify to create a clone of the data and compare the prevProps data with the new props. If the data changed, set the new forceData as the data as well as animate the bubbles.

Note   I am only showing the changes between BubbleChart.tsx and
BubbleChartWithAnimation.tsx.

First, implement componentDidUpdate.

```
// src/component/BubbleChart/BubbleChartWithAnimation.tsx

componentDidUpdate(prevProps: IBubbleChartProps, prevState:
IBubbleChartState) {
  if (JSON.stringify(prevProps.bubblesData) !== JSON.stringify(this.props.
  bubblesData)) {
    this.forceData = this.setForceData(this.props)
    this.animateBubbles()
  }
}
```

To re-animate the bubble, everything is there; all I need to do is add a button (I am
using Material-UI) and set the click event handler to use the animateBubbles() method
I already have. I am using the fat arrow inline function, so I won't need to bind my
handler.

```
import { Button } from '@material-ui/core'render()

  return (
    <div>
      <Button
        className="buttonFixed"
        variant="contained"
        color="default"
        onClick={() => {
          this.animateBubbles()
        }}
      >
        Animate
      </Button>
        ...
```

```
      </div>
    )
  }
}
```

App.tsx Update

For the parent component, let's add a button to update the data. What I can do is to sort my array data randomly so the bubble chart will imitate a change of data. The changes for App.tsx are highlighted.

Note   I am only showing the changes from the previous App.tsx file.

```
// src/App.tsx
import { Button } from '@material-ui/core'
const changeData = () => {
  setData(d.sort(() => Math.random() - 0.5))
}
return (
    <div className="App">
      <header className="App-header">
        <Button
          className="appButtonFixed"
          variant="contained"
          color="default"
          onClick={() => {
            changeData()
          }}
        >
          Change data
        </Button>
        <BubbleChartWithAnimation bubblesData={data} width={800}
        height={600} textFillColor="drakgrey" backgroundColor="#ffffff"
        minValue={1} maxValue={150} selectedCircle={selectedKeyHandler} />
```

```
        </header>
    </div>
)
```

App.scss Update

For App.scss, I will be adding styling for my button so it's in a fixed location on the top of the screen.

```
.appButtonFixed {
  position: fixed;
  left: -100px;
  top: 60px;
}
```

Take a look at the final result in Figure 8-3. Once I click the change data button, the data changes, and the component is animated.

Additionally, when I use the animate button inside the bubble chart, I can see my bubble re-animating, as expected.

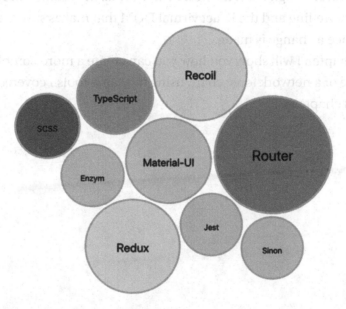

Figure 8-3. *Redrawing bubble chart*

You can download the complete project from here:

https://github.com/Apress/integrating-d3.js-with-react/tree/main/ch08/
bubble-chart

Summary

In this chapter, I showed you how to build a simple bubble chart using React, D3, and TypeScript.

We were able to create our component and we used React to help manage the state and update and redraw the DOM when needed.

This architectural design takes the best of all worlds: the module libraries from D3 that lets us do storytelling and the React virtual DOM that makes sure the page gets rendered only once a change is made.

In the next chapter, I will show you how you can create a more complex force charting example of a network force chart, using the same tools I covered in this chapter and the previous chapters.

CHAPTER 9

Force Charts: Part 2

In this chapter, I will show you how to create a Network graph (force directed graph). We will create a network visualization chart with mechanical spring behavior to represent interview questions you may want to review before your next React job interview. Let's get started.

Force Directed Graph

A force-directed graph is often used for showing relationships between nodes.

What We Will Be Building?

Figure 9-1 shows the final results; see also https://elielrom.com/ReactQuestions.

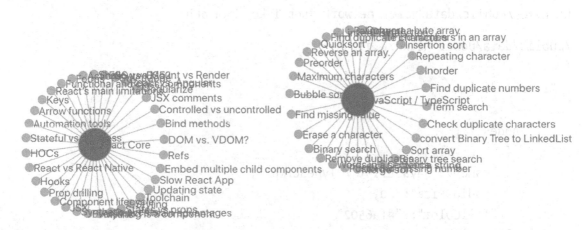

Figure 9-1. *Simple force graph final results*

E. Elrom, *Integrating D3.js with React*, https://doi.org/10.1007/978-1-4842-7052-3_9

Housekeeping

I broke down this subchapter into three steps.

- *Step 1*: Setup

- *Step 2*: Force-chart creation

- *Step 3*: Recoil widget creation

Let's get started.

Setup

Create a new project.

```
$ yarn create react-app force-chart --template must-have-libraries
```

Install the same libraries we installed in the previous project.

```
$ yarn add d3 @types/d3 d3-force @types/d3-force react-uuid
```

Force Chart Component

For the data feed, I will be using the top React and TypeScript interview questions and answers.

In terms of structure, the data feed consists of nodes and links. I am placing the data file here: /public/data/power_network.json. Take a look at it:

```
/public/data/power_network.json
{
  "results": [
    {
      "nodes": [
        {
          "name": "JavaScript / TypeScript",
          "radiusSize": 20,
          "fillColor": "#fa6502"
        }
      ],
```

```
    "links": [
      {
        "source": "Erase a character",
        "target": "JavaScript / TypeScript",
        "value": "How would you erase a character from a string?"
      }
    ]
  }
]
}
```

types.ts

The types file will hold all the TS types I will be using for `SimpleForceGraph`.

- node: These are the nodes we set up in the data feed.

- link: These are the links we set up in the data feed.

- dataObject: The data object includes both the nodes and the links.

- Point: This represents an x and a y.

- Datum: This is the internal data for D3.

Take a look at the code:

```
// src/component/SimpleForceGraph/types.ts

export namespace Types {
  export type node = {
    name: string
    group: number
    radiusSize: number
    fillColor: string
  }
  export type link = {
    source: string
    target: string
    value: string
  }
}
```

```
export type dataObject = {
  nodes: node[]
  links: link[]
}
export type point = {
  x: number
  y: number
}
export type datum = {
  x: number
  y: number
  fx: number | null
  fy: number | null
}
}
```

Graph Subcomponents

To represent the elements in the graph, I could draw everything using D3. However, mixing D3 with React is more suitable for the job, since React is more readable and has the built-in logic to update the DOM as well as the style on a refresh only.

The graph is made with multiple circles, links, and labels. I will be breaking down these elements into files accordingly.

- *Circles.tsx and Circle.tsx*: For the circle's elements

- *Links.tsx and Link.tsx*: For the link (lines between nodes) elements

- *Labels.tsx and Label.tsx*: For the text label of each node

Circles.tsx and Circle.tsx

I will be creating a component that will hold all the nodes. Each node will be represented as a circle, but this can be changed to whatever we like.

Circles.tsx

I will be creating a component that will hold all the nodes. Each node will be represented as a circle, but this can be changed to something else if you like.

To achieve that, I will be passing the nodes data and the `restartDrag` and `stopDrag` methods, so my parent component can tell when to stop this interaction. I would rather have my parent component know about what's happening in case I need to add additional logic. Take a look at the complete code:

```tsx
// src/component/SimpleForceGraph/Circles.tsx
import * as React from 'react'
import * as d3 from 'd3'
import { D3DragEvent } from 'd3'
import Circle from './Circle'
import { Types } from './types'

const uuid = require('react-uuid')

export default class Circles extends React.PureComponent<ICirclesProps, {}>
{
  componentDidMount() {
    this.setMouseEventsListeners()
  }

  componentDidUpdate(prevProps: ICirclesProps) {}

  setMouseEventsListeners = () => {
    const { props } = this
    d3.selectAll('.node')
      // @ts-ignore
      .call(d3.drag<SVGCircleElement, Types.datum>().on('start',
      onDragStart).on('drag', onDrag).on('end', onDragEnd))

    // @ts-ignore
    function onDragStart(event: D3DragEvent<SVGCircleElement>,
    d: Types.datum) {
      if (!event.active) {
        props.restartDrag()
      }
      // eslint-disable-next-line no-param-reassign
      d.fx = d.x
```

```
    // eslint-disable-next-line no-param-reassign
    d.fy = d.y
  }

  function onDrag(event: D3DragEvent<SVGCircleElement, never, never>,
  d: Types.datum) {
    // eslint-disable-next-line no-param-reassign
    d.fx = event.x
    // eslint-disable-next-line no-param-reassign
    d.fy = event.y
  }

  function onDragEnd(event: D3DragEvent<SVGCircleElement, never, never>,
  d: Types.datum) {
    if (!event.active) {
      props.stopDrag()
    }
    // eslint-disable-next-line no-param-reassign
    d.fx = null
    // eslint-disable-next-line no-param-reassign
    d.fy = null
  }
}

render() {
  const nodes = this.props.nodes.map((node: Types.node) => {
    return <Circle key={`node-${uuid()}`} node={node} />
  })
  return <g className="nodes">{nodes}</g>
}
}

interface ICirclesProps {
  nodes: Types.node[]
  restartDrag: () => void
  stopDrag: () => void
}
```

Notice that for the mouse event handlers, I am using the D3 drag event and set the new x and y for D3. There is an event that requires a change.

```
setMouseEventsListeners = () => {
  const { props } = this
  d3.selectAll('.node')
    .call(d3.drag<SVGCircleElement, Types.datum>().on('start',
    onDragStart).on('drag', onDrag).on('end', onDragEnd))

  function onDragStart(event: D3DragEvent<SVGCircleElement>, d: Types.
  datum) {
    if (!event.active) {
      props.restartDrag()
    }
    d.fx = d.x
    d.fy = d.y
  }

  function onDrag(event: D3DragEvent<SVGCircleElement, never, never>,
  d: Types.datum) {
    d.fx = event.x
    d.fy = event.y
  }

  function onDragEnd(event: D3DragEvent<SVGCircleElement, never, never>,
  d: Types.datum) {
    if (!event.active) {
      props.stopDrag()
    }
    d.fx = null
    d.fy = null
  }
}
```

For the render method, I will map through the data to draw each node and set a unique key for each node for React to perform VDOM to know which element needs an update for React to perform better.

```
  render() {
    const nodes = this.props.nodes.map((node: Types.node) => {
      return <Circle key={`node-${uuid()}`} node={node} />
    })
    return <g className="nodes">{nodes}</g>
  }
}
```

Circle.tsx

For each node, I am using a reference (ref), and once the node is mounted, I will use the data from the node data to feed and set the color and size of each node.

```
// src/component/SimpleForceGraph/Circle.tsx

import * as React from 'react'
import * as d3 from 'd3'
import { Types } from './types'

export default class Circle extends React.Component<{ node: Types.node }> {
  ref: SVGCircleElement | undefined

  componentDidMount() {
    if (this.ref) d3.select(this.ref).data([this.props.node])
  }

  render() {
    return (
      // eslint-disable-next-line no-return-assign
      <circle className="node" r={this.props.node.radiusSize} fill={this.
       props.node.fillColor as string} ref={(ref: SVGCircleElement) =>
       (this.ref = ref)}>
        <title>{this.props.node.name}</title>
      </circle>
    )
  }
}
```

Links.tsx and Link.tsx

For the links (the lines between each node), I follow the same architecture I set up for the nodes. I create a links subcomponent, attach events, and map each item to draw each link.

Links.tsx

Notice that since I only need the link data for my props, I am just setting it in the signature instead of creating a props interface.

On the render, I map through my data to draw each link.

```
// src/component/SimpleForceGraph/Links.tsx

import * as React from 'react'
import Link from './Link'
import { Types } from './types'

const uuid = require('react-uuid')

export default class Links extends React.PureComponent<{ links: Types.
link[] }> {
  render() {
    const links = this.props.links.map((link: Types.link) => {
      return <Link key={`links-${uuid()}`} link={link} />
    })
    return <g className="links">{links}</g>
  }
}
```

The link itself calls the link.tsx component for each item mapped to keep the code neat.

Link.tsx

Each link is represented with an SVG line path (the line). I am also placing events and show the data on a mouseover event. Take a look at the complete Link.tsx code:

```
// src/component/SimpleForceGraph/Link.tsx
import * as React from 'react'
```

```
import * as d3 from 'd3'
import { Types } from './types'

export default class Link extends React.PureComponent<ILinkProps> {
  ref: SVGElement | undefined

  componentDidMount() {
    if (this.ref) d3.select(this.ref).data([this.props.link])
  }

  // eslint-disable-next-line class-methods-use-this
  onMouseOverHandler(event: React.MouseEvent<SVGLineElement, MouseEvent>,
  link: ILinkProps) {
    d3.select('.linkGroup')
      .append('text')
      .attr('class', 'linkTextValue')
      .text((link.link.value as string).replace(/(.{50})..+/, '$1…'))
      .attr('x', event.nativeEvent.offsetX)
      .attr('y', event.nativeEvent.offsetY)
  }

  // eslint-disable-next-line class-methods-use-this
  onMouseOutHandler() {
    d3.select('.linkTextValue').remove()
  }

  render() {
    return (
      <g className="linkGroup">
        <line
          // eslint-disable-next-line no-return-assign
          ref={(ref: SVGLineElement) => (this.ref = ref)}
          className="link"
          onMouseOver={(event) => {
            this.onMouseOverHandler(event, this.props)
          }}
```

```
      onMouseOut={(event) => {
        this.onMouseOutHandler()
      }}
    />
  </g>
 )
}
}

interface ILinkProps {
  link: Types.link
}
```

Notice that on a mouseover event, I use D3 to select the link group element and add the text copy.

```
onMouseOverHandler(event: React.MouseEvent<SVGLineElement, MouseEvent>,
link: ILinkProps) {
  d3.select('.linkGroup')
    .append('text')
    .attr('class', 'linkTextValue')
    .text((link.link.value as string).replace(/(.{50})..+/, '$1...'))
    .attr('x', event.nativeEvent.offsetX)
    .attr('y', event.nativeEvent.offsetY)
}
```

On mouse out, I am using D3 to remove the text.

```
onMouseOutHandler() {
  d3.select('.linkTextValue').remove()
}
```

The render includes the SVG group and line with the event.

```
<g className="linkGroup">
  <line
    ref={(ref: SVGLineElement) => (this.ref = ref)}
    className="link"
```

```
        onMouseOver={(event) => {
          this.onMouseOverHandler(event, this.props)
        }}
        onMouseOut={(event) => {
          this.onMouseOutHandler()
        }}
      />
    </g>
```

Labels.tsx and Label.tsx

For the labels, I can follow the same process similar to how the nodes and links are rendered.

Labels.tsx

The labels will iterate all the labels for each node. The interface will be the nodes, and I am also setting up a selected node dispatcher to pass the data back to the parent graph.

```
// src/component/SimpleForceGraph/Labels.tsx
import * as React from 'react'
import { Dispatch, SetStateAction } from 'react'
import Label from './Label'
import { Types } from './types'

const uuid = require('react-uuid')

export default class Labels extends React.PureComponent<ILabelsProps> {
  render() {
    const labels = this.props.nodes.map((node: Types.node) => {
      return <Label key={`label-${uuid()}`} node={node}
      onNodeSelected={this.props.onNodeSelected} />
    })
    return <g className="labels">{labels}</g>
  }
}
```

```
interface ILabelsProps {
  nodes: Types.node[]
  onNodeSelected: Dispatch<SetStateAction<number>>
}
```

Notice that I map through the array to create each label.

```
<Label key={`label-${uuid()}`} node={node} onNodeSelected={this.props.
onNodeSelected} />
```

Label.tsx

For each label, I need the node data and the dispatcher to indicate the label selected.

Note   This code could be changed to use a context instead of the `props` drilling I am doing here, but I wanted to leave the code simple. Feel free to refactor it.

```
import * as React from 'react'
import * as d3 from 'd3'
import { Dispatch, SetStateAction } from 'react'
import { Types } from './types'

export default class Label extends React.PureComponent<ILabelProps> {
  ref: SVGTextElement | undefined

  componentDidMount() {
    if (this.ref) d3.select(this.ref).data([this.props.node])
  }

  render() {
    return (
      <text
        style={{ cursor: 'pointer' }}
```

```
      className="label"
      // eslint-disable-next-line no-return-assign
      ref={(ref: SVGTextElement) => (this.ref = ref)}
      onClick={() => {
        this.props.onNodeSelected(((this.props.node as unknown) as {
        index: number }).index - 1)
      }}
    >
      {this.props.node.name}
    </text>
  )
  }
}

interface ILabelProps {
  node: Types.node
  onNodeSelected: Dispatch<SetStateAction<number>>
}
```

SimpleForceGraph.tsx

The simple force graph as the name suggests will be the main graph component.

In terms of an interface, I will be exposing attributes for the alignment such as the width, height, distance, link strength, and centering.

Additionally, the data will be passed from the parent component, and lastly, I will be passing a function to pass on data once the user selects a node. Here is the complete code:

```
// src/component/SimpleForceGraph/SimpleForceGraph.tsx
import * as React from 'react'
import * as d3 from 'd3'
import './SimpleForceGraph.scss'
import { Simulation, SimulationNodeDatum } from 'd3-force'
import { Dispatch, SetStateAction } from 'react'
import Links from './Links'
import Circles from './Circles'
```

```
import Labels from './Labels'
import { Types } from './types'

class SimpleForceGraph extends React.PureComponent<ITopContentPowerChart
Props, ITopContentPowerChartState> {
  private simulation: Simulation<SimulationNodeDatum, undefined> |
  undefined

  constructor(props: ITopContentPowerChartProps) {
    super(props)
    this.state = {
      // EE: the clone data is needed to avoid:
      // TypeError: Cannot add property index, object is not extensible
      clonedData: JSON.parse(JSON.stringify(this.props.data)),
    }
  }

  componentDidMount() {
    this.simulatePositions()
    this.drawTicks()
    this.addZoomCapabilities()
  }

  componentDidUpdate(prevProps: ITopContentPowerChartProps, prevState:
  ITopContentPowerChartState) {
    this.simulatePositions()
    this.drawTicks()
  }

  simulatePositions = () => {
    this.simulation = d3
      .forceSimulation()
      .nodes(this.state.clonedData?.nodes as SimulationNodeDatum[])
      .force(
        'link',
        d3
          .forceLink()
```

```
        .id((d) => {
          return (d as Types.node).name
        })
        .distance(this.props.linkDistance)
        .strength(this.props.linkStrength)
    )
    .force('charge', d3.forceManyBody().strength(this.props.
    chargeStrength))
    .force('center', d3.forceCenter(this.props.centerWidth, this.props.
    centerHeight))

  // @ts-ignore
  this.simulation.force('link').links(this.state.clonedData?.links)
}

drawTicks = () => {
  const nodes = d3.selectAll('.node')
  const links = d3.selectAll('.link')
  const labels = d3.selectAll('.label')

  if (this.simulation) {
    this.simulation.nodes(this.state.clonedData?.nodes as
    SimulationNodeDatum[]).on('tick', onTickHandler)
  }

  function onTickHandler() {
    links
      .attr('x1', (d) => {
        return (d as { source: Types.point }).source.x
      })
      .attr('y1', (d) => {
        return (d as { source: Types.point }).source.y
      })
      .attr('x2', (d) => {
        return (d as { target: Types.point }).target.x
      })
```

```
    .attr('y2', (d) => {
      return (d as { target: Types.point }).target.y
    })
  nodes
    .attr('cx', (d) => {
      return (d as Types.point).x
    })
    .attr('cy', (d) => {
      return (d as Types.point).y
    })
  labels
    .attr('x', (d) => {
      return (d as Types.point).x + 5
    })
    .attr('y', (d) => {
      return (d as Types.point).y + 5
    })
  }
}

addZoomCapabilities = () => {
  const container = d3.select('.container')
  const zoom = d3
    .zoom()
    .scaleExtent([1, 8])
    .translateExtent([
      [100, 100],
      [300, 300],
    ])
    .extent([
      [100, 100],
      [200, 200],
    ])
```

```
    .on('zoom', (event) => {
      let { x, y, k } = event.transform
      x = 0
      y = 0
      k *= 1
      container.attr('transform', `translate(${x}, ${y})scale(${k})`).
      attr('width', this.props.width).attr('height', this.props.height)
    })

  // @ts-ignore
  container.call(zoom)
}

restartDrag = () => {
  if (this.simulation) this.simulation.alphaTarget(0.2).restart()
}

stopDrag = () => {
  if (this.simulation) this.simulation.alphaTarget(0)
}

render() {
  if (JSON.stringify(this.props.data) !== JSON.stringify(this.state.
  clonedData)) {
    this.setState({
      clonedData: JSON.parse(JSON.stringify(this.props.data)),
    })
  }
  const initialScale = 1
  const initialTranslate = [0, 0]
  const { width, height } = this.props
  return (
    <svg className="container" x={0} y={0} width={width} height={height}
    transform={`translate(${initialTranslate[0]}, ${initialTranslate[1]})
    scale(${initialScale})`}>
```

```
      <g>
        <Links links={this.state.clonedData?.links as Types.link[]} />
        <Circles nodes={this.state.clonedData?.nodes as Types.node[]}
        restartDrag={this.restartDrag} stopDrag={this.stopDrag} />
        <Labels nodes={this.state.clonedData?.nodes as Types.node[]}
        onNodeSelected={this.props.onNodeSelected} />
      </g>
    </svg>
  )
  }
}

interface ITopContentPowerChartProps {
  width: number
  height: number
  data: Types.dataObject
  onNodeSelected: Dispatch<SetStateAction<number>>
  linkDistance: number
  linkStrength: number
  chargeStrength: number
  centerWidth: number
  centerHeight: number
}

interface ITopContentPowerChartState {
  clonedData: Types.dataObject
}

export default SimpleForceGraph
```

Let's review the code.

D3 extends the data provided to it for the force graph, so I need to clone the item since D3 adds an index and I don't want to modify the original data I am passing from the parent component.

This is not just good practice; it will also avoid us getting this TypeScript error: "TypeError: Cannot add property index, the object is not extensible."

```
interface ITopContentPowerChartState {
  clonedData: Types.dataObject
}
```

For the import portion, I will be adding a React library and Links, Circles, and Labels subcomponents as well as D3, d3-force libraries, and a style SCSS file.

```
import * as React from 'react'
import * as d3 from 'd3'
import './SimpleForceGraph.scss'
import { Simulation, SimulationNodeDatum } from 'd3-force'
import { Dispatch, SetStateAction } from 'react'
import Links from './Links'
import Circles from './Circles'
import Labels from './Labels'
import { Types } from './types'
```

```
class SimpleForceGraph extends React.PureComponent<ITopContentPowerChartProps,
ITopContentPowerChartState> {
```

I am holding a copy of the force simulation as a private member so I can work with it through the component.

```
private simulation: Simulation<SimulationNodeDatum, undefined> |
undefined
```

The signature includes the props and the cloned data I will be using for D3.

```
constructor(props: ITopContentPowerChartProps) {
  super(props)
  this.state = {
    clonedData: JSON.parse(JSON.stringify(this.props.data)),
  }
}
```

Once the component mounts, I will be setting up the force simulation's position, drawing each item, and adding zoom capabilities.

```
componentDidMount() {
  this.simulatePositions()
  this.drawTicks()
  this.addZoomCapabilities()
}
```

If I want to update the data, I need to set up componentDidUpdate to ensure the DOM will get redrawn.

```
componentDidUpdate(prevProps: ITopContentPowerChartProps,
prevState: ITopContentPowerChartState) {
  this.simulatePositions()
  this.drawTicks()
}
```

For the D3 force simulation, I am setting up the attributes such as centering, strength, and link distances.

```
simulatePositions = () => {
  this.simulation = d3
    .forceSimulation()
    .nodes(this.state.clonedData?.nodes as SimulationNodeDatum[])
    .force(
      'link',
      d3
        .forceLink()
        .id((d) => {
          return (d as Types.node).name
        })
        .distance(this.props.linkDistance)
        .strength(this.props.linkStrength)
    )
    .force('charge', d3.forceManyBody().strength(this.props.
    chargeStrength))
    .force('center', d3.forceCenter(this.props.centerWidth, this.props.
    centerHeight))
```

```
  // @ts-ignore
  this.simulation.force('link').links(this.state.clonedData?.links)
}
```

I am setting up a method to draw everything, setting up a tick handle based on each time span, and resetting the new x,y values.

```
drawTicks = () => {
  const nodes = d3.selectAll('.node')
  const links = d3.selectAll('.link')
  const labels = d3.selectAll('.label')

  if (this.simulation) {
    this.simulation.nodes(this.state.clonedData?.nodes as
    SimulationNodeDatum[]).on('tick', onTickHandler)
  }

  function onTickHandler() {
    links
      .attr('x1', (d) => {
        return (d as { source: Types.point }).source.x
      })
      .attr('y1', (d) => {
        return (d as { source: Types.point }).source.y
      })
      .attr('x2', (d) => {
        return (d as { target: Types.point }).target.x
      })
      .attr('y2', (d) => {
        return (d as { target: Types.point }).target.y
      })
    nodes
      .attr('cx', (d) => {
        return (d as Types.point).x
      })
      .attr('cy', (d) => {
        return (d as Types.point).y
      })
```

```
labels
  .attr('x', (d) => {
    return (d as Types.point).x + 5
  })
  .attr('y', (d) => {
    return (d as Types.point).y + 5
  })
  }
}
```

Next, I am going to add the addZoomCapabilities method to handle mouse and trackpad zooming capabilities. I am using the minimum code to get the functionality to work. We can improve this code, but I wanted to keep this component simple. Notice that D3 needs to set up the zoom and then use the call to set up these handlers.

```
addZoomCapabilities = () => {
  const container = d3.select('.container')
  const zoom = d3
    .zoom()
    .scaleExtent([1, 8])
    .translateExtent([
      [100, 100],
      [300, 300],
    ])
    .extent([
      [100, 100],
      [200, 200],
    ])
    .on('zoom', (event) => {
      let { x, y, k } = event.transform
      x = 0
      y = 0
      k *= 1
      container.attr('transform', `translate(${x}, ${y})scale(${k})`).
      attr('width', this.props.width).attr('height', this.props.height)
    })
```

```
  // @ts-ignore
  container.call(zoom)
}
```

If you recall when I drew the nodes, I passed the restart and stop drag handlers to the parent; here they are, and I can handle the simulation and animate the force graph once the drag stops:

```
restartDrag = () => {
  if (this.simulation) this.simulation.alphaTarget(0.2).restart()
}

stopDrag = () => {
  if (this.simulation) this.simulation.alphaTarget(0)
}
```

For the render method, I am setting the data to scale (for zoom abilities). Lastly, I am adding my subcomponents so the links, circles, and labels will display.

```
render() {
  if (JSON.stringify(this.props.data) !== JSON.stringify(this.state.
  clonedData)) {
    this.setState({
      clonedData: JSON.parse(JSON.stringify(this.props.data)),
    })
  }
  const initialScale = 1
  const initialTranslate = [0, 0]
  const { width, height } = this.props
  return (
    <svg className="container" x={0} y={0} width={width} height={height}
    transform={`translate(${initialTranslate[0]}, ${initialTranslate[1]})
    scale(${initialScale})`}>
      <g>
        <Links links={this.state.clonedData?.links as Types.link[]} />
        <Circles nodes={this.state.clonedData?.nodes as Types.node[]}
          simulation={this.simulation} restartDrag={this.restartDrag}
          stopDrag={this.stopDrag} />
```

```
        <Labels nodes={this.state.clonedData?.nodes as Types.node[]}
          onNodeSelected={this.props.onNodeSelected} />
      </g>
    </svg>
  )
  }
}

export default SimpleForceGraph
```

Recoil Widget

I have the force graph ready. Now the last part is to set up the data and include the force graph component in the `App.tsx` parent component.

For data management, I will be using Recoil, just as we did in previous chapters. I will set up a selector to get the data using the minimum code and set up a widget component. Lastly, I will include the widget in `App.tsx`. This process is broken into three parts and we will work with these three components;

- powerChartSelectors
- NetworksWidget
- App

powerChartSelectors.ts

The Recoil selector will pull the JSON file and cast it as `Types.dataObject`. I could create an atom instead of using the TS types from my force graph, but I wanted to keep the code at a minimum and don't require an atom.

```
// src/recoil/selectors/powerChartSelectors.ts

import { selector } from 'recoil'
import { Types } from '../../components/SimpleForceGraph/types'

export const getPowerChartData = selector({
  key: 'getPowerChartData',
```

```
  get: () => {
    return getDataFromAPI()
  },
})
const getDataFromAPI = () =>
  new Promise((resolve) =>
    fetch('/data/power_network.json').then((response) => {
      if (response.status !== 200) {
        // eslint-disable-next-line no-console
        console.log(`Houston, we have a problem! ${response.status}`)
        return
      }
      response.json().then((data) => {
        const d = data.results[0] as Types.dataObject
        resolve(d)
      })
    })
  )
```

NetworksWidget.tsx

Now that we have all the pieces, namely, the force graph and a Recoil selector, the last step is to implement them.

As you saw in previous chapters, using a widget is great because I can add other related components and share data and provide interactivity. Take a look at the complete code:

```
// src/component/QuestionsWidget/QuestionsWidget

import React, { useState } from 'react'
import './NetworksWidget.scss'
import { useRecoilValue } from 'recoil'
import SimpleForceGraph from '../../components/SimpleForceGraph/
SimpleForceGraph'
import { Types } from '../../components/SimpleForceGraph/types'
import { getPowerChartData } from '../../recoil/selectors/powerChartSelectors'
```

```
const NetworksWidget = () => {
  const forceData: Types.dataObject = useRecoilValue(getPowerChartData) as
  Types.dataObject
  const [selectedIndex, setSelectedIndex] = useState(0)

  return (
    <>
      {forceData ? (
        <>
          <div className="selectedText">Selected Index: {selectedIndex}</div>
          <div className="wrapperDiv">
            <SimpleForceGraph
              width={800}
              height={350}
              data={forceData}
              onNodeSelected={setSelectedIndex}
              linkDistance={80}
              linkStrength={1}
              chargeStrength={-20}
              centerWidth={350}
              centerHeight={170}
            />
          </div>
        </>
      ) : (
        <>Loading</>
      )}
    </>
  )
}
export default NetworksWidget
```

Let's review.

My selector data will be captured in forceData, and I am also adding a state to pass to my force graph so I can be made aware of a selected node.

```
const forceData: Types.dataObject = useRecoilValue(getPowerChartData) as
Types.dataObject
const [selectedIndex, setSelectedIndex] = useState(0)
```

To render the component, I am setting the force graph with the props only once the forceData is set from the Recoil selector component; otherwise, it shows a loading message.

Once the user has selected a node, {selectedIndex} is binding and will show the selected node.

```
return (
  <>
    {forceData ? (
      <>
        <div className="selectedText">Selected Index: {selectedIndex}</div>
        <div className="wrapperDiv">
          <SimpleForceGraph
            width={800}
            height={350}
            data={forceData}
            onNodeSelected={setSelectedIndex}
            linkDistance={80}
            linkStrength={1}
            chargeStrength={-20}
            centerWidth={350}
            centerHeight={170}
          />
        </div>
      </>
    ) : (
      <>Loading</>
    )}
  </>
)
}
```

NetworksWidget.scss

Lastly, I set up a wrapper div to clip my graph so it doesn't bleed over other content, and then I set up the selected text I am using to display the selected index.

```scss
.wrapperDiv {
  width: 800px;
  height: 350px;
  clip-path: inset(10px 20px 30px 40px);
}

.selectedText {
  font-size: 13px;
  color: #373636;
}
```

Keep in mind that there are other ways to ensure the content does not bleed. This is just one simple option.

Parent Component App

My `App.tsx` parent component is straightforward; just add the `NetworksWidget` file.

App.tsx

Here's the code:

```tsx
// src/App.tsx

import React from 'react'
import './App.scss'
import NetworksWidget from './widgets/NetworksWidget/NetworksWidget'

function App() {
  return (
    <div className="App">
      <header className="App-header">
        <NetworksWidget />
      </header>
```

```
    </div>
  )
}

export default App
```

App.scss

For the `App.tsx` style, I change the color to white, just as I did for the bubble chart, so that the image looks nicer in this book's printed version.

```
.App-header {
  background-color: #ffffff;
  min-height: 100vh;
  display: flex;
  flex-direction: column;
  align-items: center;
  justify-content: center;
  font-size: calc(10px + 2vmin);
  color: white;
}
```

That's it! Navigate to port 3000 to check it out. Go ahead and pull the nodes and see how the force simulation pulls them back to the center.

Now, what can I do with this chart?

I can tie my chart to a flipbook that I created to show the React and TypeScript interview questions and answers, like at `https://elielrom.com/ReactQuestions` (Figure 9-2).

Answer To Question #5

A solution using TypeScript;

```
function firstRepeatingCharacter(str: string) {
  for (let i = 0; i < str.length; i++) {
    if (str.indexOf(str.charAt(i)) !== str.lastIndexOf(str.charAt(i))) {
      return str.charAt(i)
    }
  }
  return 'no results found'
}

firstRepeatingCharacter('123455') // 5
To first a non-repeated character of a given string — same as before just remove the '

function firstNoneRepeatingCharacter(str: string) {
  for (let i = 0; i < str.length; i++) {
    if (str.indexOf(str.charAt(i)) === str.lastIndexOf(str.charAt(i))) {
      return str.charAt(i)
```

Figure 9-2. Flip chart

You can download the project from here:

https://github.com/Apress/integrating-d3.js-with-react/tree/main/ch09/
force-chart

Summary

In this chapter, I showed you how to build a force directed graph chart using React, D3, and TypeScript.

I used Recoil state management to fetch the data, add logic to be able to share the state. I added a widget to include the chart.

This chapter shows you how you can create a more complex chart, using the same tools I covered in the previous chapters.

We let React manage our state and update and redraw the DOM when needed. This gives us the best of all worlds: the module libraries from D3 that let us reuse logic, calculations, force simulations, and even mouse event handling ,and React with the help of the virtual DOM to make sure the page gets rendered only once a change is made.

In the next chapter, I will be covering how to integrate popular chart libraries built on top of D3.

CHAPTER 10

Integrating Popular Chart Libraries Built on D3

As we have covered throughout this book, D3 is the standard when it comes to creating charts.

We have seen how to combine the power of React with D3. This gives an additional benefit because taking advantage of the React VDOM can ensure the DOM is only getting updated when needed. You also get the benefit of other React libraries.

In this chapter, I will be exploring some of the most popular React/D3 libraries. I will first cover the selected criteria I used to test each React D3 library and compare them. In the second part of the chapter, I will show you how to implement each library and give you some of the pros and cons of each.

Keep in mind that I have not worked very long with each library, I am covering so my opinion is limited to what I learned from implementing each example. These libraries are living things, and the information provided here may change, so I recommend checking these libraries out for yourself.

Why Use Ready-Made Components?

There are gazillions of libraries out there built on top of D3 that include ready-to-use components that have been tested. They are cross-platform and include documentation, community support, examples, mock data, and much more.

With that said, creating a truly innovative visualization chart may be a challenge using a chart "library," and there's a good chance that you may find yourself in need of either creating your chart from scratch using D3 or forking the original library you are using to achieve more control over the chart.

© Elad Elrom 2021
E. Elrom, *Integrating D3.js with React*, https://doi.org/10.1007/978-1-4842-7052-3_10

However, these third-party libraries do have their purpose and can help create a proof of concept (POC) or expedite development in cases where these vanilla flavors meet your needs.

I want to point out that using these libraries comes with a price. Many libraries may not be set up as modules and can bloat your bundle for a single simple chart. Generic charts can be seen all over the Web as they may be used by hundred or even thousands of apps, and they may have many bugs that would take a long time to solve.

Caution   I want to point out that using these D3 React libraries comes with a price. Many libraries are not set up as modules and can bloat your bundle for a single simple chart.

Popular React Charts Built on Top of D3

When I say "popular," I am basing my statement on GitHub engagement and my personal opinion.

The most popular ones I have found are listed here:

- *Recharts*: https://github.com/recharts/recharts (examples: http://recharts.org/en-US/examples)

- *Visx*: https://github.com/airbnb/visx (examples: https://airbnb.io/visx/gallery)

- *Victory*: https://github.com/FormidableLabs/victory (examples: https://formidable.com/open-source/victory/gallery)

- *Nivo*: https://github.com/plouc/nivo (examples: https://nivo.rocks/components)

- *React-vi*: https://github.com/uber/react-vis (examples: https://github.com/uber/react-vis/tree/master/docs/examples/showcases)

Comparison of Popular React Charts Built on Top of D3

Table 10-1 lists my results split into the different criteria.

Table 10-1. *Popular React Charts*

Chart	Recharts	Visx	Victory	Nivo	React-vis
Cost	432KB 👎	91KB 👍	164KB	241KB	316KB 👎
Support TS	Yes	Yes	Yes	Yes	Partially
Modules	No 👎	Yes	Yes	Yes	Yes
Mock data	No	Yes	Yes	Yes, nivo-generators	No
Simplicity	Yes	No 👎	Yes 👍	Yes	Yes
Styled already	No	Yes 👍	No	Yes	Yes
Documents	Yes	Yes	Yes	Yes	Yes
Examples	Yes	Yes	Yes	Yes	Yes
Contributors	177 👍	87	135	113	116
Popularity	15600 👍	12500	8500	7800	7500
Open issues	131	72 👍	154	133	277 👎

Let's review these criteria.

Support TS

Having TypeScript (TS) as a type checker for me is a must. Even if you don't use TS now, you might want to in the future.

Many times, all that it takes is a contributor to add the types, or you may need to set the types yourself. If you are on a strict time schedule, you may not have the luxury to do that.

Luckily, all the libraries I have covered include type support. Keep in mind that React-vis includes TS support for the main libraries, but not for many of the modules.

Modules

A Library that is based on module approach is better than including the entire library.

In Table 1-1, I used the cost per module (if that was possible). If you need a simple chart that can be created with D3 in a mere few lines of code, it does not make sense to use these libraries, especially since D3 consists of modules as of version D3 version 4 and up.

Rechart does not include modularity, and the entire library had to be included and used. React-vis has a main library that is pretty big in size and other libraries as separate modules.

The rest of the libraries I checked were organized as modules and cost little when I used only one simple chart.

Mock Data

Having mock data makes creating the chart easier instead of having to provide data and setting that up. Having mock data makes using a library much more pleasant out of the gate.

A nice little surprise from Victory is that it includes mock data so no need to bring your own data.

Simplicity

When I talk about simplicity, I mean how long it takes to get going with a ready chart. Most of the chart libraries have good documentation and examples and are easy to get started with.

Visx seems the most complex out of all of them since it is built as small pieces to put together into a composition. This is great in terms of flexibility, but it requires more time to learn and implement.

Styled Already

Having a library that looks nice and is easy to style goes a long way.

It was nice to see a style sheet included in React-vis, and Visx looks great as is, compared with some of the other libraries that look more like wireframes that need to be styled.

Documents and Examples

Having good documents and examples is crucial and can help you understand how to implement them.

Nivo was a bit of a challenge since I could not get anything to render and display on the screen, just to find out that the wrapper container needs to set the width and height for the container.

Making docs as simple as possible is key. Most libraries were easy to understand with the documents and examples.

Contributors, Popularity, and Open Issues

Popularity, open issues, and contributors are a big consideration. Rechart takes the lead in terms of popularity.

Visx comes second and gets extra credit as it has the least number of open bugs. React-vis comes last on the list in popularity as well as support.

Implementing Libraries

In this section, I will implement each library to give it a try to see how easy it is to get started with. I will be implementing the following libraries:

- Recharts

- Visx

- Victory

- Nivo

- React-vis

Starter Project

Set up a new project using CRA with the MHL template project.

```
$ yarn create react-app react-chart-libraries --template must-have-libraries
$ cd react-chart-libraries
$ yarn start
$ open http://localhost:3000
```

Rechart

Rechart (https://recharts.org/en-US/) is described as a composable charting library built on React components.

Rechart is the most popular library I have found, and it is built with React and D3. It has 15,800 stars as well as a 1.2K fork on GitHub (https://github.com/recharts/recharts).

Additionally, it has a dedicated website with examples and documentation, and it seems to be well maintained with 177 contributors, but 130 open issues.

The library is based on declarative components (presentational components only), is lightweight with only a few D3 modules included, and supports SVG.

Setup

Install Rechart and the TS types.

```
yarn add recharts @types/recharts
```

Implement Rechart

I am going to implement a simple line chart and use SVG as a custom x-axis and y-axis.

For the types I will be setting one file that holds the data object I will set up.

types.ts

Here is the file:

```
// src/component/SimpleLineChart/types.ts

export namespace Types {
  export type Data = {
    date: string
    value: number
  }
}
```

SimpleLineChart Component

I am implementing a simple line chart. Take a look at the complete code:

```tsx
// src/component/SimpleLineChart/SimpleLineChart.tsx
import React from 'react'
import { LineChart, Line, XAxis, CartesianGrid, Tooltip, YAxis } from
'recharts'
import { Types } from './types'

const CustomizedAxisTick = (props: { x: number; y: number; payload: {
value: string } }) => {
  return (
    <g transform={`translate(${props.x},${props.y})`}>
      <text fontSize={12} x={0} y={0} dy={16} textAnchor="end" fill="black"
      transform="rotate(-35)">
        {props.payload.value}
      </text>
    </g>
  )
}

const CustomizedYAxisTick = (props: { x: number; y: number; payload: {
value: string } }) => {
  return (
    <g transform={`translate(${props.x},${props.y})`}>
      <text fontSize="12px" x={0} y={0} dy={0} textAnchor="end"
      fill="black">
        {props.payload.value}
      </text>
    </g>
  )
}

const EmptyDot = () => {
  return <></>
}
```

```
const SimpleLineChart = (props: ISimpleLineChartProps) => {
  return (
    <>
      <LineChart
        width={500}
        height={300}
        data={props.data}
        margin={{
          top: 5,
          right: 30,
          left: 20,
          bottom: 5,
        }}
      >
        <CartesianGrid strokeDasharray="3 3" />
        <XAxis
          height={60}
          dataKey="date"
          // @ts-ignore
          tick={<CustomizedAxisTick />}
        />
        <YAxis
          // @ts-ignore
          tick={<CustomizedYAxisTick />}
        />
        <Tooltip />
        <Line type="monotone" dataKey="value" stroke="#8884d8"
        dot={<EmptyDot />} />
      </LineChart>
    </>
  )
}
```

```
interface ISimpleLineChartProps {
  data: Types.Data[]
}
```

```
export default SimpleLineChart
```

Let's review.

I am setting up a function component that will have the custom text, and I will render my x-axis rotated 35 degrees. Take a look:

```
const CustomizedAxisTick = (props: { x: number; y: number; payload: {
value: string } }) => {
  return (
    <g transform={`translate(${props.x},${props.y})`}>
      <text fontSize={12} x={0} y={0} dy={16} textAnchor="end" fill="black"
      transform="rotate(-35)">
        {props.payload.value}
      </text>
    </g>
  )
}
```

As for the custom y-axis, I am just setting up some custom text using SVG:

```
const CustomizedYAxisTick = (props: { x: number; y: number; payload: {
value: string } }) => {
  return (
    <g transform={`translate(${props.x},${props.y})`}>
      <text fontSize="12px" x={0} y={0} dy={0} textAnchor="end"
      fill="black">
        {props.payload.value}
      </text>
    </g>
  )
}
```

The chart comes as default with dots on every point, since I have many dots I don't want to see them on the chart, so I will be setting an empty render, not to show them.

```
const EmptyDot = () => {
  return <>
}

const SimpleLineChart = ( props : ISimpleLineChartProps ) => {
  return (
    <>
```

For the line chart, I am using the Rechart LineChart component and setting up my custom SVG for the x-axis, y-axis, and dots.

```
<LineChart
  width={500}
  height={300}
  data={props.data}
  margin={{
    top: 5,
    right: 30,
    left: 20,
    bottom: 5,
  }}
>
  <CartesianGrid strokeDasharray="3 3" />
  <XAxis
    height={60}
    dataKey="date"
    // @ts-ignore
    tick={<CustomizedAxisTick />}
  />
  <YAxis
    // @ts-ignore
    tick={<CustomizedYAxisTick />}
  />
  <Tooltip />
```

```
      <Line
        type="monotone"
        dataKey="value"
        stroke="#8884d8"
        dot={<EmptyDot />}
      />
    </LineChart>
  </>
  )
}
```

lineDataSelectors.ts

For the data, I am using the Recoil selector to fetch the data using D3.

```
// src/recoil/selectors/lineDataSelectors.ts

import { selector } from 'recoil'
import * as d3 from 'd3'

export const getLineData = selector({
  key: 'getLineData',
  get: () => {
    return getData()
  },
})
const getData = () =>
  new Promise((resolve) =>
    d3
      .dsv(',', '/Data/line.csv', (d) => {
        const res = d as { date: string; data: string }
        const value = parseFloat(res.data as string)
        const { date } = res
        return {
          date,
          value,
        }
      })
```

```
      .then((data) => {
        resolve(data)
      })
  )
```

App.tsx

The last part is having the parent component App.tsx use Recoil to get the state and pass it to the chart component.

```
// src/App.tsx

import React from 'react'
import './App.scss'

import { useRecoilValue } from 'recoil'
import SimpleLineChart from './components/SimpleLineChart/SimpleLineChart'
import { Types } from './components/SimpleLineChart/types'
import { getLineData } from './recoil/selectors/lineDataSelectors'

function App() {
  const data = useRecoilValue(getLineData) as Types.Data[]

  return (
    <div className="App">
      <header className="App-header">
        <SimpleLineChart data={data} />
      </header>
    </div>
  )
}

export default App
```

You can see the final results in Figure 10-1.

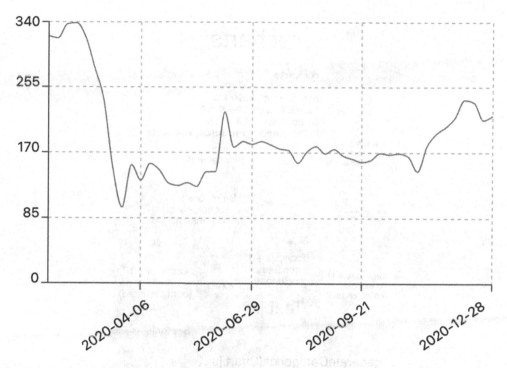

Figure 10-1. Rechart line chart component

Cost

The cost of Rechart for one chart is 186.5KB parsed; see Figure 10-2. This is not as small as I would think a popular library would be; however, this size is acceptable considering what we are getting.

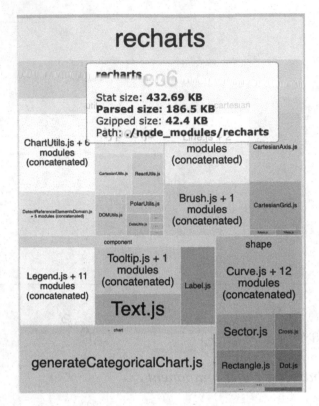

Figure 10-2. Rechart library cost

Pros

I liked how easy it was to customize my chart using SVG. I was also impressed by the number of charts available, the popularity, and the community engagement. It's easy to understand the popularity of this library.

Cons

Each component is not modular, so I needed to bring in the entire library. With that said, 186.5KB is a not too big price to pay if you need to use multiple charts from Rechart.

Visx

Visx (`https://airbnb.io/visx/`), created by Airbnb, is described as a collection of expressive, low-level visualization primitives for React.

Visx is the second most popular library. The Airbnb team really seemed to make some extra effort with this library, its visual appeal, and its support.

Setup

I will be using a bar chart from Visx's examples.

Visx is built as modules, so I can just install what I need and not the whole library.

```
yarn add @visx/mock-data @visx/group @visx/shape @visx/scale
```

Implementing Visx

I used the example from the Visx GitHub location, with a few changes to overcome some of the ESLint errors that were generated instead of just casting them away or ignoring all of them.

Here are my main changes:

- The bar keys were based on the array index (which is a big no-no!).

- The variable data was used twice.

- I removed unused code.

- I refactored the name to SimpleBarGraph.

Take a look:

```
// src/component/SimpleBarGraph/SimpleBarGraph.tsx

import React from 'react'
import { letterFrequency } from '@visx/mock-data'
import { Group } from '@visx/group'
import { Bar } from '@visx/shape'
import { scaleLinear, scaleBand } from '@visx/scale'

const uuid = require('react-uuid')

// We'll use some mock data from `@visx/mock-data` for this.
const data = letterFrequency
```

```
// Define the graph dimensions and margins
const width = 500
const height = 500
const margin = { top: 20, bottom: 20, left: 20, right: 20 }

// Then we'll create some bounds
const xMax = width - margin.left - margin.right
const yMax = height - margin.top - margin.bottom

// We'll make some helpers to get at the data we want
// eslint-disable-next-line @typescript-eslint/no-explicit-any
const x = (d: { letter: any }) => d.letter
const y = (d: { frequency: React.Key }) => +d.frequency * 100

// And then scale the graph by our data
const xScale = scaleBand({
  range: [0, xMax],
  round: true,
  domain: data.map(x),
  padding: 0.4,
})
const yScale = scaleLinear({
  range: [yMax, 0],
  round: true,
  domain: [0, Math.max(...data.map(y))],
})

// Compose together the scale and accessor functions to get point functions
// @ts-ignore
const compose = (scale, accessor) => d => scale(accessor(d))
const xPoint = compose(xScale, x)
const yPoint = compose(yScale, y)

// Finally we'll embed it all in an SVG
function SimpleBarGraph() {
  return (
```

```
    <svg width={width} height={height}>
      {data.map((d, i) => {
        const barHeight = yMax - yPoint(d)
        return (
          <Group key={`bar-${uuid()}`}>
            <Bar
              x={xPoint(d)}
              y={yMax - barHeight}
              height={barHeight}
              width={xScale.bandwidth()}
              fill="grey"
            />
          </Group>
        )
      })}
    </svg>
  )
}

export default SimpleBarGraph
```

For App.tsx, just include the component: <SimpleBarGraph />.
You can see the final results in Figure 10-3.

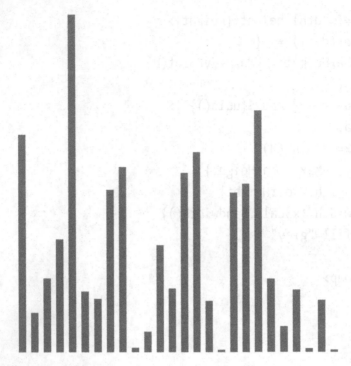

Figure 10-3. *Visx bar chart component*

Cost

The parsed size of 42KB is small (see Figure 10-4).

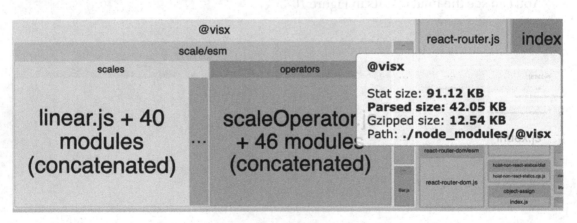

Figure 10-4. *Visx module size for the bar chart*

Pros

Overall, I am highly impressed by Visx. It has a small footprint, and as promised, Visx consists of low-level components, which is a great option when you want to get a final product and the Visx functionality is close to what you are looking for. I liked that it has built-in mock data. It's great to have that so I can focus on the front-end development of the component.

Cons

As you can see from the code, the components are broken into small, low-level components that the developer needs to patch together. There is a learning curve in order to use the Visx library. For simple charts, it seems like overkill, and it's better to just invest your time on mastering D3.

Victory

Victory (`https://formidable.com/open-source/victory/`) is described as React.js components for modular charting and data visualization.

It has almost the same number of stars on GitHub compared to Visx. With that said, there are double the contributors and double the bugs.

Setup

We need to install Victory.

```
$ yarn add victory
```

Implementing Victory

I will be implementing a pie chart based on the code at `https://formidable.com/open-source/victory/docs/victory-pie`.

Victory is easy to implement. Just import the library and include the component. It doesn't even need data to be passed; the mock data is there as the default data.

```tsx
// src/component/SimplePie/SimplePie.tsx

import React from 'react'
import { VictoryPie } from 'victory'

const SimplePie = () => {
  return (
    <div className="SimplePie">
      <VictoryPie />
    </div>
  )
}

export default SimplePie
```

You can pass data just as in any other data viz libraries.

```tsx
// src/component/SimplePie/SimplePie.tsx

import React from 'react'
import { VictoryPie } from 'victory'

const SimplePie = () => {
  return (
    <div className="SimplePie">
      <VictoryPie
        data={[
          { x: 'Cats', y: 35 },
          { x: 'Dogs', y: 40 },
          { x: 'Birds', y: 55 }
        ]}
      />
    </div>
  )
}

export default SimplePie
```

Take a look at the final results (see Figure 10-5).

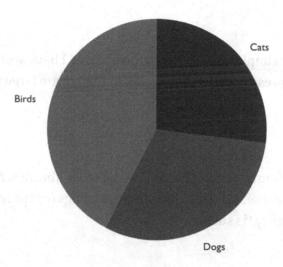

Figure 10-5. *Victory pie chart component*

Cost

The cost parsed is 164KB (see Figure 10-6).

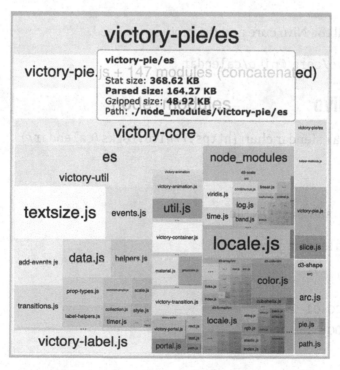

Figure 10-6. *Victory library cost for the pie chart*

Pros

Victory is the easiest to implement out of all the libraries I have seen. The examples are easy, there are impressive gallery examples, and there are large followers, fans, and backers.

Cons

Victory doesn't have as many charts as some of the other libraries. Additionally, at the time of writing, there seems to be too many open bugs (`https://github.com/FormidableLabs/victory/issues`).

Nivo

Nivo (`https://nivo.rocks/`) provides a rich set of data viz components built on top of the D3 and Reactjs libraries.

Setup

We can just install the Nivo core and the module we need.

```
$ yarn add @nivo/core @nivo/calendar
```

Implement Nivo

I will be creating a calendar chart (`https://nivo.rocks/calendar/`).

calendar.json

For the data, let's create a JSON file.

```
/public/data/calendar.json
[
  {
    "day": "2020-01-01",
    "value": 100
  },
]
```

calendarDataSelectors

I will be using a Recoil selector to retrieve the data.

```
// src/recoil/selectors/calendarDataSelectors.ts

import { selector } from 'recoil'

export const getCalendarData = selector({
  key: 'getCalendarData',
  get: () => {
    return getData()
  },
})
const getData = () =>
  new Promise((resolve) =>
    fetch(`${process.env.PUBLIC_URL}/data/calendar.json`).then((response) => {
      if (response.status !== 200) {
        // eslint-disable-next-line no-console
        console.log(`Houston, we have a problem! ${response.status}`)
        return
      }
      response.json().then((data) => {
        resolve(data)
      })
    })
  )
```

SimpleCalendarChart

Now it's time for the main calendar component. Here is the complete code:

```
// src/component/SimpleCalendarChart/SimpleCalendarChart.tsx

import React from 'react'
import { ResponsiveCalendar } from '@nivo/calendar'
```

```
const SimpleCalendarChart = (props: ISimpleCalendarChartProps) => {
  return (
    <div style={{ width: 800, height: 500 }}>
      <ResponsiveCalendar
        data={props.data}
        from="2019-01-01"
        to="2021-12-31"
        emptyColor="#eeeeee"
        colors={['#61cdbb', '#97e3d5', '#e8c1a0', '#f47560']}
        margin={{ top: 40, right: 40, bottom: 40, left: 40 }}
        yearSpacing={40}
        monthBorderColor="#ffffff"
        dayBorderWidth={2}
        dayBorderColor="#ffffff"
        legends={[
          {
            anchor: 'bottom-right',
            direction: 'row',
            translateY: 36,
            itemCount: 4,
            itemWidth: 42,
            itemHeight: 36,
            itemsSpacing: 14,
            itemDirection: 'right-to-left',
          },
        ]}
      />
    </div>
  )
}

interface ISimpleCalendarChartProps {
  data: { day: string; value: number }
}

export default SimpleCalendarChart
```

Let's review.

To set the width and height of the parent component, I am using the Nivo ResponsiveCalendar component.

```
return (
  <div style={{ width: 800, height: 500 }}>
    <ResponsiveCalendar
      data={props.data}
      from='20110-01-01'
      to='2021-12-31'
      emptyColor='#eeeeee'
      colors={[ '#61cdbb', '#97e3d5', '#e8c1a0', '#f47560' ]}
      margin={{ top: 40, right: 40, bottom: 40, left: 40 }}
      yearSpacing={40}
      monthBorderColor='#ffffff'
      dayBorderWidth={2}
      dayBorderColor='#ffffff'
      legends={[
        {
          anchor: 'bottom-right',
          direction: 'row',
          translateY: 36,
          itemCount: 4,
          itemWidth: 42,
          itemHeight: 36,
          itemsSpacing: 14,
          itemDirection: 'right-to-left'
        }
      ]}
    />
  </div>
)
}
```

For the type I can extract that data into its own TS type (just like we did in previous example in this book). I left it in the interface to keep our example simple.

```
interface ISimpleCalendarChartProps {
  data: { day: string, value: number }[]
}
```

App.tsx

App.tsx will retrieve the data using the Recoil selector I created and pass the data to the SimpleCalendarChart component.

```
import React from 'react'
import './App.scss'
import { useRecoilValue } from 'recoil'
import SimpleCalendarChart from './components/SimpleCalendarChart/
SimpleCalendarChart'
import { getCalendarData } from './recoil/selectors/calendarDataSelectors'

function App() {

  const data = useRecoilValue(getCalendarData) as { day: string, value:
  number }[]

  return (
    <div className="App">
      <header className="App-header">
        <SimpleCalendarChart data={data} />
      </header>
    </div>
  )
}

export default App
```

Take a look at the final results in Figure 10-7.

Figure 10-7. *Nivo calendar component*

Cost

The Nivo library is based on modules; however, using one module requires the core library, which costs 241KB, and includes libraries such as React-spring (`https://www. npmjs.com/package/react-spring`), D3, lodash, and a few Nivo libraries.

Pros

I am impressed by the selection of unique charts that Nivo offers; they are nice looking and easy to implement. The library has a server-side rendering (SSR) API, which is great when working with large data sets.

Cons

The examples are not as straightforward as they can be; when I tried to use some of the examples provided by the docs, I could not get them to render, so I had to figure out that the wrapper container needs to have a width and height set; otherwise, nothing will show. It would have been easier if they has set some default values to get something to render and allow us to override the default settings.

React-vis

React-vis (https://uber.github.io/react-vis/), created by Uber, is described as a composable charting library.

It's the least popular library on the list. There are 116 contributors and 277 open bugs.

Setup

We need to install the library and the types.

```
$ yarn add react-vis @types/react-vis
```

Implementing React-vis

I will be creating a simple line chart. I used the example from https://github.com/uber/react-vis/blob/master/docs/getting-started/getting-started.md with some modifications. Take a look:

```
// src/component/SimpleReactVizChart/SimpleReactVizChart.tsx

import React from 'react'
import './BasicRadarChart.scss'
import '../../../node_modules/react-vis/dist/style.css'
import { XYPlot, LineSeries, XAxis, YAxis, HorizontalGridLines,
VerticalGridLines } from 'react-vis'

const SimpleReactVizChart = () => {
  return (
    <>
      <div className="App">

        <XYPlot height={300} width={300}>
          <LineSeries
            data={[
              { x: 0, y: 8 },
              { x: 1, y: 5 },
              { x: 2, y: 4 },
              { x: 3, y: 9 },
              { x: 4, y: 1 },
```

```
            { x: 5, y: 7 },
            { x: 6, y: 6 },
            { x: 7, y: 3 },
            { x: 8, y: 2 },
            { x: 9, y: 0 },
          ]}
        />
        <VerticalGridLines />
        <HorizontalGridLines />
        <XAxis />
        <YAxis />
      </XYPlot>

    </div>
  </>
 )
}

export default SimpleReactVizChart
```

See Figure 10-8.

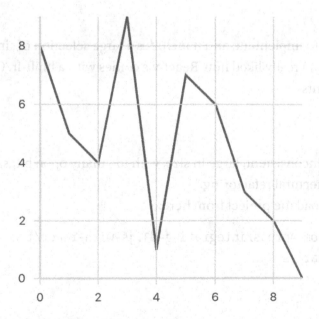

Figure 10-8. *React-vis line chart component*

Cost

The library includes one core library and additional modular libraries. At 635KB unparsed (316KB parsed), that's a high number. See Figure 10-9.

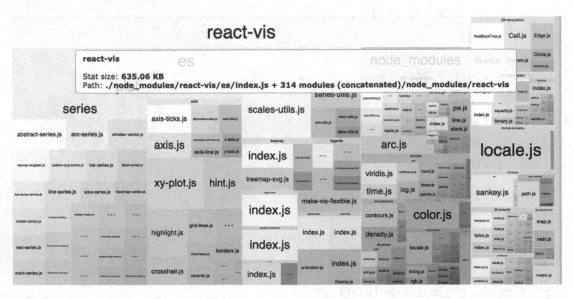

Figure 10-9. *React-vis*

Pros

React-vis was easy to implement, and it includes a large selection of simple and custom charts. Additionally, I really liked how React-vis comes with a built-in CSS file to help style the components.

Cons

The library seems inconsistent, large in size, with too many open bugs, and the library could use an architectural refactoring.

You can download the project from here:

```
https://github.com/Apress/integrating-d3.js-with-react/tree/main/ch10/
react-chart-libraries
```

Summary

In this chapter, I covered some of the most popular React D3 libraries. In the first section of this chapter, I compared the different libraries using specific criteria.

In the second part of the chapter, I showed you how to set up, implement, and use each library and included the cost of each library and the pros and cons.

As you have seen, using a ready-made component built on D3 with the use of React is a no-brainer. We get hours of work done for us effortlessly; many of the charts are open source and cross-platform; and they come with mock data, documentation, examples, and even community support.

With that said, there are too many open bugs in all these libraries, and the release bundle increases significantly in many of the libraries I used. If all you need is a simple chart, they seem like overkill. Continuing to invest time in D3 appears to be the better option.

As you have seen, each library includes different sets of charts and has pros and cons. Here are some examples:

- – Rechart is the most popular with the largest number of contributors.

- – Visx is an impressive library with the unique charts being offered, the support, and the level of organization. It does require effort to understand and work with all the module pieces.

- – Victory is great because it is simple to implement and has many different charts to offer.

What it boils down to is finding the chart you are looking for. If you find one that is close to what you need, then it is worth it to start from zero and implement it using D3.

With that said, D3 also has a learning curve. I think that knowing these libraries and keeping them in mind is useful; however, if you are serious about charts, there is no escaping learning D3. Once you understand D3, that knowledge will help you to customize these ready-made components. Plus, you can always fork the open source components if they don't have what you need.

Keep in mind that I focused only on six libraries, but there are many other libraries out there such as the following:

- *Semiotic*: https://github.com/nteract/semiotic (examples: https://semiotic.nteract.io/examples)

- *react-d3-components*: https://github.com/codesuki/react-d3-components (examples: https://github.com/codesuki/react-d3-components#examples)

Keep these others in mind, and even if you don't use them, these libraries can be used as inspiration for your customized chart.

CHAPTER 11

Performance Tips

Many times data visualization requires lots of resources to run. For instance, consider the features that a common chart includes: animations, a live data feed updating at runtime, a chart with thousands of records or a few charts placed on a single page, and so on.

These requirements can cause a sluggish experience, especially when the user is using a less capable device such as an old mobile device or a computer with low memory or a slow network connection.

In this chapter, I will show you some performance tips you can implement to provide a better user experience.

The chapter is broken down into different topic areas.

- Data loading
- Installing modules instead of global imports
- Server-side rendering
- Tree shaking
- Updating the DOM only when needed
- Using CSV over JSON
- Optimizing CRA with prerendering, prefetching, and precaching
- Memorizing functions with useCallback

The complete chapter code can be found here:

```
https://github.com/Apress/integrating-d3.js-with-react/tree/main/ch11/
knick-knacks
```

© Elad Elrom 2021
E. Elrom, *Integrating D3.js with React*, https://doi.org/10.1007/978-1-4842-7052-3_11

Setup

Let's set up a project to implement the performance enhancements I will be showing you in this chapter.

```
$ yarn create react-app knick-knacks – template must-have-libraries
$ cd knick-knacks
$ yarn start
```

Data Loading

The core of working with charts is the data. Optimizing the data being sent across the wire can make a significant impact on the time it takes to load the chart.

You should only transmit the metrics you need instead of loading the entire data set. For instance, in our previous chapter, we drew a calendar chart with Nivo using a data set of calendar.json.

That data set included data from 2018; however, the chart I used was set to display the data from 2019–2021, so all that data from 2018 was not needed in our app, and it would have slowed down the user experience unnecessarily.

Similarly, when we created the network force chart in the previous chapter, we used the power_network.json file, which included the fillColor field with the color of the node.

That was great that we could control the color of each node; however, that is not needed, because we can change that to a type and create an enumeration class that points to the type that we can then use later in the code.

Each small change may not seem significant, but combine them, and these small measurements will decrease the data size and increase performance.

```
export enum ColorsTypeEnum {
 ONE = '#fffff',
 TWO = '#00000'
}
```

The general rule to reduce overhead is to avoid duplications in the data and in the code.

Similarly, if you send data over the wire, there are many ways to decrease the size and send only what you need. A good example is GraphQL (`https://graphql.org/`), which gives clients the power to ask for exactly what is needed and nothing more.

To measure how long it takes to make these service calls, you can use the browser tools or other third-party tools.

For instance, in Chrome, right-click, select Inspect, and then go to the Network tab. In Figure 11-1, you can see that the response timing breakdown took 17.39 milliseconds; that's not much, but on a large data set that can be a matter of half a second or even a few seconds that the user has to wait for the chart to load.

Figure 11-1. *Chrome network response timing breakdown for calendar.json*

Lastly, there are three quick cardinal rules when working with services, as recently shown by `https://catchjs.com/Blog/PerformanceInTheWild` after rendering a million web pages.

- *Make as few requests as possible*: Keeping a low number of requests is more important than the number of kilobytes transferred, and that goes for any resources. That was proven by performance tests.

- *HTTP 3 over HTTP2 and avoid HTTP*: HTTP 3 is the best option, and it's about 100 time more common. Why? It's because most sites link to the same resources such as `analytics.js` and `fbevents.js`.

- *Async over blocking requests*: Use async and avoid blocking requests as much as possible.

Install Modules Instead of Global Imports

With D3 (version 4 and up) as well as many other libraries, it is possible to import certain modules instead of the entire library. Doing that can reduce the bundle size needed to run the app significantly.

To see this in action, you can analyze the production build. I already set up the CRA MHL template with the run script, so you just have to install `cra-bundle-analyzer` as a developer dependency.

```
$ yarn add --dev cra-bundle-analyzer
```

Now, you can run the analyze tool and check for yourself, as shown in Figure 11-2.

```
$ yarn analyzer
```

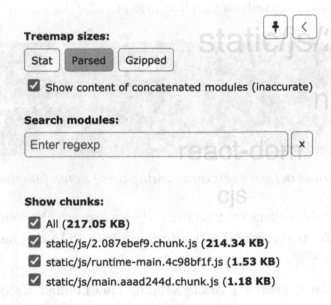

Figure 11-2. *CRA MHL template initial bundle size*

As you can see, the parsed tree map size of CRA MHL is 214KB. That includes React and React DOM v17 (129.17KB) as well as Recoil (54KB).

To better understand what the different sizes stand for, take a look at this list:

- *Stat size*: This is the size of the input after webpack bundling but before optimizations (such as minification).

- *Parsed size*: This is the size of the file on disk after optimizations. It is the effective size of the JavaScript code parsed by the client browser.

- *gzip size*: This is the size of the file after gzip is usually transmitted over the network. Keep in mind that gzip will need to unzip once it reaches the client (browser).

First, let's create some simple React D3 code that will draw a rectangle.

```
$ npx generate-react-cli component Rectangle --type=d3
```

Next, let's install both the D3 global library as well as the only the module we need (d3-selection).

```
$ yarn add d3-selection @types/d3-selection
$ yarn add d3 @types/d3
```

If we create the same code, we can just change it to first use the global D3 library and then use the d3-selection module we are using. The code is almost identical; however, the footprint changes.

Here is the version of the Rectangle.tsx function component when importing the entire D3 library (import * as d3 from d3'):

```
// src/component/Rectangle/Rectangle.tsx

import React, { useEffect, RefObject } from 'react'
import * as d3 from 'd3'

const Rectangle = () => {
  const ref: RefObject<HTMLDivElement> = React.createRef()

  useEffect(() => {
    draw()
  })

  const draw = () => {
    d3.select(ref.current).append('p').text('Hello World')
    d3.select('svg')
      .append('g')
      .attr('transform', 'translate(250, 0)')
      .append('rect').attr('width', 500)
      .attr('height', 500)
      .attr('fill', 'tomato')
  }
```

```
  return (
    <div className="Rectangle" ref={ref}>
      <svg width="500" height="500">
        <g transform="translate(0, 0)">
          <rect width="500" height="500" fill="green" />
        </g>
      </svg>
    </div>
  )
}

export default Rectangle
```

Run the analyzer again to check the bundle size, as shown in Figure 11-3.

```
$ yarn analyzer
```

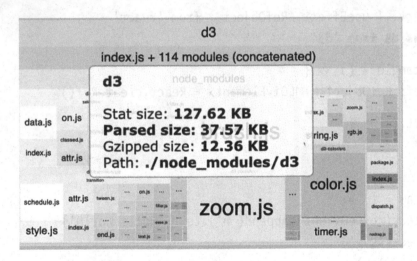

Figure 11-3. *D3 global library parsed size*

As you can see, the D3 library is 37.57KB parsed.

Now, let's change the code to only include the d3-selection module, which we are using since we don't need any other code from D3.

```
// src/component/Rectangle/Rectangle.tsx
```

```
import React, { useEffect, RefObject } from 'react'
import { select } from 'd3-selection'
```

```
const Rectangle = () => {
  const ref: RefObject<HTMLDivElement> = React.createRef()

  useEffect(() => {
    draw()
  })

  const draw = () => {
    select(ref.current).append('p').text('Hello World')
    select('svg')
      .append('g')
      .attr('transform', 'translate(250, 0)')
      .append('rect').attr('width', 500)
      .attr('height', 500)
      .attr('fill', 'tomato')
  }

  return (
    <div className="Rectangle" ref={ref}>
      <svg width="500" height="500">
        <g transform="translate(0, 0)">
          <rect width="500" height="500" fill="green" />
        </g>
      </svg>
    </div>
  )
}

export default Rectangle
```

Run the analyzer again to check the bundle size. See Figure 11-4.

As you can see (Figure 11-4), the D3 parsed size was reduced from 37.57KB to 11.97KB by using d3-selection instead of doing a global import. That's significant!

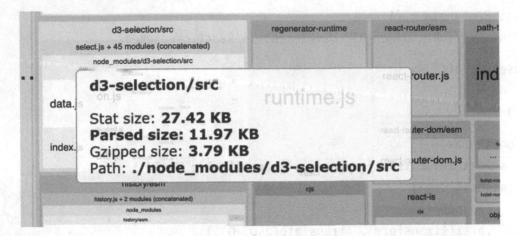

Figure 11-4. D3 module library parsed size

Server-Side Rendering

The CRA (SPA) paradigm is great for certain cases because you don't get any page refreshes, so the experience feels like you are inside a mobile app.

The pages are meant to be rendered on the client side. In addition to SPA, there is another option that I mentioned before in the book: server-side rendering (SSR).

CRA doesn't support SSR out of the box. However, there are ways to configure the routing, etc., and to get CRA to work as SSR, but that may involve ejecting and maintaining the configuration on your own and may not be worth the effort.

Note   Ejecting means you're taking on the responsibility of updating the configuration build code that you may not fully understand. If the build breaks, CRA may not be able to support the custom configuration you set up, and updating the build files may break.

If you're building something that needs SSR to increase performance, it's better to just work with a different React library that is already configured out of the box with SSR such as the Next.js framework, Razzle, or Gatsby (which include a prerender website in HTML at build time).

Tip   If you want to do server rendering with React and Node.js, check out Next.js, Razzle, or Gatsby.

Tree Shaking

Tree shaking (`https://webpack.js.org/guides/tree-shaking/`) is a term used in JavaScript to mean removing dead code.

When I say dead code, it can be two things:

- *Never executed code*: The code is never executed during runtime.

- *The result never used*: The code is executed, but the result is never used.

In our current project configuration, we have Recoil state management, but we are not using the Recoil feature for anything.

Now, if we dig inside our JS bundles and see what's happening, we can see that Recoil is using almost 54.24KB, as shown in Figure 11-5.

Figure 11-5. *Recoil library size footprint*

The reason Recoil is even included in my publish build code is that I am using Recoil for a suspense fallback to show a loading message until the component is loaded, but my code loads quickly, and that code is not needed, because I am not using a selector or any async call that would need that code.

```
// src/AppRouter.tsx

import React, { FunctionComponent, Suspense } from 'react'
import { BrowserRouter as Router, Route, Switch } from 'react-router-dom'
import { RecoilRoot } from 'recoil'
import App from './App'

const AppRouter: FunctionComponent = () => {
  return (
    <Router>
      <RecoilRoot>
```

```
  <Suspense fallback={<span>Loading...</span>}>
    <Switch>
      <Route exact path="/" component={App} />
    </Switch>
  </Suspense>
  </RecoilRoot>
</Router>
)
}
```

To optimize the code, refactor AppRouter.tsx and remove the Recoil reference.

```
// src/AppRouter.tsx

import React, { FunctionComponent } from 'react'
import { BrowserRouter as Router, Route, Switch } from 'react-router-dom'
import App from './App'

const AppRouter: FunctionComponent = () => {
  return (
    <Router>
      <Switch>
        <Route exact path="/" component={App} />
      </Switch>
    </Router>
  )
}
```

You could even remove Recoil from your package.json file to clean things up by running the yarn remove command, but if it's not used, that wouldn't be necessary if you think you would need Recoil later.

```
$ yarn remove recoil
```

Having imports for libraries we are not using increases the size of our code (JS bundles). These imports should be removed.

Run the analyzer again, and you can see that the bundle went down in size to 175KB.

```
$ yarn analyzer
```

Update the DOM Only When Needed

When working with D3 and React, as we have seen, the biggest advantage is that we can let React control the DOM. React VDOM needs to update only once a change is made. We need to ensure we are rerendering only when a change is needed.

The D3 code is considered a side effect because it adds content to the DOM outside of React's VDOM mechanism. Because of that, we want to let the VDOM know when to redraw.

In a function component, the useEffect hook is used for any side effects, and after the component is unmounted, any events that are not React-based need to be cleaned manually to ensure there will be no memory leaks.

But that's not enough. The other concern we may have is to ensure our chart is updated only when needed, instead of on every component update.

For example, if you look at the HelloD3Data.tsx function component we used in the book's first chapters, you'll see we can pass data through the function props and draw each data string as a text label.

```
// src/component/HelloD3Data/HelloD3Data.tsx

import React, { useEffect } from 'react'
import './HelloD3Data.scss'
import { select, selectAll } from 'd3-selection'
interface IHelloD3DataProps {
  data: string[]
}
const HelloD3Data = (props: IHelloD3DataProps) => {
  useEffect(() => {
    draw()
  })

  const draw = () => {
    console.log('draw!')
    select('.HelloD3Data')
      .selectAll('p')
      .data(props.data)
      .enter()
      .append('p')
```

```
      .text((d) => `d3 ${d}`)
  }
  return <div className="HelloD3Data" />
}
```

```
export default HelloD3Data
```

The parent component `App.tsx` holds the data array string as the state. On a button click, I am changing the state with the same array string value as the original initial values: `['one', 'two', 'three', 'four']`. Take a look:

```
import React, { useState } from 'react'
import './App.scss'
import { Button } from '@material-ui/core'
import HelloD3Data from './components/HelloD3Data/HelloD3Data'

function App() {
  const [data, setData] = useState<string[]>(['one', 'two', 'three', 'four'])
  return (
    <div className="App">
      <HelloD3Data data={data} />
      <Button onClick={() => setData(['one', 'two', 'three', 'four'])}>
        Click
      </Button>
    </div>
  )
}

export default App
```

Now if we run this code and keep clicking the click button, the child component `HelloD3Data.tsx` will be redrawn on each click. See Figure 11-6.

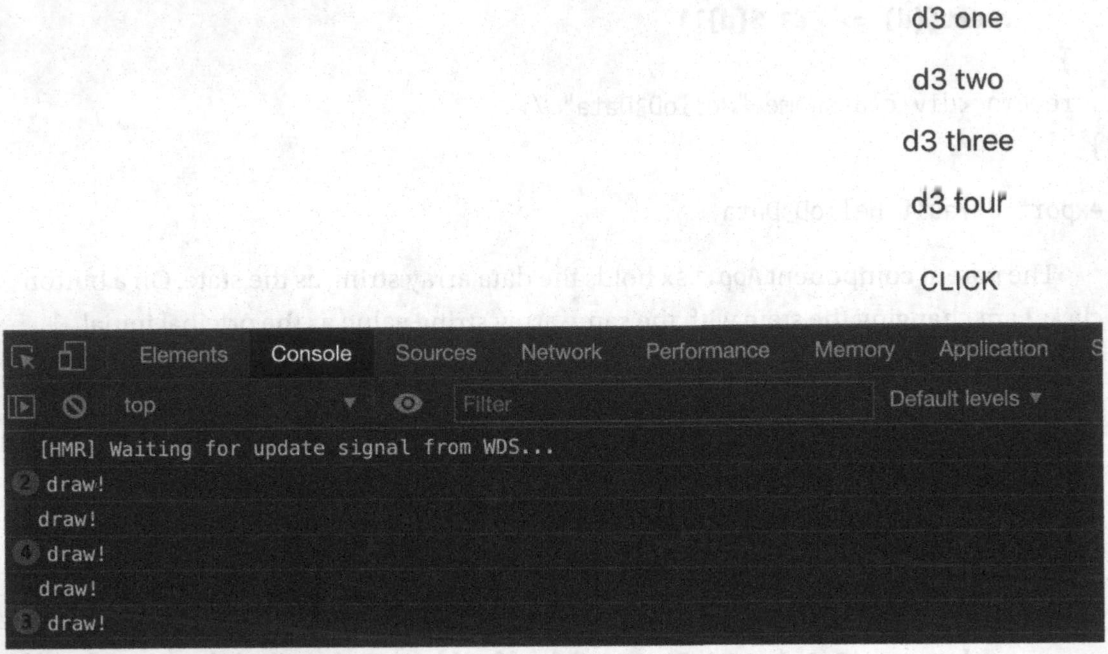

d3 one

d3 two

d3 three

d3 four

CLICK

Figure 11-6. *HelloD3Data.tsx component*

What happens here is that React calls `useEffect` on every update, and since D3 draws the DOM, it causes a redraw of the same code.

What we need to do is check for a data update.

There are a few ways to do that. Here are three:

- *Check D3 data*: Check the data inside D3 elements.

- *Clone*: Clone the data locally.

- *Create React class component*: React class components already have logic built in that passes previous values.

Check the D3 Data

To check the data in our D3 elements, we can select all the p elements we are using and then iterate through the array to create a previous data object that we can compare.

```
// src/component/HelloD3Data/HelloD3Data.tsx

import React, { useEffect } from 'react'
import './HelloD3Data.scss'
```

```
import { select, selectAll } from 'd3-selection'

const HelloD3Data = (props: IHelloD3DataProps) => {
  useEffect(() => {
    draw()
  })

  const draw = () => {
    const previousData: string[] = []
    const p = selectAll('p')
    p.each((d, i) => {
      previousData.push(d as string)
    })
    if ( JSON.stringify(props.data) !== JSON.stringify(previousData) ) {
      console.log('draw!')
      select('.HelloD3Data')
        .selectAll('p')
        .data(props.data)
        .enter()
        .append('p')
        .text((d) => `d3 ${d}`)
    }
  }
  return (
    <div className="HelloD3Data">
    </div>
  )
}

interface IHelloD3DataProps {
  data: string[]
}

export default HelloD3Data
```

With that data check in place, we can update the results and not worry about the DOM redrawing our elements more than needed.

```
<Button onClick={() => setData(['one', 'two', 'three', 'four', 'five'])}>
  Click
</Button>
```

Clone the Data

The second approach is to clone the data, and then we can compare the props value with our state value.

```
// src/component/HelloD3DataCloned/HelloD3DataCloned.tsx

import React, { RefObject, useEffect, useState } from 'react'
import './HelloD3Data.scss'
import { select } from 'd3-selection'

const ref: RefObject<HTMLDivElement> = React.createRef()

const HelloD3DataCloned = (props: IHelloD3DataProps) => {

  const [data, setData] = useState<string[]>([])

  useEffect(() => {
    if (JSON.stringify(props.data) !== JSON.stringify(data)){
      setData(props.data)
      console.log('draw!')
      select(ref.current)
        .selectAll('p')
        .data(data)
        .enter()
        .append('p')
        .text((d) => `d3 ${d}`)
    }
  }, [data, props.data, setData])

  return <div className="HelloD3Data" ref={ref} />
}
```

```
interface IHelloD3DataProps {
  data: string[]
}
```

```
export default HelloD3DataCloned
```

This approach is great, but it is less desirable than checking the data in D3, since we now have the same data being stored in memory or a reference three times (`props`, state, and HTML element).

With that said, cloning data is a sometimes necessary step, since the D3 logic changes data inside an object and React `props` would not tolerate that. TypeScript will actually spit out an error message: "TypeError: Cannot add property index, the object is not extensible." As you remember, we did that when we created the bubble and power charts.

React Class Component

The third option is to create a class component instead of a function component since it already has the lifecycle hooks (such as `componentDidUpdate`) to handle when the component is mounted and updated. We can just use that to compare the previous `props` data with the current one.

```
// src/component/HelloD3DataClass/HelloD3DataClass.tsx
```

```
import React, { RefObject } from 'react'
import { select } from 'd3-selection'
```

```
export default class HelloD3DataClass extends React.PureComponent<IHelloD3D
ataClassProps, IHelloD3DataClassState> {
  ref: RefObject<HTMLDivElement>

  constructor(props: IHelloD3DataClassProps) {
    super(props)
    this.ref = React.createRef()
  }

  componentDidMount() {
    this.draw()
  }
```

```
componentDidUpdate(prevProps: IHelloD3DataClassProps, prevState:
IHelloD3DataClassState) {
  if (JSON.stringify(prevProps.data) !== JSON.stringify(this.props.data)) {
    this.draw()
  }
}

draw = () => {
  // eslint-disable-next-line no-console
  console.log('draw!')
  select(this.ref.current)
    .selectAll('p')
    .data(this.props.data)
    .enter()
    .append('p')
    .text((d) => `d3 ${d}`)
}
render() {
  return (
    <div className="HelloD3DataClass" ref={this.ref} />
  )
}
}

interface IHelloD3DataClassProps {
data: string[]
}

interface IHelloD3DataClassState {
// TODO
}
```

As you can see, all the options I have shown you (Check d3 data, clone, and React Class component) are valid, and they allow us to control that the D3 update takes place only when the data is changed to avoid unnecessarily updating the DOM constantly.

Note   As you can see and I mentioned earlier in the book, I use `React.PureComponent` over `React.Component` when possible, since it gives a performance boost in some cases in exchange for losing the `shouldComponentUpdate` lifecycle event. Both `React.PureComponent` and `React.memo()` are preferred over `React.Component`.

Use CSV Over JSON

When creating D3 charts, it's common to use CSV and JSON for the data feed, and indeed we have used CSV and JSON in many of the examples in the book.

Keep in mind that if you have a choice in the matter, CSV is preferred over JSON.

- *CSV uses less bandwidth*: CSV uses the character separator, and JSON needs more characters just for the syntax format.

- *CSV processes data faster*: The CSV character separator is quicker to split, and in JSON the syntax needs to be interpreted.

Optimize CRA with Prerendering, Prefetching, and Precaching

The CRA (SPA) paradigm is great for certain cases, because you don't get a page refresh, and the experience feels like you are inside a mobile app.

The pages are meant to be rendered on the client side. CRA doesn't support server-side rendering out of the gate.

However, there are ways to configure the routing, etc., and get CRA to work as SSR, but that may involve ejecting and maintaining the configuration on your own and may not be worth the effort.

If you're building something that needs SSR, it's better to just work with a different React library that is already configured out of the box with SSR such as the Next.js framework, Razzle, or Gatsby.

Tip   If you want to do server rendering with React and Node.js, check out Next.js, Razzle, or Gatsby.

CRA is agnostic on the back end and produces only static HTML/JS/CSS bundles. With that being said, with CRA we can do prerendering, which is the closest you can get to SSR at this time. See the CRA documentation at `https://create-react-app.dev/docs/pre-rendering-into-static-html-files/`.

There are many options for generating HTML pages for each route or relative link. Here are a few:

- react-snap
- react-snapshot
- Webpack Static Site Generator Plugin

I recommend React-snap (`https://github.com/stereobooster/react-snap`) as it is more popular on GitHub and works seamlessly with CRA.

React-snap uses Puppeteer to create prerendered HTML files of different routes in your application automatically.

The biggest benefit is that once we use React-snap, the app doesn't care if the JS bundle is successfully loaded or not because each page we set would be on its own.

Keep in mind that for each page to load on its own, some bundle may have redundant code, so it does come with a price.

Step 1: To get started, use this:

```
$ yarn add --dev react-snap
```

Step 2: Next, add the post build run script of `package.json`.

```
// package.json
"scripts": {
  ...
  "postbuild": "react-snap"
},
```

Step 3: The static HTML rendered almost immediately; it is unstyled by default and can cause an issue of showing a "flash of unstyled content" (FOUC). This can be especially noticeable if you are using a CSS-in-JS library to generate selectors since the JavaScript bundle will have to finish executing before any styles can be set.

React-snap uses another third-party library under the hood called `minimalcss` (`https://github.com/peterbe/minimalcss`) to extract any critical CSS for different routes.

You can enable this by specifying the following in your `package.json` file:

```
// package.json"scripts": {
  ...
  "postbuild": "react-snap"
},
"reactSnap": {
  "inlineCss": true
},
```

Step 4: Now in `src/index.tsx` is where we will be hydrating, and we can also register for precaching there as well with this: `serviceWorker.register()`. You'll learn more about precaching in the next section.

```
// src/index.tsx
import React from 'react'
import { hydrate, render } from 'react-dom'
import './index.scss'
import AppRouter from './AppRouter'
import * as serviceWorker from './serviceWorker'

const rootElement = document.getElementById('root')
if (rootElement && rootElement!.hasChildNodes()) {
  hydrate(<AppRouter />, rootElement)
  serviceWorker.register()
} else {
  render(<AppRouter />, rootElement)
}
```

Step 5: Now build your production version of the app.

```
$ yarn build
```

Post build script will be called automatically via the NPM script that is configured in CRA. You should see successful results.

```
$ react-snap
✅ crawled 1 out of 1 (/)
```

Add the Rectangle as a Page

If you open AppRouter.tsx, you can see there is one route to App.tsx.

```
// src/AppRouter.tsx

import React, { FunctionComponent, Suspense } from 'react'
import { BrowserRouter as Router, Route, Switch } from 'react-router-dom'
import { RecoilRoot } from 'recoil'
import App from './App'

const AppRouter: FunctionComponent = () => {
  return (
    <Router>
      <RecoilRoot>
        <Suspense fallback={<span>Loading...</span>}>
          <Switch>
            <Route exact path="/" component={App} />
          </Switch>
        </Suspense>
      </RecoilRoot>
    </Router>
  )
}
```

Now let's add another page router and add that to the router tag (Rectangle).

```tsx
// src/AppRouter.tsx

import Rectangle from './components/Rectangle/Rectangle'

const AppRouter: FunctionComponent = () => {
  return (
    <Router>
      <RecoilRoot>
        <Suspense fallback={<span>Loading...</span>}>
          <Switch>
            <Route exact path="/" component={App} />
            <Route exact path="/Rectangle" component={Rectangle} />
          </Switch>
        </Suspense>
      </RecoilRoot>
    </Router>
  )
}
```

Now if you navigate to the Rectangle URL shown here, you can see the component we built:

```
http://localhost:3000/Rectangle
```

Run yarn build again.

```
$ yarn build
```

It still gives the same results of one page crawled, but why?

```
✅ crawled 1 out of 1 (/)
```

The reason is that the Rectangle page is not linked anywhere, so it can't be crawled. To get the page crawled, we need to add a router link in our App.tsx file.

```tsx
<NavLink to='/Rectangle' key='Rectangle'>
  Navigate To Rectangle
</NavLink>
```

Now run the build again, and now both pages are crawled.

```
$ react-snap
✓  crawled 1 out of 3 (/)

✓  crawled 2 out of 2 (/Rectangle)
```

You can also see this in the public folder; see Figure 11-7.

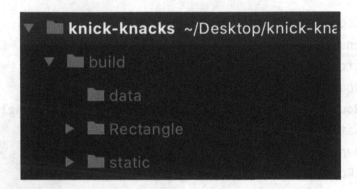

Figure 11-7. *Rectangle folder created inside build folder*

Prefetching

You might have used higher-order components (HOCs) in React to enhance a component capability (`https://reactjs.org/docs/higher-order-components.html`). We can take a similar approach when it comes to our JS bundle.

We want to first load the page and then retrieve the JS bundle, so we get to display the page ASAP.

Let's take a look. You can build a prod version and use the `serve` command to see the build.

```
$ yarn build:serve
```

Check the build (`http://localhost:5000/Rectangle`) in Chrome DevTools. Take a look at the JS bundle chunks hierarchy; they are at the top (see Figure 11-8).

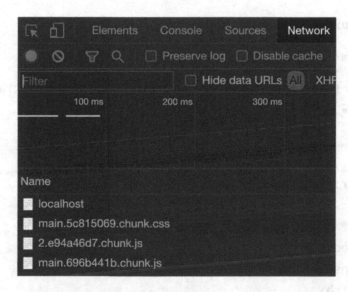

Figure 11-8. *Hierarchy not set for JS bundle*

We want to move these chunk bundles to the bottom. To do that, we can use Quicklink (https://github.com/GoogleChromeLabs/quicklink).

Quicklink attempts to make navigations to subsequent pages load faster by using techniques to decide what to load first. Let's install Quicklink.

```
$ yarn add -D webpack-route-manifest
$ yarn add quicklink
```

Notice that your package.json file was updated with this code:

```
"devDependencies": {
  "webpack-route-manifest": "^1.2.0"
}
```

In our case, we use the React CRA SPA; we will be using the React HOC where we want to add prefetching functionality to the pages we lazy load. To do that, we just use an empty option object and wrap our component with the with the Quicklink HOC.

```tsx
// src/AppRouter.tsx

import React, { FunctionComponent, lazy, Suspense } from 'react'
import { BrowserRouter as Router, Route, Switch } from 'react-router-dom'
import { RecoilRoot } from 'recoil'
import { withQuicklink } from 'quicklink/dist/react/hoc.js'

import App from './App'

const MyPage = lazy(() => import('./components/Rectangle/Rectangle'))
const options = {
  origins: [],
}

const AppRouter: FunctionComponent = () => {
  return (
    <Router>
      <RecoilRoot>
        <Suspense fallback={<span>Loading...</span>}>
          <Switch>
            <Route exact path="/" component={App} />
            <Route exact path="/Rectangle" component={withQuicklink(MyPage,
            options)} />
          </Switch>
        </Suspense>
      </RecoilRoot>
    </Router>
  )
}

export default AppRouter
```

Note Running `prerender` and serving static pages is not necessarily always the best approach; it can actually create an undesired experience for your users as each page will load and the component load will be distributed across pages. For light apps, it may be better to wait half a second for all the content to load, with no more wait time, than waiting a bit on each page load. You need to test and see for yourself, but be aware of this feature.

Step 5: To spin off a production build locally, run the CRA template and then and then the run script (`yarn build:serve`). It's using the serve library, so you don't even need to install or configure `package.json` if you are using the CRA MHL template.

Run the `serve` run script to add a local server and view the production build.

```
$ yarn build:serve
```

After implementing the logic, as you can see, the HOC worked, and now our bundle chunks are at the bottom, as shown in Figure 11-9.

```
http://localhost:5000/Rectangle
```

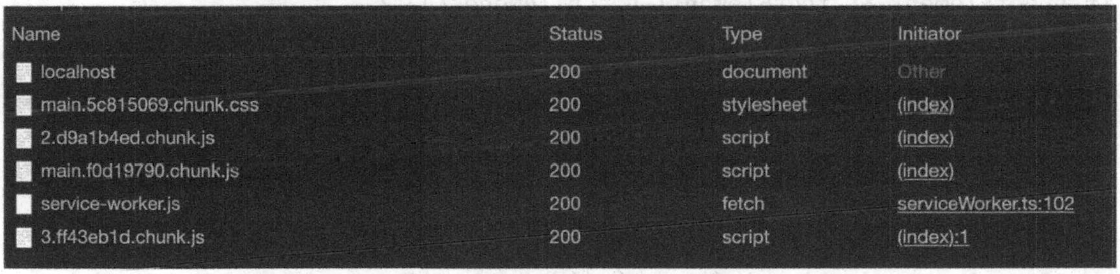

Name	Status	Type	Initiator
localhost	200	document	Other
main.5c815069.chunk.css	200	stylesheet	(index)
2.d9a1b4ed.chunk.js	200	script	(index)
main.f0d19790.chunk.js	200	script	(index)
service-worker.js	200	fetch	serviceWorker.ts:102
3.ff43eb1d.chunk.js	200	script	(index):1

Figure 11-9. HOC worked bundle chunks are at the bottom

I want to point out that another big reason to use `prerender` is the need for static pages beyond optimizing with search engine optimization (SEO). If you prerendering pages and want to generate a different title, description, metadata, etc., for each page due to SEO reasons, or need to share individual pages via social media, check out `react-helmet` that can help to set a unique header for each React page component.

Precache: Work Offline

Being able to go offline is a core functionality of a progressive web application (PWA). We can do that with a serviceWorker.

CRA includes serviceWorker inside the index.tsx file.

```
serviceWorker.unregister()
```

What Does It Mean?

CRA includes a "workbox for production" build out of the box (https://developers. google.com/web/tools/workbox/modules/workbox-webpack-plugin).

To enable the feature, just change the serviceWorker state to register.

```
serviceWorker.register()
```

We already added the serviceWorker to our index.tsx component when we build for production, in the previous section.

```
const rootElement = document.getElementById('root')
if (rootElement && rootElement!.hasChildNodes()) {
  hydrate(<AppRouter />, rootElement)
  serviceWorker.register()
} else {
  render(<AppRouter />, rootElement)
}// serviceWorker.unregister()
```

Now when you build again ($yarn build), a new file appears:
build/precache-manifest.[string].js.

See Figure 11-10.

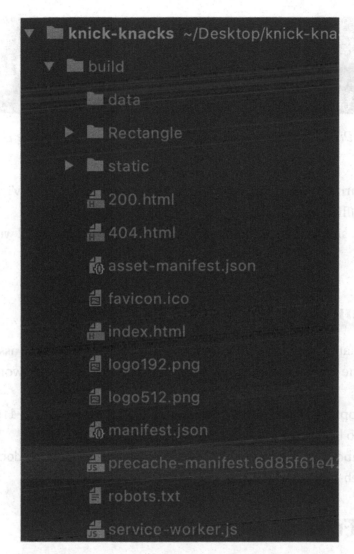

Figure 11-10. *The runtime-main bundle file was added to our static folder*

To see the worker in action, you need to run the publish build script again.

```
$ yarn build:serve
```

Take a look at the Chrome DevTools Network tab; in the Size column, you can see it says ServiceWorker, as shown in Figure 11-11.

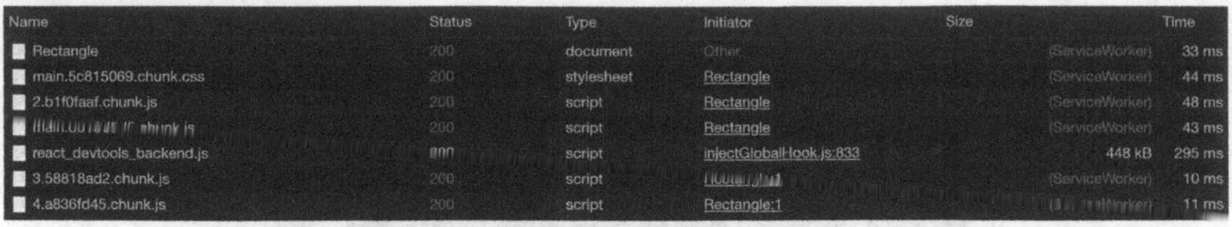

Figure 11-11. *Precaching ServiceWorker shows up in the Chrome DevTools Network tab*

Go ahead, turn off your network connection, or on the Chrome DevTools Network tab, check the Offline checkbox.

You can now simulate an offline experience. Refresh the app; it still works as if you are online!

How Is Your App Working Offline?

The workbox default precaching strategy for CRA is `CacheFirst`. Static assets are retrieved from the service worker cache mechanism, and on fail, a network request is made.

Workbox supports different strategies such as `CacheOnly`, `NetworkFirst`, etc., but CRA may need to be ejected to use a different strategy than the default.

Read more about this feature at `https://create-react-app.dev/docs/making-a-progressive-web-app/`.

Memorize Function with useCallback

I showed you previously in this chapter and throughout the book how to use `useEffect` and `draw`. Take a look:

```
useEffect(() => {
    draw()
}const draw = () => {
  // TODO
}
```

However, that code is problematic because it can cause an infinite loop! `useCallback()` can help prevent this.

useCallback() can be used with useEffect() to help prevent the re-creation of functions. (See https://reactjs.org/docs/hooks-reference.html#usecallback.)

```
useEffect(() => {
  memoizedDrawCallback()
}, [memoizedDrawCallback]const memoizedDrawCallback = useCallback(() => {
  // TODO using data as dependency
}, [data])
```

As you can see, functions such as memoizedDrawCallback are nothing more than objects in JS. Wrapping them around a function declaration and defining the dependencies of the function can ensure the function is re-created only if its dependencies have changed. For example, you can list data or props that you need in the dependencies array.

```
[props.bottom, props.data, props.fill, props.height, props.left, props.
right, props.top, props.width]
```

The memoizedDrawCallback function will not get rebuilt on every render DOM cycle update, so we have broken out of a potential infinite loop! In my d3 and React interactive course you can see how to implement many of the examples in this chapter with the memorizedDrawCallback approach. https://elielrom.com/BuildSiteCourse.

Summary

Applying the methods in this chapter and measuring the results can help reduce the application footprint and the load time in precious seconds.

Many of these tips will be used while you profile and debug your app. If you are a bit rusty about profiling and debugging the React app, check out my React book (https://www.apress.com/gp/book/9781484266953). Additionally, I have two articles that can help.

- https://medium.com/react-courses/4-ways-to-profile-your-react-app-75b740e39ab2

- https://medium.com/react-courses/six-best-debugging-options-to-crush-your-reacts-bugs-like-a-champion-70b11b6a1a2d

In the next and last chapter, I will be covering publishing your React D3 chart as both a SPA and with SSR.

CHAPTER 12

Publishing Your React D3 App

Congratulations for making it to the last chapter in the book. You should be proud of your commitment, and I am pleased you have reached this chapter. Now that we have some charts ready, it is time to publish the React and D3 code.

There are many factors to consider, and many options are available. As a team lead, startup advisor, CTO, or any technology professional, you may need to make a decision about which tool to use. So, which should you pick?

In this chapter, you will be learning about some of the best options you can select for your React starter project. Additionally, I will walk you through the process of creating one example of a SPA React app as well as an SSR React app and publishing the code.

This chapter is split into the following sections:

- Selecting your startup project

- Creating and publishing an SSR app with Next.js

- Creating and publishing an SPA with CRA

- Helpful debug profile tools

Let's get started.

Selecting Your Startup Project

In many cases, selecting a technology stack for the development environment has already been done for you. However, if you need to recommend a technology stack (even if you don't need to publish your app yet), it's good practice to create a published build.

© Elad Elrom 2021
E. Elrom, *Integrating D3.js with React*, https://doi.org/10.1007/978-1-4842-7052-3_12

Why Publish a Build During the Development Phase?

Creating a published build is important because it gives you a more realistic build than with the libraries that are already optimized and ready for deployment.

While you work on your project. Changes in the code could be significant, and it's important to constantly create published builds and not to wait for the last minute at the end of your sprint to find out that the build is broken or not working as expected.

I am a true believer that you should be publishing fast and publishing often, even twice a day.

What Tool Should You Pick?

When it comes to deciding what tool to pick, there are many paid and free solutions and options out there in terms of publishing your work that it can become overwhelming.

Additionally, you have options for using React as a SPA than choose SSR, with fully configured servers such as Ubuntu or Windows, or as serverless with no configuration solutions.

What it boils down to is what other technologies you need to integrate with, usage, costs, maintenance, langagues be deployed, your personal preference, team experience, community support, and many other facts.

To try to give you a way to look at it, I created the high-level activity diagram in Figure 12-1. This diagram can help you decide how to plan your publishing options from start to finish. Note that this activity diagram is simplified and doesn't go into all the details that should be considered.

Within each option, there are so multiple options. For example, the free solutions usually start to cost money when you scale up, so that should be checked and considered.

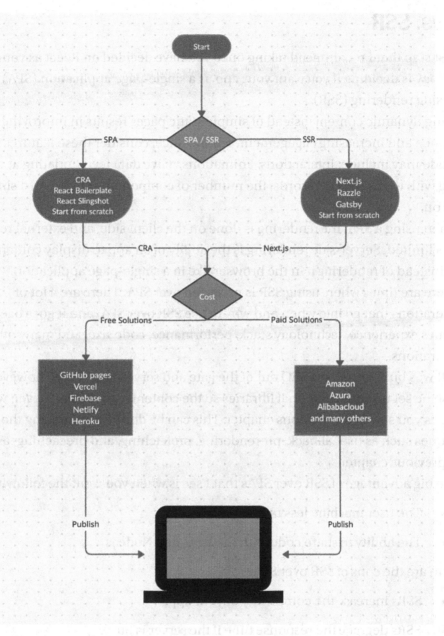

Figure 12-1. *Activity diagram for selecting a startup React project and publishing*

SPA vs. SSR

The first step that I recommend taking once you have decided on React as your web technology is deciding if you want your app as a single-page application (SPA) or to have server-side rendering (SSR).

Using dynamic content instead of simple static pages results in improving user experience and increasing engagement. For instance, consider these features that your code may include: interactions, animations, a live data feed updating at runtime, dealing with thousands of records, the number of components placed on a single page, and so on.

When using a SPA, the rendering is done on the client side, and external resource usage is limited. Server-side rendering is the ability of an app to display content on the server instead of rendering it in the browser like in a single-page application.

There are times where using SSR is preferred over SPA. There are a lot of considerations that go into when and why to use SSR over SPA, and it goes back to the team's experience, technology stack, performance, code size, and many other considerations.

SSR was built to support SEO out of the gate and serve static pages; however, SPAs can also be set up with additional libraries so the content is cached and even works offline, as you saw in the previous chapter. This can be done by optimizing the SPA with techniques such as useCallback, prerendering, prefetching, and precaching, as you saw in the previous chapter.

The big advantage of SSR over SPAs that I see is when you want the following:

- The user machine less taxed

- The ability to share code with the back-end Node.js

Here are the cons of SSR over SPA:

- SSRs increase the complexity of your app.

- SSRs degrade the response time if the server is busy.

You may already be using SSR or SPA, so how can I convert between the two?

Even if you picked an SPA and need to convert the project to an SPA or vice versa, React component's first paradigm is built for dragging and dropping components if they were built right, so you should be able set up your project by moving the components over.

SPA and SSR Startup Projects

Once you decide on SSR and SPA, you need to decide on the startup library you want to use. Using a starter project is great because you don't need to configure the project, and you can get started right away. You saw how easy we were able to start projects quickly with CRA MHL during our book examples.

However, since the templates are vanilla flavor, it's one size fits all, and you need to put effort into adding and/or removing whatever React-based libraries you use or need.

CRA (`https://github.com/facebook/create-react-app`) is Facebook's recommended starter project, and with 86,000 likes on GitHub and Facebook's seal of approval, you know you are in good hands. However, that starter project is based on SPA technology.

Turning that project into a pure SSR app is possible, but it will require ejecting (you will need to manage the configurations yourself) and setting it up on your own. I would not recommend that approach unless you are very savvy with your knowledge of the moving pieces.

If you need an SPA, I would go with Next.js (`https://nextjs.org/`). Next.js is the most popular SSR-based React starter project (with 63,000 stars on GitHub), at the time of writing, and is being used by many successful companies such as Netflix, GitHub, Hulu, and Uber.

Besides CRA and Next.js, many other starter libraries are gaining momentum and were built to enhance a specific need. Here are some examples:

- *Gatsby*: This offers serverless rendering used by companies such as PayPal, Spotify, IBM, and more. See `https://www.gatsbyjs.com/`. (This is very close in popularity to Next.js.)

- *React Boilerplate*: This focuses on offline mode and scalability (`https://github.com/react-boilerplate/react-boilerplate`).

- *React Slingshot*: This is built with some opinionated libraries such as Redux, Babel, hot reloading, and more (`https://github.com/coryhouse/react-slingshot`).

- *Razzle*: This is SSR based, with no configuration (`https://github.com/jaredpalmer/razzle`).

Additionally, you can start your project from scratch and install the libraries you need on your own as well as manage the configurations on your own. It does require more effort to set up, but you can ensure your project fits your needs like a glove.

Publish Your React Code

There are so many solutions and options out there in terms of publishing your work that it can become overwhelming if you need to pick the technology yourself.

For example, there are free solutions (free at the time of writing) that are ideal for a proof of concept (POC) or a small or uncommercial project.

- GitHub pages

- Vercel

- Firebase

- Netlify

- Heroku

- And many others

In addition to platforms that are free to get started with, there are the traditional paid solutions, such as setting up a traditional server as well as serverless solutions. Here are few examples:

- Amazon AWS (see Lambda for serverless)

- Azura (see Azure Functions for serverless)

- Alibaba cloud (see Function Compute for serverless)

- And many others

Keep in mind that today many solutions are free to get started with based on using a trial, based on your early usage, or both; however, once you start using the resources, the bills start coming in.

You should estimate your resource usage for when you scale up or the trial period ends, so make sure to read the fine print and read it often. Also, set alerts in the billing section (if this exists). I am not in any way recommending any tool here; do your own research before picking a solution.

How can companies afford to give services for free? Most cloud services realize that collecting cents turns into millions, and usually the needs grow beyond the minimum usage. The effort of moving to a different solution is hard if the setup process was not documented well.

Tip   I highly recommend you document how you set up your project to avoid being married to a solution. Prices and terms change often.

In the next section of this chapter I will show you how to set up a starter project with Next.js and publish the work.

Create and Publish SSR with Next.js

So far in the book, we have used CRA for our projects. In this section, we will create a starter project with Next.js. The only prerequisite is having Node.js and Yarn installed, which we do.

Set Up a Next.js Starter Project

Let's set up a simple Next.js React project with a D3 library using the minimum code.

```
$ yarn create next-app
```

When it asked me in Terminal "what is your project named?" I selected nextjs-ts-chart, but of course you can use any name you like. Once installation is complete, you can change the directory to `nextjs-ts-chart`.

```
$ cd nextjs-ts-chart
```

Once the libraries are downloaded, run the app.

```
$ yarn run dev
$ open localhost:3000
```

Install TypeScript

Next.js is set by default with JS; however, I highly recommend setting up your project with TypeScript for the type checker, just as we have with CRA.

```
$ yarn add -D typescript @types/react @types/node
```

When we run these libraries, notice that the tsconfig.json file will be added to your project automatically.

Install D3

The last library I am going to install is D3 to help me draw some graphics. Since I am only using the select module, I can just install what I need to install of the whole D3 global library.

```
$ yarn add d3-selection @types/d3-selection
```

Rectangle.tsx

Now the project is set. I will be setting up the project with simple D3 code using React's function component. Create a components folder and add the Rectangle.tsx component we used in previous chapters.

```
// components/Rectangle/Rectangle.tsx

import React, { useEffect, RefObject } from 'react'
import { select } from 'd3-selection'

const Rectangle = () => {
  const ref: RefObject<HTMLDivElement> = React.createRef()

  useEffect(() => {
    draw()
  })

  const draw = () => {
    select(ref.current).append('p').text('Hello World')
    select('svg').append('g').attr('transform', 'translate(250, 0)').
    append('rect').attr('width', 500).attr('height', 500).attr
    ('fill', 'tomato')
  }
```

```
  return (
    <div className="Rectangle" ref={ref}>
      <svg width="500" height="500">
        <g transform="translate(0, 0)">
          <rect width="500" height="500" fill="green" />
        </g>
      </svg>
    </div>
  )
}

export default Rectangle
```

Update index.ts

Next, to include the `Rectangle.tsx` component and work with TS, change the index
from `index.js` to `index.ts` and add the `Rectangle.tsx` component we just created.
Lastly, remove the rest of the code that was there. Here is the complete `index.tsx`
component:

```
// src/component/pages/index.tsx

import Rectangle from "../components/Rectangle/Rectangle"
import styles from '../styles/Home.module.css'
import React from "react";

export default function Home() {
  return (
    <div className={styles.container}>
      <Rectangle />
    </div>
  )
}
```

Take a look at the final results, as shown in Figure 12-2.

Hello World

Figure 12-2. *My custom React + D3 component on Next.js starter project*

Publish Next.js with Express

Now that we have our app ready, one approach is to publish that app on an Express server.

To do that, install the express library (https://github.com/expressjs/express) as a developer dependency.

```
$ yarn add -D express
```

server.js

Next, let's create an express server file that can serve our app. On the code level, I am allowing you to pass the port that will be used or set it as port 9000 (feel free to change to port 3000 or whatever you prefer).

I am also allowing to pass a NODE_ENV so the app aware if it's running in development or production.

```js
// server.js
const express = require('express')
const next = require('next')const port = process.env.PORT || 9000;
const dev = process.env.NODE_ENV !== 'production'
const app = next({ dev })
const handle = app.getRequestHandler()app.prepare()
    .then(() => {
        const server = express()        server.get('*', (req, res) => {
            return handle(req, res)
        })        server.listen(port, (err) => {
            if (err) throw err
                console.log(`Server Ready on http://localhost:${port}`)
        })
    })
    .catch((ex) => {
        console.error(ex.stack)
        process.exit(1)
    })
```

Now that we have Node.js express server code set up, we need to build a published build version of the app. That's done using the run script set up for us in the package. json file.

```
$ yarn build
```

Since we are deploying the app on our local box, we need to set an environment variable in Terminal. This is how you would do it on Windows:

```
$ SET NODE_ENV=development
```

This is how you would do it on macOS/Linux:

```
$ export NODE_ENV=development
```

Run the express server using Node and open localhost on port 9000 to see the results.

```
$ node server.js
$ open http://localhost:9000/
```

If we want to deploy this app on any server that supports express, such as Ubuntu, just copy the files and run the server script with the NODE_ENV variable set to production.

```
$ export NODE_ENV=production
```

Publish Next.js Serverless with Heroku

We have seen our SSR React app running with the help of internal Next.js scripts as well as with my custom Node.js Express server script. Getting from here to production with the serverless option that doesn't require configurations is easy once you understand the process and do it a couple of times to practice.

As I mentioned, there are plenty of solutions out in the wild, free and paid.

Heroku is one of them. First, you would need to create an account: https://signup.heroku.com/.

You also need the Heroku CLI.

For macOS users using brew, just run this command in Terminal:

```
$ brew tap heroku/brew && brew install heroku
```

For Windows users, download the installer.

https://devcenter.heroku.com/articles/heroku-cli

Next, in Terminal you would need to log in to that account. The login command will open your browser and ask you to log in and confirm.

```
$ heroku loginLogging in... done
Logged in as [your email address]
```

Now we are ready to create the Heroku project. In the project path, type Heroku with your project name. That will create the project and set your public address and a Git location.

```
$ heroku create nextjs-ts-chart
Creating ● nextjs-ts-chart... donehttps://nextjs-ts-chart.herokuapp.com/ |
https://git.heroku.com/nextjs-ts-chart.git
```

Before we publish, there is one more step. We need to set our run script on package.json with a start run command that points to the server file we created. That start command will be used by Heroku automatically.

Change package.json from this:

```
// package.json"scripts": {
  "start": "next start"
  ..
}
```

to the following:

```
// package.json"scripts": {
  "start": "node server.js"
  ..
}
```

Next, let's create the build using the package.json run build command script and push to the Heroku server.

```
$ yarn run build
$ git remote
$ git push heroku master
```

As you can see, creating a starter project with Next.js, running a published version, and publishing your code was straightforward with little work on our end and is similar to what we have done with CRA.

Common Helpful Commands for Working with Heroku

Once you make changes, just do what you do normally do with Git.

```
$ git add && git commit -m 'change' && git push heroku master
```

If you are on a Git branch other than the master (such as dev, main, or production), you can avoid this error: "master does not match any error failed to push some refs to Heroku" by setting the branch name.

```
$ git push heroku [branch name]:master
```

Here's an example:

```
$ git push heroku HEAD:master
```

Lastly, let's say you want to remove the repo we just created. Just use the following:

```
$ git remote rm heroku
```

If you need to check for any errors, use the `tail` flag.

```
$ heroku logs --tail
```

Create and Publish an SPA with CRA

Using the CRA MHL, let's create a new project with `cra-ts-chart`.

```
$ yarn create react-app cra-ts-chart --template must-have-libraries
$ cd cra-ts-chart
$ yarn start
$ open http://localhost:3000
```

Rectangle.tsx

Next, use the same `Rectangle.tsx` component we created previously and place it here: src/components/Rectangle/Rectangle.tsx.

App.tsx

Just as we did with Next.js, add `Rectangle.tsx`, the component in our parent component `App.tsx`, and remove the rest of the boilerplate code.

```
// src/App.tsx

import React from 'react'
import './App.scss'
import Rectangle from './components/Rectangle/Rectangle'
```

```
function App() {
  return (
    <div className="App">
      <Rectangle />
    </div>
  )
}

export default App
```

Publish CRA with serve

The easiest way to publish CRA code would be to use CRA `serve` and let it handle the rest.

Use the `package.json` CRA MHL template project's run scripts that I added with one command.

```
$ yarn build:serve
```

If you check `package.json`, you can see that this run script runs these two other run scripts:

```
$ yarn build && serve -s build
```

Keep in mind that the same script works in Next.js as well. That will open your browser with a published script.

That script creates an optimized version of the app and sets it on port 5000 (if not taken), as shown in Figure 12-3.

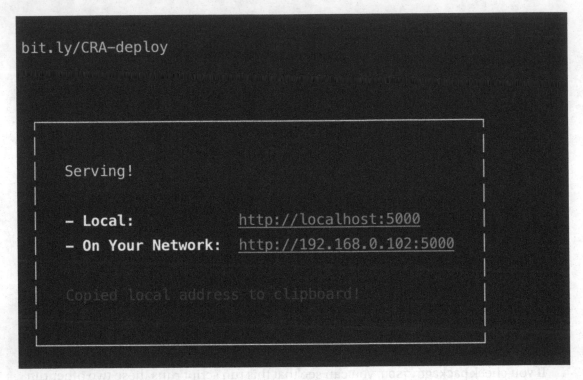

Figure 12-3. *Running published build with serve*

To shut down the server, press Command+C on a Mac (or Control+C on PC) to close the server.

Publish CRA with Express

Next, we can set up CRA with Express in the same manner that we set up Next.js.

Install Express as a developer dependency.

```
$ yarn add -D express
```

Server.js

Next, let's create an express Node.js file similar to the one we created for Next.js. I am using process.env.PORT or port 9000 and pointing to the build directory with index.html as an entry point.

```
const express = require('express')
const path = require('path')
const server = express()
```

```
const publicFolder = path.join(__dirname, 'build')
const port = process.env.PORT || 9000;

server.use(express.static(publicFolder))
server.get('*', (req, res) => {
  res.sendFile(path.join(publicFolder, 'index.html'))
});

server.listen(port, (err) => {
  if (err) throw err
    console.log(`Server Ready on http://localhost:${port}`)
})
```

Run it to test.

```
$ node server.js
```

Publish CRA Serverless with Heroku

To publish our CRA serverless with Heroku, it's the same steps as Next.js. We already have the Heroku CLI, so there's no need to re-install. Start from the login portion, as shown here:

```
$ heroku login
```

The command should open a browser and allow you to log in and accept.

Next, create the project name, and you will see the same Git and public URL as in the steps for Next.js.

```
$ heroku create cra-ts-chartCreating ● cra-ts-chart... donehttps://cra-ts-
chart.herokuapp.com/ | https://git.heroku.com/cra-ts-chart.git
```

We need to add a start run script for Heroku.

```
// package.json"scripts": {
  "start": "node server.js",
  ..}
```

The last part is the same as before. Run the build and push the code to a Heroku repo.

```
$ yarn build
$ git remote
$ git push heroku master
```

Now, see that `https://cra-ts-chart.herokuapp.com/` is deployed to Heroku.

```
$ heroku open
```

See Figure 12-4.

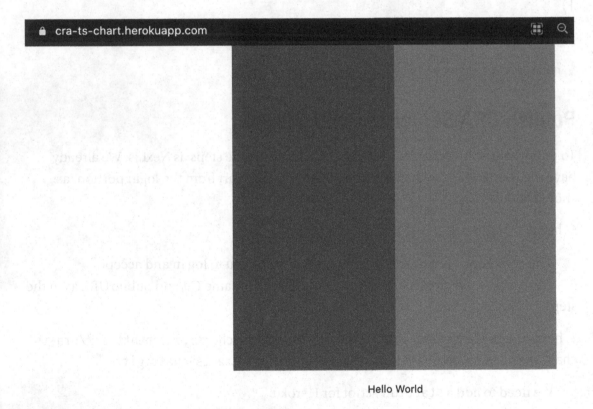

Figure 12-4. *Project published on Heroku*

CRA has a publishing options page at `https://create-react-app.dev/docs/deployment/`.

Helpful Debug Profile Tools

Now that you have published your app, you may find a bug or two and need to fix your app. Debugging is a common practice for detecting and removing errors (also called *bugs*) in your code that can cause undesired behavior.

When you work with a React app, there are some specific useful tools you can use to debug and profile your app when you run into problems. Having the right tools for the job and knowing how to use them can remove pain points and expedite the process.

React is based on JavaScript, and all the same tools that work for any JS-based app work on React. Techniques such as inspecting DOM elements, IDE debugging, and setting up alerts and console messages are all valid.

I am not going to show the simple and common ways to debug and profile your app as this book assumes you have some working knowledge of React, HTML, and JavaScript; however, feel free to check out my other React book:

```
https://www.apress.com/gp/book/9781484266953
```

Additionally, you can check out my two articles online:

- ```
  https://medium.com/react-courses/six-best-debugging-options-
  to-crush-your-reacts-bugs-like-a-champion-70b11b6a1a2d
  ```

- ```
  https://medium.com/react-courses/4-ways-to-profile-
  your-react-app-75b740e39ab2
  ```

These resources highlight a few methods that you may not be unaware of.

In this last section of the chapter, I want to point out additional tools that can help you get the job done once you publish your code.

The following are the debugging and profiling tools I will be covering:

- Debug and profile with Chrome DevTools

- React Chrome DevTools extension

- React Profiler API

Debug and Profile with Chrome DevTools

Chrome DevTools extensions is the standard and one of the most common tools used to debug and profile an app. If you need to test an app in other browsers, keep in mind they also provide development tools similar to Chrome.

349

What Is the Chrome DevTools Extension?

The React team, as well as the React community, built a Chrome DevTools extension that can help.

Here are three helpful React development DevTools extension management tools:

- React Developer Tools: `https://chrome.google.com/webstore/detail/react-developer-tools/fmkadmapgofadopljbjfkapdkoienihi`

- Realize for React: `https://chrome.google.com/webstore/detail/realize-for-react/llondniabnmnappjekpflmgcikaiilmh`

- Recoil: `https://chrome.google.com/webstore/detail/recoil-dev-tools/dhjcdlmklldodggmleehadpjephfgflc`

React Developer Tools Chrome DevTools Extension

React Developer Tools lets you inspect React component hierarchies in the Chrome Developer Tools. We get two new tabs in your Chrome DevTools: ❀ Components and ❀ Profiler.

To test the tool, I am using my site and navigating to `https://elielrom.com/Books`.

We can see a lot of information about the component and React specifically such as the version of React (in my case `v17-rc.0`), `Os`, router information, and component hierarchies, as shown in Figure 12-5.

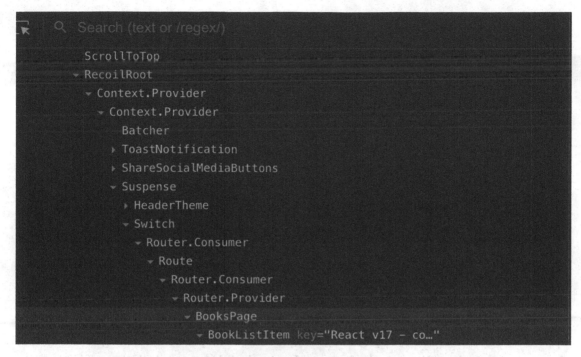

Figure 12-5. React developer tools—components window

The second tab is for Profiler, where we can record a production profiling build.

Profiler in React Developer Tools Chrome DevTools Extension

The React Developer Tools Chrome DevTools extension has two tabs: Components and Profiler. The Profiler tab gives insight into what is called Flamegraph.

Flamegraph is an ordered chart tool that shows the total time it took each component to render. The colors point to the render time (the greener, the better) and how long it took to render or rerender these changes from the VDOM to the "real" DOM. It includes tabs for rankings as well as interactions. See Figure 12-6.

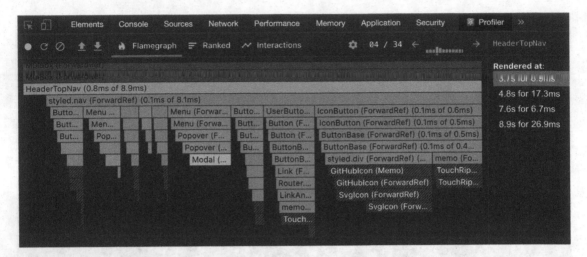

Figure 12-6. *Flamegraph results for my development build*

Remember, we created a run script for profiling a production build. You can compare the different results from the optimized build to the development build. Figure 12-7 shows the ranked profiling results for a production build ($ `yarn build:profile`).

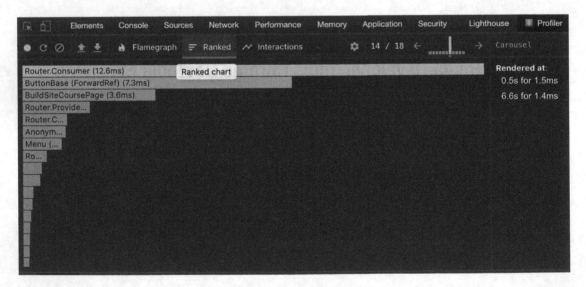

Figure 12-7. *Ranked results for my production build*

You can also opt in to your production build to get profiling working. Keep in mind that setting up profiling on a production build does come with a small overhead.

Realize for React Chrome DevTools Extension

Components are at the core of React. Once you have React Dev Tools installed, there is a great tool to help you visualize the React components tree. The tool helps track the state and gives you a holistic overview of the component hierarchy. See Figure 12-8.

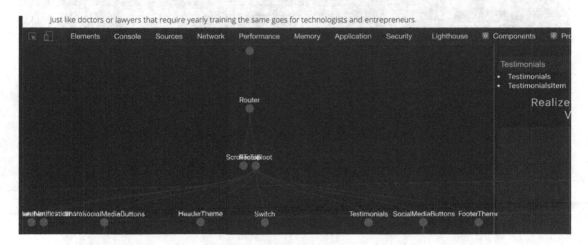

Figure 12-8. *Realize for React Chrome DevTools on* `https://EliElrom.com`

This holistic overview is breaking down the `AppRouter.tsx` file on my personal site neatly.

Recoil Chrome DevTools Extension

When working with state management such as Redux or Recoil, it would be neat to be able to track the internal workings of the state. There is plenty of writing about the Redux Chrome DevTools extension, but I want to point out a new tool for Recoil that we used in the book for state management. The tool gives information about atoms, selectors, and subscribers. See Figure 12-9.

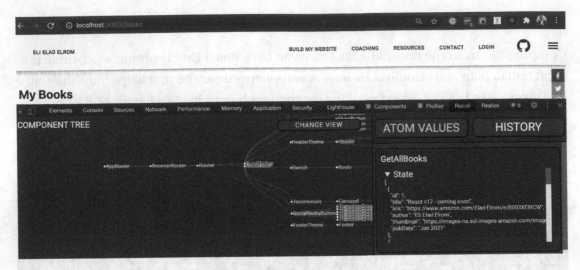

Figure 12-9. *Recoil Chrome DevTools on* `https://EliElrom.com`

In my case, the atom is based on `bookObject`, and I can inspect the state value and changes in the browser.

```
export interface bookObject {
  title: string
  author: string
  pubDate: string
  link: string
  thumbnail: string
}
```

React Profiler API

The React Profiler API (`https://reactjs.org/docs/profiler.html`) includes a `<Profiler/>` component that helps customize the metrics from the source code to measure the component's lifecycle time.

To test the component, you can set up a new project with the CRA template project.

```
$ yarn create react-app your-project-name --template must-have-libraries
```

Next, refactor the router AppRouter.tsx and wrap it with the <Profiler/> component; see Figure 12-10.

```tsx
// src/AppRouter.tsx

import { Profiler } from 'react'

const AppRouter: FunctionComponent = () => {
  return (
    <Profiler onRender={(id, phase, actualTime, baseTime, startTime,
    commitTime) => {
      console.log(`${id}'s ${phase} phase:`);
      console.log(`Actual time: ${actualTime}`);
      console.log(`Base time: ${baseTime}`);
      console.log(`Start time: ${startTime}`);
      console.log(`Commit time: ${commitTime}`);
    }}>
    <Router>
      <RecoilRoot>
        <Suspense fallback={<span>Loading...</span>}>
          <Switch>
            <Route exact path="/" component={App} />
          </Switch>
        </Suspense>
      </RecoilRoot>
    </Router>
    </Profiler>
  )
}
```

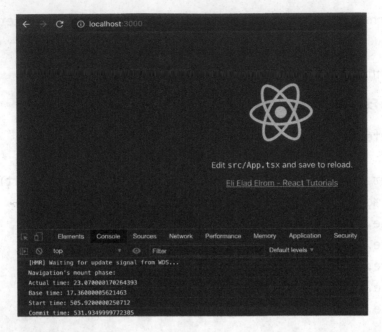

Figure 12-10. *Profiler API results on CRA-MHL template development build*

In this example, I am logging everything, but we can create a script that will filter results and handle them in different ways.

Summary

As you have seen, you have plenty of options when it comes to selecting your startup project and publishing your React app. First, decide whether you want to use an SPA or SSR, next select the startup project, and then select server or serverless. What it boils down to is what other technologies you need to integrate your React project with, usages, costs, maintenance, languages, your personal and team experience, and many other facts.

In the last part of this chapter, I showed you some helpful debugging and profiling tools that can help you in your development journey. I want to thank you for purchasing this book, and congratulations for completing it.

Check my d3 and React interactive course to see other ways you can implement all the examples in this book with different approaches plus insights and more explanation.

The interactive course is packed with material that covers more topics, such as, taking more control over the DOM, color spaces, interactivity, design, as well as expanding on what's in this book. The interactive course compliment this book and can help you master React and D3; `https://elielrom.com/BuildSiteCourse`.

Send me social media post of you and the book and receive a discount code for the interactive course.

If you manage to build a cool D3 with React chart using this book, I would love to hear from you and see your chart. Please drop me a note and share:

- `https://elielrom.com/Contact`

- `https://twitter.com/EliEladElrom`

- `https://www.linkedin.com/in/eladelrom`

Index

© Elad Elrom 2021
E. Elrom, *Integrating D3.js with React*, https://doi.org/10.1007/978-1-4842-7052-3

H, I

Y, Z

Printed in the United States
by Baker & Taylor Publisher Services